Books by Fran Stewart

<u>The Biscuit McKee Mystery Series</u>:

Orange as Marmalade
Yellow as Legal Pads
Green as a Garden Hose
Blue as Blue Jeans
Indigo as an Iris
Violet as an Amethyst
Gray as Ashes
Red as a Rooster
Black as Soot
Pink as a Peony
White as Ice

A Slaying Song Tonight

<u>The ScotShop Mysteries</u>:

A Wee Murder in My Shop
A Wee Dose of Death
A Wee Homicide in the Hotel

Poetry:

Resolution

For Children:

As Orange As Marmalade/
Tan naranja como Mermelada
(a bilingual book)

Non-Fiction:

From The Tip of My Pen: a workbook for writers
BeesKnees #1: A Beekeeping Memoir (#1 of 6 volumes)
BeesKnees #2: A Beekeeping Memoir (#2 of 6 volumes)
BeesKnees #3: A Beekeeping Memoir (#3 of 6 volumes)
BeesKnees #4: A Beekeeping Memoir (#4 of 6 volumes)
BeesKnees #5: A Beekeeping Memoir (#5 of 6 volumes)
BeesKnees #6: A Beekeeping Memoir (#6 of 6 volumes)
Clear as Mud
Coming Soon - *Clearly Me*

Clear as Mud

Fran Stewart

Clear as Mud

Fran Stewart

© 2020 Fran Stewart

All rights reserved. No part of this book may be used or reproduced in any manner whatsoever without written permission from the author, except by a reviewer who may quote brief passages in a review.

ISBN: (Softcover) 978-1-951368-22-7

This book was printed in the United States of America.

Published by

My Own Ship Press
PO Box 490153
Lawrenceville GA 30049
myownship@icloud.com

franstewart.com

Introduction

I spent several years being a bit wishy-washy about Facebook. I'd check it occasionally, but was never too enthusiastic about it. Even when I put together a separate FB page for my posts as an author, I didn't adhere to any particular schedule.

Gradually, though, the author posts became a good way for me to keep in touch with my friends and readers, so I started paying more attention to what I wrote and when I wrote it.

Throughout 2014, my health went gradually downhill—not that I noticed it really, but I began to get more and more tired as each day passed. For someone who has for years been attuned to the messages my body gives me, I was being particularly dense.

Finally, I decided to book a trip to Mexico to see the Monarch butterflies. "Maybe I need some time away," I thought. Only trouble was, that trip had to be cancelled because of increasing violence in that area of Mexico, which left me with a credit from the airline. The caveat was that I had to take another trip within one year.

So I called my friend Jan in Hawai'i and asked if I could come visit.

"Three weeks," she said. "You have to come for three full weeks. Otherwise you'll end up recovering from jetlag just in time to turn around and head home."

I scheduled a three-week trip. Jan took the opportunity to book a speaking engagement for me at her local library in Hilo.

So I went.

"Jetlag," I thought the first few days.

"Maybe something you contracted on the plane," Jan suggested when I couldn't get my energy level up. We took a lot of very slow walks. I took a lot of pictures. And I posted almost every single day on my FB author page. I loved seeing Jan, but I felt lousy the whole time.

The you-know-what didn't truly hit the fan, though, until I was on my flight home. Don't worry, you'll read all about it in a few pages.

The upshot of this whole experience is that I began to see my posts as a mini-memoir. And since nobody wants to scroll down and down and down, and then up and up and up, just so they can read the thing in chronological order, I decided to make it easier for you.

My gift to you—my memoirs. I hope you enjoy them.

I dedicate this book to Eli, Veronica, Savannah, Aiden, Diana, Erica, Darlene, and Marcia—eight people who have enriched my life immeasurably.

Fran Stewart

January 2015

Arrival in Hilo

January 10, 2015 – Had to say hello to the gorgeous ocean. Once we were home, a little friend climbed onto Jan's arm.

~ ~ ~

Hilo Library

January 15, 2015 -- Did you wonder where I've been for the past five days? Dying (or feeling like it) in Paradise is not what I'd recommend for the first week of a vacation. Must have caught something on the plane. I did make it to the Hilo Library yesterday, where I was scheduled to speak for an hour. It was a small but enthusiastic audience, and I'm so glad I made it through without coughing too much. Feeling slightly better today.

Cassie Hernandez was one of the audience members who had a great time. And the lei I wore (not too visible against the bright muumuu) has incredible detail.

Peridot's Pregnancy

January 16, 2015 – Jan and I took Peridot, Jan's pregnant toy poodle, to the vet today for an X-ray of the babies. Four definite spines and 1 or 2 maybe spines in that little tummy. Loved looking at the delicate vertebra.

Between two poodles, two cats, and multiple geckos and anoles that live on the ceiling and the screens and the walls . . . there's lots of wonderful life in this house!

p.s. I delighted in watching the entire birth process—and helping Jan when she had to cut through the third baby's enveloping membrane. The mom was just too pooped by that point to chew it away from the baby. And here's the first baby (Pearl) a few days later and a snuggle-bundle of three, resting up from having birthed.

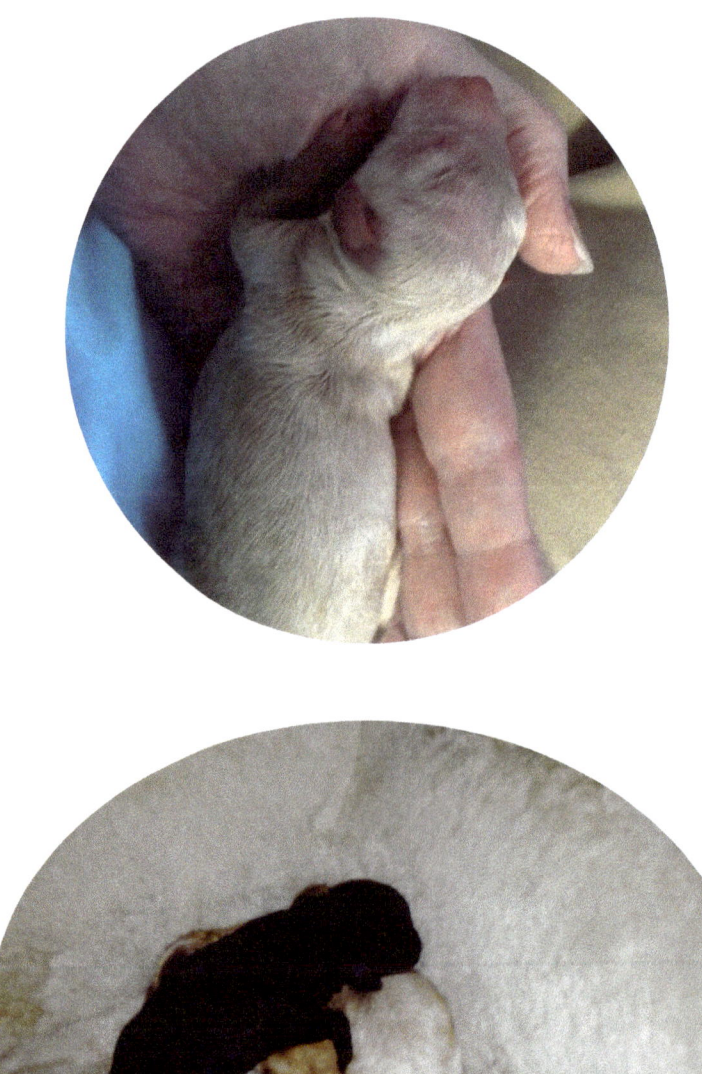

~ ~ ~

Hula lesson

January 20, 2015 – Headed to a hula lesson in about half an hour…

They offered to let me dance along with them, but after about ten minutes I was too pooped, so I sat on the floor and watched.

Then we went home, and I watched the puppies. They're so squiggly squirmy.

~ ~ ~

Kilauea's Silence

January 23, 2015 – Visited the Kilauea Volcano today. The caldera is enormous. We were inside the caldera, but couldn't approach too close to the active lava crater. We were there close enough to sunset that I got photos of what it looks like in the daytime (nothing much except lots of steam rising from a hole in the ground) and at night when the lava way at the bottom of the crater reflects on the clouds of steam rising from it.

The visitor's center was crowded, but I managed to have a brief conversation with one of the park rangers who told me that on quiet evenings, if the wind is from the right direction, she can sometimes hear the lava bubbling.

So, wonder of wonders, as night fell and the steam over the crater glowed, I stood up on a stone bench, called for everyone's attention, and told them what the ranger had said. "Would you be willing," I asked them, "to be absolutely quiet for about three minutes? Maybe we'll be able to hear the lava."

Fran Stewart

Those who didn't speak English somehow or other found people to translate for them, and everyone—yes, every single one of us—zipped our mouths and quit shuffling around. The silence was intense. The expectation was palpable.

It couldn't last, of course. But we got in at least three minutes. The wind must not have been quite right, so we never really heard the bubbling, but it wasn't for lack of our trying. And simply watching the shifting reflections of the molten rock in utter silence was truly magical. So was the cooperation between people who moments before had been total strangers to each other.

~ ~ ~

The Start of the Drama

January 31, 2015 – So - I can hear you asking, where did Fran disappear to for the last week? Good of you to ask. I've been in a hospital in Houston – the ER, the ICU, and finally, a high-risk ward. Just returned home today. I'm trying to get my energy back. Will tell the whole story in a day or two (or three). Give me some time – and please continue the positive thoughts / prayers / good vibes / candles – whatever works for you.

February 2015

United Flight Attendant Saved My Life

2/1/2015 – This banyan tree at Wailuku River State Park is easily 500 years old, maybe much more. That one tree has formed a grove – all attached, all one tree, but when I threw up my hands in sheer glory, I was standing between the root-joined trees in a clearing that was a hundred or so feet in diameter. It was the holiest ground I've ever stood on. I'm glad I contacted that energy on that particular day.

A few hours later, I was on an airplane headed to Houston. I couldn't sleep well throughout that night flight, and about two hours outside of Houston I began to be very uncomfortable. When the flight attendants came around with morning juices, I told one of them that I was having trouble breathing. He brought me a tank of oxygen. With the mask on my face, I began to feel much better.

Another attendant came by and asked if I'd like to be checked by paramedics when we landed. "No, I'm breathing just fine now." You see, I knew a paramedic visit would mean nobody else could get off the plane until the "problem" had been handled. I didn't want anyone to miss a flight because of me – and I had only an hour layover before my flight home.

She came back a few minutes later. "The pilot says we'll be arriving 15 minutes early. Are you sure you don't want to see a paramedic?"

"No, really." I took two deep breaths. "I'm doing okay now."

A few minutes later she was back. "May I take your pulse?" I lifted my arm. Within seconds she had both her hands on mine. "If you've had trouble on this big plane," she said, "you won't enjoy the next flight. It's on what we in the industry call a Barbie Doll plane – it's real skinny and bounces all over the place." Before I could object (again), she said, "Honey, I'd feel a whole lot better if you let me call the paramedics. Would you do it just for me? Please?"

So I said yes.

Turns out my pulse was bouncing between 174 and 90, back up to 128, 70, 163, 35. And the EKG looked like an earthquake had hit.

That flight attendant had figured out exactly how to get me to do what she felt was necessary. She saved my life. I don't know her name, but she was on United Flight 252 Honolulu to Houston on January 26/27 (overnight). If you know any of the crew on that flight, please pass the word on. Better yet, please share this post with anyone you know – the word is bound to get to her eventually.

I have to go take a nap now. I'll be back sometime to tell you the rest of the story.

~ ~ ~

Yellow Angel

2/3/2015 – As soon as the paramedics saw my heart going crazy on the EKG, one of them said, "We're taking you to the hospital, ma'am."

"No! I have a flight to Atlanta to catch in less than an hour."

He looked at me long and hard, all the while packing up his little EKG machine. "No, ma'am. You have an ambulance to catch in less than two minutes."

The ER at Memorial Hermann Northeast Hospital was a scramble of activity, but I lay in a fog as they X-rayed my heart, did a CT scan, took blood and urine, and who knows what else. At that point, I didn't care. I felt so exhausted and hurt so much, I didn't see how I could keep going.

Eventually, there came a lull, in which I was left alone in a blessedly quiet room. With no warning sounds whatsoever, I felt a being, a presence, a *something* standing at my left knee. I opened my eyes and saw a column of the most unearthly yellow, swirling gently all the way up to the ceiling and beyond. I felt a sense of ineffable peace. There was no face, there were no arms, no human form whatsoever, but it said to me—did I actually hear it with my ears? I don't think so—but it somehow said, "Don't be afraid. You are at a crossroads in your life, as you have been four previous times. You are completely at choice. You may go with me, or you may stay."

Oh.

I lay there, watching the gently undulating yellow column, and thought about it. I thought perhaps that if I went, I might not hurt so much. I wondered what sort of legacy, if any, I would leave behind. I have two wonderful, loving, happy children, five loving grandchildren, and many dear friends. My 11 published books—soon to be 12—would live on after me. Not a bad record.

I felt content.

Then, just by my left shoulder, I saw a column of the brightest, most vivid purple—as otherworldly a color as the yellow was. It began to roll lists of names upward, like the credits on a movie screen. My children and grandchildren came first, my closest friends, people whose company I enjoy thoroughly, people I knew many years ago, like Diane Marie Hart, my best friend in 4th grade (whom I've never seen or heard from since then). The list went on and on.

Off to one side of the "credits," the names of my books began to appear, and I saw below them a blank space. Which meant to me that I have a lot more books to write.

I looked back at the yellow angel, who simply waited. There was no feeling of hurry whatsoever. I have no idea whether this process took 2 seconds or 2 hours—it felt timeless.

"I think I'll stay."

A surge of absolute acceptance flooded around and through me. I knew in that moment, that no matter which choice I'd made, the yellow angel would have seen it as exactly right. I have never felt so completely loved in all my life.

The colors dissolved away, and a doctor knocked on the door and entered the room. "We've found the source of your problem," she said. "Your thyroid has gone haywire, which is what's made your heart race for so long, but we can control them both with medication."

I know, I thought.

She held her thumb and index finger almost touching. "When you got here, you were that far away from a fatal heart attack."

I know, I thought again, and noticed a tiny yellow prick of light over her shoulder. A reflection? Or a reminder?

* * *

I should note that: a) nothing like this has ever happened to me before; b) I'm fairly sure the angel that appeared to me as a column of bright yellow might appear to someone else with wings or a sword, a face or a halo; and c) If I'd seen somebody with wings, I'm sure I would have thought I was hallucinating.

Please share this post with your Facebook friends if you feel it's appropriate.

~ ~ ~

Emergency Room Pizza

2/4/2015 – After the flight attendant saved my life (see banyan tree post on February 1st) and the angel came (see yellow angel post yesterday), I'd been in the ER for more than half a day. Memorial Hermann Northeast Hospital in Houston was full – they didn't have a bed for me (other than the one I was lying on). My daughter called me repeatedly throughout the day. When she called late that evening, I happened to mention that I must be better because I was hungry.

"They haven't fed you?"

"It's an ER, Veronica. I don't think they do meal service here."

"You tell your nurse right now that you need something to eat."

"Okay, okay. I will." At that point I'd already been there in the ER for almost eleven hours, but I truly hadn't thought about food until Veronica's call.

Just a moment after we ended the call, my nurse walked in. "We're transferring you to the ICU in about an hour—or maybe two—or possibly three. As soon as a bed there is available. I'm sorry you've had to stay down here in the ER for so long."

"Thanks, Joe," I said, "but I'm kinda hungry. Is there any food around?"

He brought me some apple juice and a turkey sandwich, opened the juice, unwrapped the sandwich for me (my hands were still too shaky to manage those tasks), and turned to do something else. As I took my second bite, someone with a phone to her ear walked into the room.

"She's right here … she's eating … she has a sandwich … don't worry, we're feeding her … okay." And she ended the call. "That was your daughter," she said [like I hadn't already figured that out!] "She called to ask for the number of the closest pizza place so she could order you a pizza."

"I'm sorry she took up your time," I said.

"Not at all," she replied. "I think it's sweet. There are so many people here who don't have anyone to worry about them."

So, for the next few days, I told that story to everyone who had a moment to listen. My daughter's loving concern brought smiles to so many faces.

I can't tell you how much I appreciate her love and her support. Thank you, Veronica.

* * *

As before, I ask you to share this story with your friends. We all need some light in our lives, whether it comes from caring strangers (like the flight attendant), from caring professionals (like the paramedics and everyone I dealt with at the hospital), from friends (of which I'm thankful to have so many), or from family (who are dearer to me than I could possibly express).

~ ~ ~

Murder in the Magic City

[**2020 note**: I was still awfully shaky after my somewhat harrowing experience over the previous week, but for quite a while I'd been scheduled to appear at "Murder in the Magic City," a fabulous author event put together for mystery fans by the Birmingham Library. I was bound and determined not to fink out on the wonderful folks who'd invited me to be a part of this conference. I talked a friend into driving me to Birmingham in exchange for my footing her bill. Thank goodness. I never could have made it otherwise. As it was, I probably shouldn't have gone, since, as you can see from the pictures, I was totally wiped out the whole time. But I made it through, met some wonderful fans, and came home totally exhausted. I tried, though, to downplay my exhaustion when I wrote about the experience.]

February 7, 2015 – Murder in the Magic City (Birmingham) has been great fun. Each of the 20+ authors here had a chance to be on a panel and talk about murder in its various manifestations. Four of us clowned around after our panel discussion – Mary Anne Edwards, Cynthia Lott, and Stacy Allen all got the gray memo. I missed it. And then I talked with Hank Phillippi Ryan. Tomorrow we're all headed to Wetumpka, Alabama for "Murder on the Menu," a fundraiser for the Wetumpka Library.

~ ~ ~

Blurb by Ryan

February 17, 2015 – Here's an amazing blurb Hank Phillippi Ryan wrote for my first ScotShop mystery, A WEE MURDER IN MY SHOP. I absolutely love her tag *Outlander goes cozy*. 13 days till the release.

Completely charming—Outlander goes cozy.

This lilting mystery-fantasy series, with its dashing fourteenth-century Scotsman ghost and its engaging contemporary heroine, is intelligent, original, and irresistible.

--Hank Phillippi Ryan

Agatha, Anthony, Macavity & Mary Higgins Clark award winning author of TRUTH BE TOLD

~ ~ ~

United's Reply

April 6, 2015 – Remember when I posted in early February about how a flight attendant saved my life? I thought those of you who followed that story might be interested in the thoughtful email response I receive from United Airlines after I sent them a "feedback" form:

Dear Ms. Stewart:

Fran Stewart

Thank you for taking the time to let us know about the service and assistance provided by our inflight staff when you traveled on United flight 252 from Honolulu, HI to Houston, TX on January 26, 2015.

I am glad our representatives were able to assist with your specific needs and provide all necessary assistance. This acknowledgement means a great deal to our employees and reinforces the fact that our customers value the efforts we make in providing quality service. We applaud our representatives who show true concern for our customers.

In the service industry, nothing is more important than the impression we make with our customers. I sincerely appreciate your thoughtfulness in taking the time to let us know about this show of excellence by our representatives. Your comments will be documented in our corporate report and shared with Inflight management and the flight staff for flight 252.

We value you as our customer and I am so glad that you are doing well.

We look forward to our next opportunity to welcome you onboard United Airlines.

Sincerely,
Calethia Thompson
Complaint Resolution Official (CRO)
Disability Specialist - Corporate Customer Care

~ ~ ~

Science Through Forensics

April 17, 2015 – I spent the day at Parkview High School today, speaking to the Forensics classes and was delighted with the good reception from the students. We laughed a lot together, particularly over Jackie White's song "Just Kill Him, Girl," which Jackie wrote in response to the first chapter of A WEE MURDER IN MY SHOP. The students learn science through studying forensics – I sure wish I'd had that as an option when I was in high school.

One of the students from today's forensics class presentation shared the following, but I obviously can't figure out Facebook, as it showed up on my personal FB page rather than here on my author page. Ah well, I did a copy and paste. Maybe someday someone can teach me how this system works …

Alex Bond   April 17 at 2:26pm

Fran Stewart just came to Parkview High School. She talked about her career as an author and the whole presentation was simply inspiring. As a songwriter, I was very intrigued with her stories. She also said something that caught my attention. She said that she wanted her audience to be entertained by the stories, but she also wanted them to finish the book understanding her message and reason for writing the stories. That was one of the many things I could relate to. I want my audience to finish my songs with a new perspective and a comprehension of the message in the song. Ms. Stewart's visit was much needed for me personally and I plan to read her books in the future. Thanks Fran Stewart, you're truly inspiring!

~ ~ ~

The Perfect Book Club

May 27, 2015 -- Yestereen (a word that's been in the English language for more than 400 years–it means yesterday evening), I was invited to speak about A WEE MURDER IN MY SHOP to one of the most successful book clubs I've ever had the pleasure of attending. Many of the members are teachers, and everyone there was a joy for me to meet.

The questions they asked were insightful—they'd ALL read the book, which felt like something of a miracle.

The Scot-themed book club event began with scones and shortbread, of course, as well as Scotch eggs and a wee dram or two.

[**2020 Note**: I enjoyed these women so much, I asked if I could join their book club – and they said yes, so I've been a member for five years now.]

~ ~ ~

Fran Stewart

My July 4th Tradition

July 4, 2015 – How many times have you read the Declaration of Independence and/or the U.S. Constitution? I'd be willing to bet that, unless you were a history major, you read the Declaration of Independence once in high school along with bits and pieces of the Constitution.

As a writer, living in a country with freedom of the press is vital to me, so I'd like to encourage you to join me in reading those two documents (or at least the D of I) today, as I've been doing every July 4th for the past three decades.

I generally struggle through reading this facsimile of the declaration, but it's slow going with the archaic penmanship. Unless you're a stickler for authenticity, I'd recommend getting a transcript at archives.gov. My book of the Constitution is this beautiful one inscribed and illustrated by Sam Fink, which I bought in 1985, when it was first published. The insights in it about the writing of the Constitution, and the introduction by James Michener, have taught me a lot over the years.

~ ~ ~

ScotShop in Audio

July 5, 2015 -- Well, the audio version of A WEE MURDER IN MY SHOP is available for pre-order through Tantor Media! The whimsical cover surprised (and disappointed) me, but that's the type of illustration they use for the cozy mysteries they record. The GREAT news is that I've listened to another book recorded by Tanya Eby, the chosen narrator for WEE MURDER, and she has a GREAT voice – very expressive. I think she'll be able to do justice to Peggy and Dirk and all the other inhabitants of Hamelin VT.

And yippee! There's an audio sample of the audiobook on the Tantor Website! I love it so far. Can't wait to hear the whole thing.

~ ~ ~

[2020 Note]

Now, the question is – what happened to the rest of my posts from 2015?

I'm glad you asked.

Wish I had an answer for you.

Facebook swallowed them somehow or other. I have to assume they weren't all that memorable. No, wait! Maybe I'll assume they were incredibly written, decidedly moving, obviously vital, and so phenomenal, they blew 2015 FB right off the screen.

There. I feel better now.

On to 2016. Whoops! It's missing too, along with three-fourths of 2017.

You'll notice that November of 2017 is when I started posting a blog entry on my website every Friday. It didn't last long, but I've included those posts here in *Clear as Mud*.

October 2017

Odometer Fun

2017-10-08 Do you ever sit in a parking lot or your driveway (NOT on the road) and take a picture of your odometer, or am I the only one who does that sort of thing? I love it when the numbers play like this. Sort of the way I play with words in my books.

~ ~ ~

Ghoti

2017-10-28 – Did you ever see the word ghoti?

English is such a crazy language – particularly our spelling. So, for today and the next two days I'm going to be posting about some of the stranger aspects of our language, which is said to be the second hardest language to learn to speak.

For today, try figuring out what ghoti sounds like, and I'll give you the answer tomorrow.

What does this bug picture have to do with ghoti? Absolutely nothing, except that I can't figure out what kind of bug it is. I took the photo last summer in the north Georgia mountains.

It kind of reminds me of the trundle bugs in Anne McCaffrey's Dragons of PERN series.

~ ~ ~

Weird

2017-10-29 So, here's the answer from yesterday's question: What is ghoti?

Spoken aloud, use the sound of gh in enough, o in women, and ti in elation.

Therefore, ghoti is . . . (drumroll, please) . . . fish.

Now, on to another weirdness. Check out this mug. I can't give a photo credit because there were billions of matches to this image when I did a search through tineye.com.

Which means you've probably already seen this mug. If so, I hope you enjoy it seeing it again!

~ ~ ~

OUGH

2017-10-30 – And here is yet another fun exploration into the wonders of English. How many different pronunciations of "ough" do you see here?

Again, with billions of matches on tineye.com, I can't figure out who to credit for the photo <<sigh>>

~ ~ ~

Monster

2017-10-31 – Happy Halloween! May all your monsters be gentle ones.

November 2017

Dad in the Mirror

2017-11-01 - I don't like selfies very much. They always tend to distort the face. At least, they do when I take one. And then, I found this old, old version of a selfie, and I love it.

My dad had quite an artistic eye, something I never really appreciated until after he died, and my sister and I went through old photos. This one, where he used a mirror (in place of the selfie technology which wasn't possible back in the 1940s) caught my eye. I love the composition of it.

Then, lo and behold, a couple of years ago, one of my granddaughters took a very similar picture of herself with her siblings in a mirror.

She must have inherited the artist's eye from her great-granddad.

Fran Stewart

~ ~ ~

Defiant

2017-11-02 – I'm getting ready to send out a sneak preview this Saturday of **RED AS A ROOSTER** to everyone who's signed up on my website (franstewart.com) to receive my newsletter.

RED will be the first of the quartet of books that will wrap up the Biscuit McKee mystery series. Here's a picture of the wood stove that is featured in all four books. I picked it because: a) I love the idea of a wood stove from Vermont, where I used to live, b) it's powerful enough to heat Biscuit and Bob's whole house, and c) I think it's beautiful.

Can't you just imagine Marmalade curled up in a basket next to it?

~ ~ ~

BLOG #001 **2017-11-03 – teeny frog**

Scrolling through old photos from Sapelo Island, I came across this one. One rainy afternoon in July of 2014, my friend Mozelle Funderburk spotted this little fella sitting on the step. Naturally, she had to reach down and make contact while I took a picture. He just sat there and checked us out. He wasn't frozen in fear. After the contact with her finger, he puttered around the step for several minutes, enjoying the drizzle.

I got to wondering how often I walk right past somebody like this, not even noticing him/her. I tend to notice lizards, most likely because they generally move, but when somebody sits perfectly still and doesn't try to hop or slither or run or walk away, it sure is easy not to see, whether it's a frog, a snake, a rabbit, a deer, or a person.

Have you ever stood perfectly still in a crowded room and noticed how you become almost invisible?

~ ~ ~

Translucence

2017-11-04 – I'm headed to a funeral today and felt like I needed this reminder that there is always a dawn, and in the spring, the flowers always come back. I love the way this picture, which I took in the north Georgia mountains a couple of years ago, shows that some layers don't seem to admit light. But when I look closer, I see that they all do. It's just that when there are many layers, the light has a harder time getting through. I'm in the process of lightening the number of layers in my life, releasing anything that doesn't let my light shine.

Fran Stewart

Now, if I could just get my desk cleared off…

~ ~ ~

Cabin Dawn

2017-11-05 – It's misty outside, and I was struck by how soft all the houses in my neighborhood looked when I took my pre-dawn morning walk.

Barbara Brown Taylor wrote a book called *Learning to Walk in the Dark*. I've referred to it often in the Memoirs class I teach, because it goes beyond just telling "what happened" and delves into the "why" and the "what I learned from it."

I love books like that. As I walked this morning, passing from places where the outside lights of various houses gave way to the darker sections where I had to feel carefully with my feet, I was reminded of Taylor's book.

There will always be times of darkness in our lives. Instead of fearing them, can we not learn to walk through them with confidence?

~ ~ ~

Shakespeare puzzle

2017-11-6 – Are you a jigsaw puzzle kind of person? I love them, and the more complicated they are, the better I enjoy piecing them together.

Unfortunately, Wooly Bear thinks the puzzle table is her perching spot. Years ago, I had a cat who liked to help me with puzzles. She would hop very delicately onto the table, barely disturbing the position of a single piece. If she decided to lie down, she did so primly, lifting her tail off the surface before curling it around her. If I needed to access the pieces under her, I would say, "Excuse me, please," and she would lift herself up without messing any of my carefully arranged pieces. She's the cat I used as a model for Marmalade in my Biscuit McKee mysteries.

Wooly Bear is another story altogether. I thought I'd NEVER get this Shakespearean puzzle (which I bought at the gift shop in Atlanta's Shakespeare Tavern) finished. Wooly is prone to taking flying leaps at the table, sending puzzle pieces flying. Or she'll jump up carefully and then lie down on her side and S-T-R-E-T-C-H, skewing everything that had been lined up properly.

<<sigh>> But she gives wonderful cat hugs.

~ ~ ~

2017-11-7 —NO INTERNET - NO POST

~ ~ ~

Daisy Toes

2017-11-8—Okay. It's time for some "cute." These are Daisy's feet. And a picture of her back in August of 1998 when she was just a teeny kitten.

If these pictures don't brighten your day, find a puppy picture somewhere, like the ones I posted on October 21st. [**2020 Note:** Too bad that post—and a whole lot of other ones—were lost in cyberspace. You'll just have to imagine it.]

Go ahead, smile.

There. Don't you feel better now?

I know I do.

And the internet problem? It's just a puff of dust in the wind.

Clear as Mud

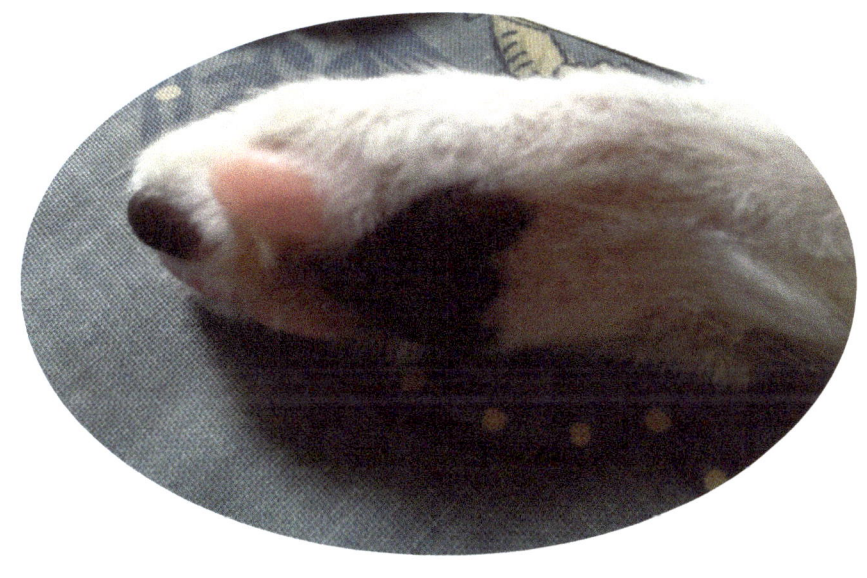

Spread-Eagled

2017-11-9 —How do you relax?

My grand-dog, Max, knows how to relax. He stretches out on the couch or the floor, the way he's doing in this photo. If I tried to duplicate his pose, I'd throw my back out of alignment for the next three months.

But how do I relax after a day of writing? I think that's a pretty good question. When I first posed it to myself, I ran over a number of possibilities — I knit, I listen to audio books, I read, I diddle around at the piano, I drum or sing or take walks.

I'm not so sure any of these choices are that relaxing. When I knit, I'm as likely to have to rip out a row and re-do it. When I listen to audio books, I'm either driving or knitting. Reading? I unconsciously edit as I go. Piano-playing—I spend the time berating myself for wrong notes. Drumming and singing? Well, I guess those are pretty relaxing. Ditto the walking.

But the absolutely most relaxing thing I ever do is sit on my front porch and watch the birds. I've spent more on birdseed this year than I have on food for myself.

But it feeds my soul, so I'd say that's a pretty fair trade.

BLOG #002 - Friday 11/10/2017 at 5:42 a.m.

The memoirs class I've been teaching at my local library wrapped up last Tuesday. The assignment from the previous class was to write a memory that involved conversation of some sort. I decided I might as well fulfill the assignment myself, so I got around to writing about something that happened well more than a dozen years ago.

The class members enjoyed it, so I thought I'd share it with you as well.

Whiskers - by Fran Stewart © 2017

Sixteen or seventeen years ago, I decided (for some bizarre reason) to attend an Atlanta sewing expo. I, who am not a fan of crowds, found myself engulfed by thousands of women. I, who am a mediocre seamstress at best, was surrounded by women wearing phenomenal outfits they had created for themselves.

I wandered, eyes agog, for several hours until I found a display that must have been thirty feet long, made up of wide tables end to end, covered in sewing implements, scissors, knives, pliers, tweezers. Ha! Stop right there. Tweezers! Just what I needed!

The man behind the display was busy with another customer about twenty feet from me. I waited until he was free and then motioned him toward me. When he was close, I leaned as far across the display table as I could and said in as low a voice as I could, "I'm looking for a really good pair of tweezers. I have this … uh … this whisker that I can't seem to grab hold of."

"You have a whisker?" His voice boomed across the crowds.

I cringed. Was the man deaf? Did he have no consideration for my embarrassment?

"I have the perfect tweezer for whiskers!" He motioned me to follow him a bit farther down the table, booming all the way. "This'll pull out any whisker you can imagine!"

By the time we reached the section he had in mind, at least a dozen women surrounded me, and more kept pouring in. A tall, emaciated-looking woman to my left spoke up. "Tweezers? That's just what I need."

"They'll work wonders on your whiskers," he shouted.

Another woman reached across in front of me. "I'll take a pair."

"Give me two pairs." A gaudily garbed older woman held up her hand. "Both my daughters could use them. No, wait! Give me three!"

Fortunately, after he sold maybe two dozen tweezers to all the other women, he handed a pair to me and winked. Talk about a salesman.

And the tweezers? I still have them, and they still work wonders.

So how about writing a memory you'd like to preserve? There's no time like the present!

[**2020 Note**: I'm now teaching memoirs classes online. If you want help getting started with writing the stories of your life, check out my website franstewart.com]

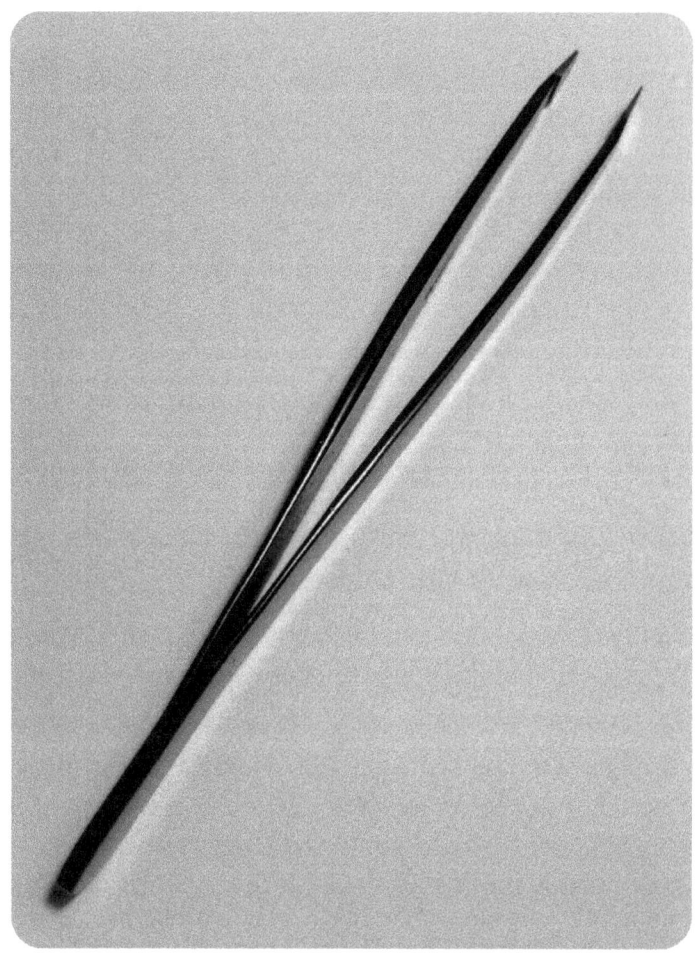

~ ~ ~

Garage Faces

2017-11-10 – I've developed something of a reputation in my neighborhood for being the crazy lady. You know, multiple cats, no apparent job (writing and editing seem to baffle many people), and those faces on the garage door.

I finally had to cover them up, so I painted the garage bright purple with green trim (to match my front door).

One more reason for neighbors to think I'm nuts.

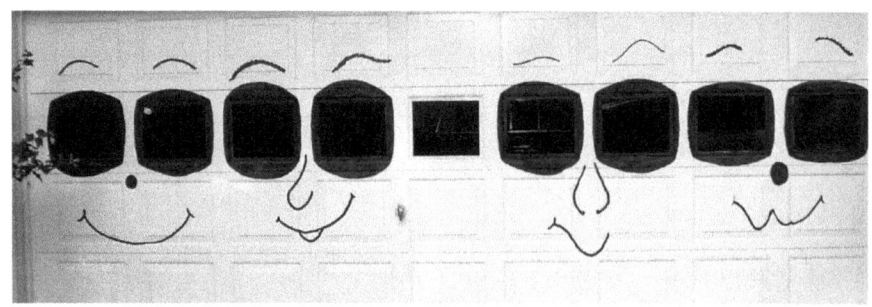

~ ~ ~

Sunset over Sapelo

Saturday November 11th — The sun doesn't disappear when it sets; it simply lights another area of the earth.

In memory of my dad, who was an Air Force man. His sun set a little more than fifteen years ago, but I still feel his light.

Eli and the Tiger

2017-11-12 – Whether he's SCUBA diving with eels or stingless jellyfish or taking the time to get to know a tiger as in this photo, my son surprises me often with his various adventures. He's traveled all over the world, and I get to enjoy the countries vicariously without having to deal with long plane flights, upset tummies, or unexpected horrors (like the tsunami, the bombing, and the earthquake he dealt with).

Of course, I also don't get to talk with the delightful people he meets, see the sights in person, or muddle through trying to say "thank you" and "where's the loo?" in a language I don't understand.

And I certainly don't get to pat a tiger!

~ ~ ~

Abney Park Detail

Monday 2017-11-13 — Lines and circles that intersect, cross, loop around, come back again. I've always been intrigued by such patterns, as depicted in this picture of part of a Celtic cross in Abney Park by Gigi Pandian, who gave me permission to use her photo here.

I got to thinking, though. Such patterns are evolving under my fingertips as I write the last four books of the Biscuit McKee mystery series.

I've been in a quandary for months now, trying to figure out just how to work (or re-work) a particular part of the plot so it makes sense. I've felt like I was up against a maze with no solution. Or a jigsaw with missing pieces. Last night I went to bed wondering how on earth to handle it.

This morning, I awoke with the answer so clearly in my mind it was like a roadmap — another one of those marvelous creations with all the intersecting lines.

Now, all I have to do is go back and rewrite 40 or 50 chapters so all the pieces will fit.

Piece of cake!

And, sometime in 2018, you'll get to read the result…

Photo Used with Permission 1

~ ~ ~

Moon Through Trees

Tuesday 2017-11-14 — I almost never take a photo that looks like it could be from a professional. In part, that's because I don't have a fancy camera. But the real reason is that I don't have "the eye" — that ability to frame a shot to its best advantage.

Several mornings ago I went on my usual walk and couldn't resist trying for the full moon.

Fran Stewart

I love the way the dark outline of trees always seems to highlight the beauty of the moon. All by itself in a bare clear sky, the moon is lovely, of course. But when it's surrounded by trees, mist, clouds, even the outline of a skyscraper, something magical seems to happen.

It reminds me of the way a scene of bare dialogue in a book can be very meaningful, but when enveloped in a sense of place, with descriptions or actions that are vivid but not overwhelming, the words come alive.

One of the examples I use in the memoirs class I teach is the difference between these two lines:

"I don't think so," he said.

and

He moved his fork one quarter of an inch to the right. "I don't think so."

Don't you see this fussy, exacting man more clearly when his words are outlined by that action?

Just as I pay more attention to the moon when there's a tree nearby.

~ ~ ~

Something's Missing

Wednesday 2017-11-15 — Sometimes things just don't go the way you intended.

Take, for instance, the last time Eagle Eye Book Shop in Decatur GA ordered a case of my ScotShop mysteries. *A Wee Murder in My Shop* was perfect. So was *A Wee Homicide in the Hotel*. The second book in the series, *A Wee Dose of Death*, somehow or other ended up with the cover spine misprinted. Here are two pictures. One the way they're supposed to look, and one the way they arrived at Eagle Eye.

Naturally, Penguin/Random House replaced the books at no charge to Eagle Eye. When a company prints and ships out more than a million books a day (or so I've been told) there are bound to be some goofs, but I've been wracking my brain trying to figure out how a saved computer file can leave off half of a title and half of the author's name and still have the rest of the cover unaffected.

Makes the little disruptions in my daily life look insignificant.

Although I really do want to get my broken garage door opener working before icy weather sets in.

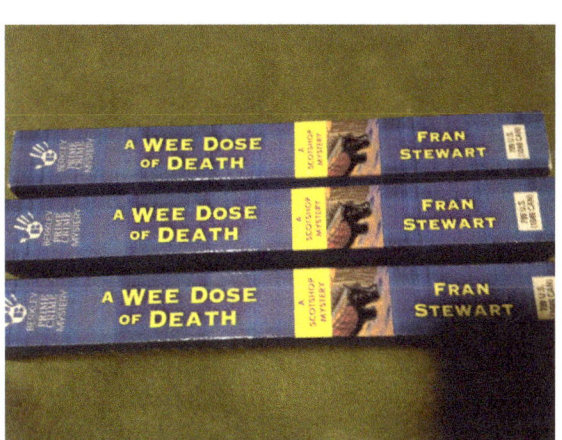 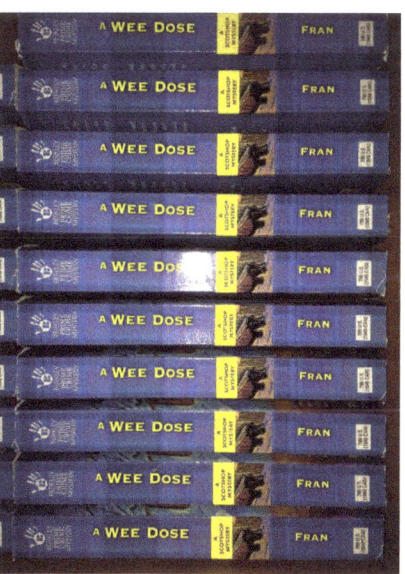

~ ~ ~

Denali and Portage Glacier

Thursday 2017-11-16 — It looks like I've been doing a lot of recycling.

Am I talking paper and cardboard and plastics? No, although I DO recycle those religiously.

I'm talking photographs. In writing these daily Facebook posts, I've been going through my photo files, using pictures taken through the last decade. Ever since I bought a smart phone, all my photos are on my computer, but the ones for today are pictures I just took of photographs from when I visited my son in Alaska in 1996.

I like browsing through old photo albums. The physical ones where you have to turn the pages and sometimes the photos stick together, or the label written on the back bleeds through to mar the face of the person in the picture.

When Eli took me to Denali, I stood in one place and rotated slowly from left to right, snapping pictures as I went. Once the film was developed, I taped seven of them together to turn them into a fold-out marvel for my three-ring Alaska binder. I did the same thing at the Portage Glacier where I posed in one of the life preserver rings.

Nowadays, all you have to do is set a button on your smart phone to give you an instant panorama.

It may be faster, but it's not nearly as much fun.

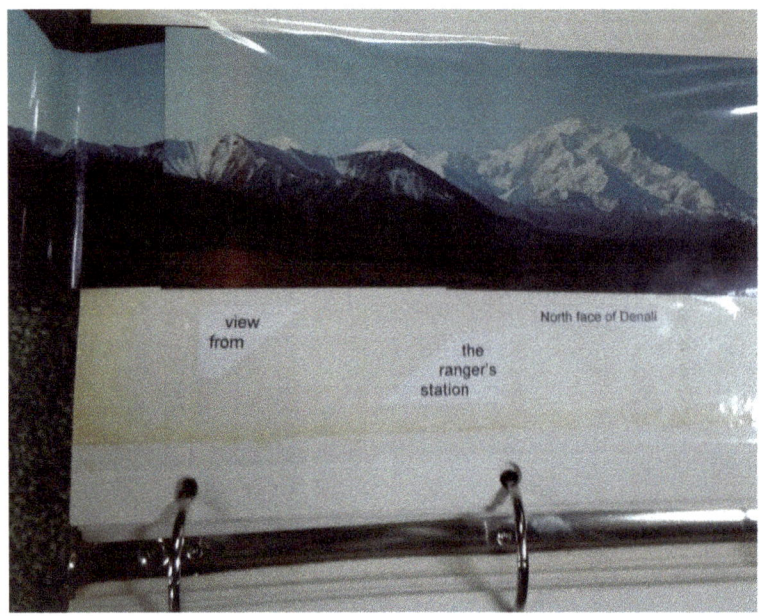

[**2020 Note:** I just looked up Portage Glacier and found that it's described as being 10 stories tall. A story is generally considered to be around 14 feet high. That means that the glacier has shrunk from being 210 feet tall in 1996 (see my note in the photo above) to about 140 feet now in 2020. I'm sure it's still very impressive looking, but what a loss. Why on earth do people think climate change is not a reality?]

~ ~ ~

Rock Climbing

Friday 2017-11-17 — Here it is. Proof that I actually did some rock climbing on a real cliff. These pictures are ones I took of two photos in my Alaska Trip album from 1996. I used this rock-climbing adventure in GREEN AS A GARDEN HOSE, my third Biscuit McKee Mystery, where Biscuit is trying out rock climbing with the help of her son, when a body plummets over the cliff, nearly colliding with her on the way down.

No, there was no dead body falling off my Alaska cliff.

But I'm a writer. What can I say? The ideas just spring up wherever I go and whatever I do.

Fran Stewart

~ ~ ~

BLOG #003 Friday November 17, 2018

Yes, Yes, YES!!! I finally sent RED AS A ROOSTER to my beloved and well-trusted beta-readers. It's getting closer! Still no publication date, since I have to complete writing the other three books first, just in case something develops in one of them that will require me to tweak RED a bit.

As I shared on my Facebook author page last Monday (11/13/2017), one major plot problem got solved in the middle of the night, for I woke with the answers firmly cemented in my head. Fortunately, I wrote myself a long note with details. Why do I say "fortunately"? Because when I reviewed the note several hours later, my mind had already fuzzed over some of the ideas. After the wake-up eureka, it was just a matter of writing like crazy to integrate the solution into RED. (I still have to work it into the other three books, but—like a good road map—I have the answer in my hands.)

In Monday's post, I used a picture of zoomorphic interlacing (otherwise known as Celtic Knots) taken by Gigi Pandian, to describe the workings of my mind. Did I know the term zoomorphic interlacing at the time? Nope. It was supplied in a comment by my marvelous niece, Erica. She's the one who supplied me with Chaucerian words for Dirk to use in my ScotShop mysteries.

Anyway, the interweaving stories in these last four Biscuit McKee mysteries are like a zoomorphic interlacing. Characters introduced in RED AS A ROOSTER show up at different times and places in BLACK AS SOOT, PINK AS A PEONY, and finally, in WHITE AS ICE, where all the questions are answered, all the hanging threads are woven into place, and all my goals as a writer will be fulfilled.

~ ~ ~

Snowflake Tea House

Saturday 2017-11-18 — Okay, I admit it. I pigged out yesterday.

Two of my fans asked if we could meet for tea at the Snowflake Tea House in Duluth GA. Sure! I'd never been there, but it sounded like fun. And it was. Thanks, Emily and Isabelle, for a delightful afternoon.

We got there early, so we practically had the place to ourselves, although it began to get busier an hour and a half later as we left. It took us that long because we had so much to talk about — books and travel and education and writing and the value of reading, and on and on. We laughed about a stationery store whose sign read Stationary Store. "Obviously it's not going anywhere," we quipped.

Snowflake has these marvelous desserts called Shaved Snow, which is basically a very light icy ice cream. We each ordered a different kind, although Emily and I both had Oreos and M&Ms as toppings on ours. Mine, which looks the biggest of the three in this photo, started with dark chocolate ice and caramel sauce.

Emily and Isabelle both began with original (i.e. vanilla) shaved snow.

We all agreed that, along with the oolong tea, this formed a complete meal.

Heck — why not? As long as it doesn't become a habit…

~ ~ ~

Pigeon Visitors

Sunday 2017-11-19 — Do you like drop-in visitors? Do you even ever have drop-in visitors?

I can remember years ago when people felt comfortable stopping by for a quick visit. If the people they wanted to see weren't at home, they'd just come back another day. And often they'd leave a note stuck on the door. "Sorry I missed you."

Nowadays, my only drop-in visitors are birds, like these pigeons on my skylights and the multiple species on the bird feeders and in my yard. Nowadays, all the people call and schedule first. Or, even more often, they seem to do their "visiting" via text messages. All that means to me is that there's less incentive to keep the house picked up. I can pile my 'to be read' books around the floor of my favorite chair and not have to worry about anybody tripping on them. I can let the cat hair accumulate on that same chair, because I'm the only one who's going to pick up hair on my pants.

Now, holidays — that's different. Families or friends gather, giving a darn good incentive for cleaning a bit more than usual.

My book club recently read *The Year of Living Danishly* about a couple who moved from New York to a small town in Denmark. One of the MANY differences was that people in Denmark keep their houses immaculately clean and tidy all the time. It's an esthetic mentality that we American's just don't seem to have absorbed. Okay—maybe YOU keep your house picked up all the time, but I guess I'm not in your league.

So, if you want to drop in for a visit, give it a try. If you don't mind sitting on cat hair and stepping over piles of wondrous books.

And, in the meantime, have a lovely time getting ready for Thanksgiving.

~ ~ ~

Callie's Help

Monday 2017-11-20 — When I send a manuscript off to my beta readers, I generally put my writing on hold until I hear back from them. So I don't mind when Callie sits on top of whatever I've been working on.

Since yesterday afternoon, though, I've been scooting her away, encouraging her to sit on my lap rather than my laptop. I've gotten responses from two of my three beta readers, and—HURRAY!—they've given me exactly the sort of feedback I need in order to tighten the story, get rid of any deadwood, explain a few things better so the reader doesn't get confused, and stick in a few missing quotation marks.

Now all I have to do is decide how to revise two puzzling scenes in RED AS A ROOSTER, then write one last scene in BLACK AS SOOT so it will be ready to go off for its beta read.

This time in the writing of a book is always so impelling. I love doing the final edits, but it wouldn't be possible—at least not for me—without my wonderful beta readers who give so generously of their time to help me make my Biscuit McKee books ready for YOU to read.

Therefore, here's a huge "thank you" to Diana Alishouse, Darlene Carter, and Millie Woollen!

~ ~ ~

Sky with Clouds

Tuesday 2017-11-21 — Remember playing the "Face in the Clouds" game when you were a kid? Or maybe you still do it. I know I do. Amazing what you can find floating around up there.

This picture for instance shows a dog chasing a mouse, about to nip its tail, a gargoyle peeking out from between two groups of branches, and a very pregnant seahorse (as well as a heart in the lower left corner). There's a blue-beaked duck, too.

Head outside and look up. No telling what you'll see!

~ ~ ~

Teach Us

Wednesday 2017-11-22 — On a trip to visit friends in Florida a few years ago, I snapped this picture of a tiny yellow flower. It was the only one in a wide patch of green leaves, and I wondered why it had popped open when there were no companion flowers nearby.

Brave little soul! Teach us how to bloom.

~ ~ ~

Diana in 1946

Thursday 2017-11-23 — There are so many reasons I'm thankful this year, but I thought I'd show you the picture of one that is a foundation stone in my life. My big sister, Diana, who wrote *Depression Visible: The Ragged Edge*. http://depressionvisible.com

Growing up, she paved the way for me. She fought the battles that I wouldn't have to fight later. She is one of my greatest fans. She provides a ready ear if I need to cry or vent or just laugh.

I love her dearly, and I delight in this chance to tell you how special she is to me.

Wishing you a joy-filled Thanksgiving Day.

Fran Stewart

~ ~ ~

Nose and Tail

Friday 2017-11-24 — I'm spending the next few days after the holiday completely engrossed in my writing. Fuzzy Britches keeps me company, curled in a circle against the cold, her tail touching her nose, reminding me that sometimes hibernation works just fine.

It's not my nose that's cold, though. It's my hands. So I put my wrist warmers on to keep from shivering when I touch the laptop — these are basically just narrow tubes I knitted that reach from the middle of my palm to halfway up my forearm. It's surprising how much warmer I am in this drafty house when I take care of myself this way.

Take care of yourself this weekend.

~ ~ ~

BLOG #004 Monkey Label

Friday 2017-11-24 — Researching a book during the writing phase is so much fun.

http://www.peachridgeglass.com/2012/08/merchants-gargling-oil-good-for-man-and-beast/

Young Gideon Hastings and his family figure prominently in the quartet of books that will complete the Biscuit McKee mysteries. Although his father dislikes the idea, Young Gideon is determined to be a veterinarian, so he apprentices himself to the elderly town vet and eventually takes over the practice when the old doctor dies.

One of the scenes I loved writing was one in which Young Gideon tries out a new liniment on one of the horses, while the mother of the horse's owner watches him. Of course, I wanted to use an actual liniment that was popular in the early 1800s. Blessings on the Internet. I found Merchant's Gargling Oil (really!). Why the word "gargling" got into the title is a complete mystery, for it was not to be gargled, but to be applied externally.

As soon as I saw the monkey on the label and read the description of the oil's long list of uses (everything from skin rashes to hemorrhoids), I knew I had to use it in my book.

Be sure to sign up for my newsletter, because the next one I send out will include this favorite scene.

~ ~ ~

Wrapped-up Grandchild

Saturday 2017-11-25 — A number of summers ago, the weather was hot and muggy, so my grandkids and I stayed inside and looked for something to do. Cellphones were off limits at Grannie's house, and I don't have a TV, so it's amazing what we could come up with each week when they visited me.

I'd just gotten a shipment of books, packed in long, wide swaths of newsprint. What better use than to let my grandkids make presents out of themselves.

It's easy to tell this photo was taken a number of years ago, just by looking at Aiden's arms. Now he's on his high school's wrestling team, with biceps that bulge with power.

I love watching how people grow and change.

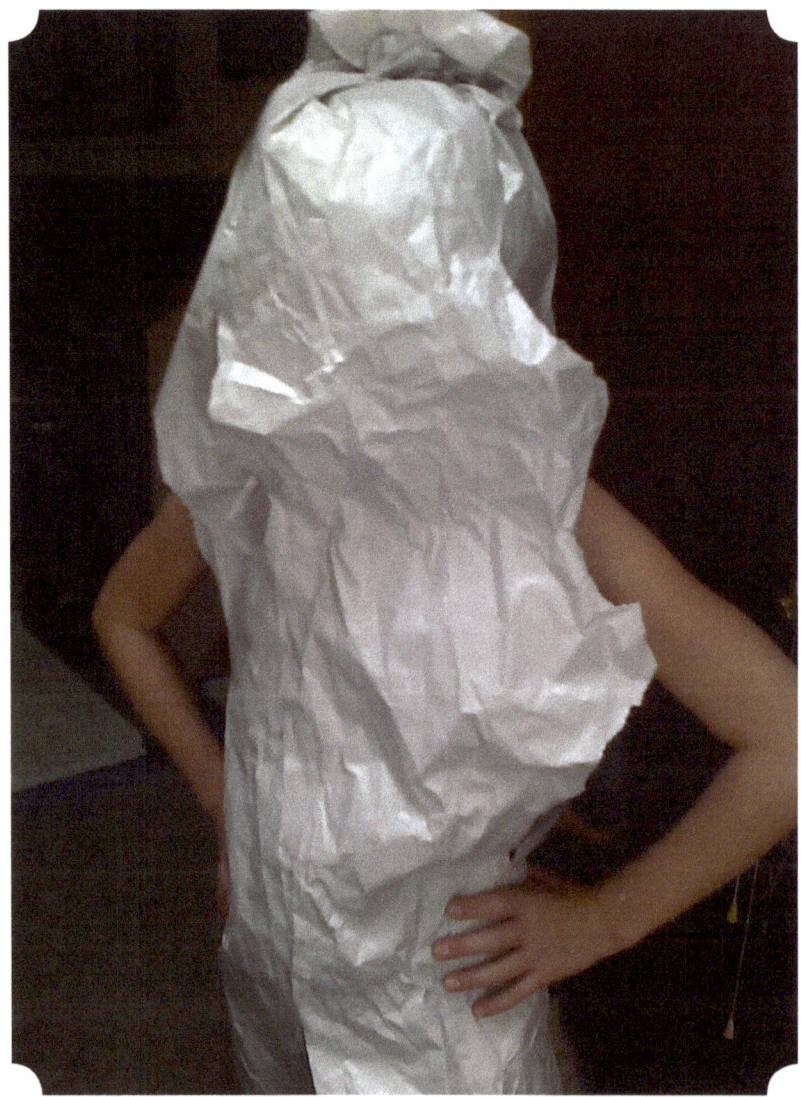

~ ~ ~

Julie Porath's Chickens

Sunday 2017-11-26 — It's just as well that I got over my fear of chickens before I started writing RED AS A ROOSTER.

Why was I afraid of chickens? Because when I was four or five, my grandmother sent me down to the hen house to collect a basket of eggs. The hens' nests were on a built-up tier that was taller than I was, which meant the hens loomed over me as they sat on their eggs. And they pecked the heck out of my hands when I tried to reach into their nests.

So, I grew up convinced that chickens were at least six feet tall.

When I mentioned that to Julie Porath, who was selling eggs at a farmer's market half a dozen years ago, she said, "Well, you obviously haven't met my sweet chickens."

The upshot of it was that I visited her spread, met her hens (and Rocky the rooster), and ended up actually holding Lacey, one of the gentle young hens, and kissing her on the top of her soft head.

I'm a convert. Chickens are great.

~ ~ ~

Wooly Bear in the Sink

Monday 2017-11-27 — Don't you love the way cats and dogs and just about every other animal I know can simply curl up anywhere and be absolutely comfortable?

Can you do that?

Small children can, but I lost the ability a number of decades ago. Porcelain and wood floors and even carpeted floors just aren't squishy. I want my couch to be comfy, my bed to be comfy, my chair to be comfy.

If a sink were large enough, would I curl up in it the way Wooly Bear curls up to watch me when I brush my hair at night? Well, no, I probably wouldn't.

Would you?

~ ~ ~

Pink

Tuesday 2017-11-28 — It's not even full winter yet, and here I am gazing at pictures of flowers. Brrrr!

Spring really is my favorite season.

~ ~ ~

No Frigate Like a Book

Wednesday 2017-11-29 — "There is no Frigate like a Book / To take us Lands away," Emily Dickinson wrote in a letter in 1873. Her words are just as true today as they were 144 years ago.

Have you gone sailing away into a good book lately?

If so, which book?

If not, why not?

~ ~ ~

Genie's green ornament

Thursday 2017-11-30 — Serendipity: the development of events by chance in a happy or beneficial way. I love serendipity. I come across it all the time. Such as the day I saw a young mother walking around the cul-de-sac with her little girl and a baby carriage. I went out to say hello, expecting just to meet a neighbor. After that day, I often saw Heather (the mom) and Hannah (the child) and Holden (the baby).

Then, one day, it was the grandmother instead of the mom walking with little Hannah. Naturally, I went out to say hello.

Genie Guthrie has turned out to be one of the delights of my life. Last year she gifted me with a light catcher she made that combines all the colors of my Stewart tartan, along with two tiny Scottie dog charms. I have a chandelier over the table where I write, so I suspended her gift there where it catches the afternoon sun pouring through one of my skylights.

Have you met any new neighbors lately? No telling how wonderful that might turn out to be.

Fran Stewart

December 2017

BLOG #005 - Postcard Story from Folly Beach—Friday December 1st

Whenever I travel, I compose a short fun story for my five grandchildren, write it on fifteen or twenty postcards without numbering them, address three or four cards to each of the five (plus a couple for Mom and Dad), and mail them.

When the cards arrive, all out of order, my daughter saves them until I return from my trip, at which point everybody gathers in the living room, the postcards are distributed to the addressees to be read aloud. Of course, they have to figure out what the order is. The first card always starts with "Once upon a time," and the last one always ends with "Love, Grannie."

Since each card generally ends in the middle of a sentence, it can take a while to muddle through the possibilities, but we always have a good laugh as various sentence endings are tried out and rejected until somebody comes up with the right one.

This particular story is about a seagull named Gullwana who lived in the kingdom of Folly Beach. I was there in the fall of 2013 with a number of artist friends who would all disperse during the day to paint, draw, or photograph while I stayed in the beach house and wrote. In the evenings, we'd eat a meal together and then talk for hours. By the last evening, I had my postcard story written, so I handed out the cards and let them try to figure out the sequence.

I've written about an alligator named Willagator, five moose children who saved a cow whose leg was stuck between two rocks, a gathering of small animals on Nanny Goat Beach who were accompanied by a witch, two royal frogs named Plop and Fromena, … and so on.

Writing a postcard story is good experience for an author because:

    it definitely gets the creative juices flowing;

    it has to be succinct;

    it hones one's "beginning, middle, end" skills; and

it provides a good alternative to sitting there wondering how to deal with the next scene in the latest work-in-progress.

Once I finish the postcard story, I'm usually raring to get back to whatever writing project I'm working on.

You didn't know writers had such sneaky tricks, did you?

You did?

Oh. Well then, why don't you try writing a postcard story yourself? It's loads of fun.

****

Tomorrow, I'll be appearing at the Athens Regional Library for their "How Outlandish" Festival, where I've been asked to compare Diana Gabaldon's ghost of Jamie Fraser to my ghost, Dirk Farquharson. If you're anywhere near Athens GA, come enjoy all the Scottish exhibits from 10 to 4:30—and hear me speak at 11am.

~ ~ ~

K-9s

Friday 2017-12-1 — Did I ever tell you about the time I took the Gwinnett County Citizen Police Academy? One of our classes dealt with the K-9 officers. We had a chance to learn about the way they're trained, we got to ask loads of questions, we saw the dogs run through some of their routines.

Then, we were asked, "Does anybody want to put on the padded suit and actually get attacked by a dog?"

Growing up in a military family, one thing I learned was the hard and fast rule NEVER VOLUNTEER.

So, naturally, I volunteered.

I've been bitten by dogs twice—once when I was in my twenties, once in my thirties. I must admit to a fair amount of terror at the thought of having a highly trained Belgian Malinois charge me at full speed.

It didn't take him ten seconds to wrest me to the ground.

Once they called off the dog and he loosened his grip on my (well-padded) arm, I couldn't bend in the middle, so I couldn't stand up.

The very polite young officer grabbed the "Michelin Man Suit" at the back of my neck and a foot or so farther down and levitated me to an upright position. My academy classmates never let me live that down.

Fran Stewart

~ ~ ~

Saturday 2017-12-2 — Although I never sleep in very late (because of three hungry cats who meow or butt my head—BREAKFAST TIME, MOM!), there are some mornings when this is my reaction to the daylight: YAWN…

After I witnessed the birth of three tiny toy poodles at my friend Jan's house in Hilo, Hawaii a couple of years ago, during which process I was completely in awe, Jan kept me apprised of their growth with photos like this one.

Did you ever watch the birth of puppies or kittens?

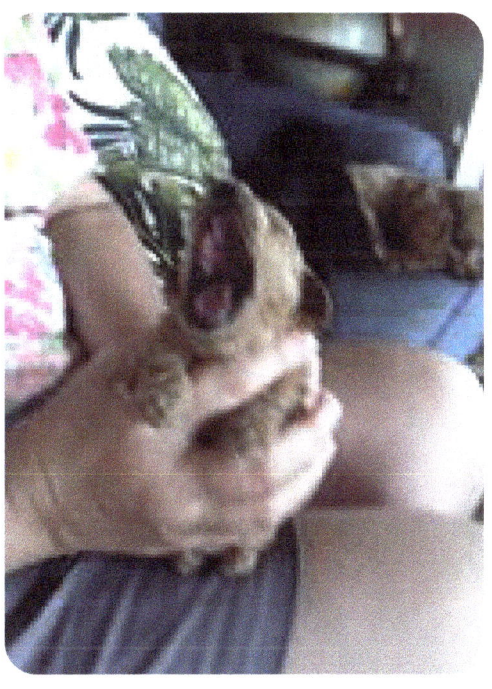

~ ~ ~

With Claire and Jamie

Sunday 2017-12-3 — What fun I had yesterday at the "Outlandish in Athens" Festival at the Athens Area Regional Library. I had a great time reading from Diana Gabaldon's books and comparing Jamie Fraser to Dirk, my ghost in my ScotShop Mysteries.

We were told that there would be a very exciting announcement coming soon related to the library — but Joy, the coordinator of the event, wouldn't breathe a word about the details. I'll be sure to let you know as soon as the "whatever" is made public.

~ ~ ~

Super Moon

Monday 2017-12-4 — Did you see the supermoon last night or early this morning? I did, and it was spectacular. The good news is that there will be two more chances for you to see it next month—on Dec 30 – Jan1 and Jan 30 – Jan 31.

You can read all about it in this article from Forbes, which is where I found these two photos.

https://www.forbes.com/sites/trevornace/2017/12/03/tonight-supermoon-supermoon-2017/#18ec77a33fac

Clear as Mud

~ ~ ~

Great Big Bear

Tuesday 2017-12-5 — Some time ago I shared this photo, but it bears repeating (pun intended). I was at my friend Peggy's mountain cabin when this huge bruin ambled along the gravel path, stopped and looked in the window at us (although I've read that bears are rather near-sighted, so I wonder just how much he saw as we stood there breathless), and then walked on. We gave him plenty of time not only to disappear into the woods but to keep going. Then we went outside and checked out his footprints.

Later we learned that bears tend to travel regular paths, often stepping exactly into the footprints they made the last time(s) they walked that way.

Fran Stewart

Creatures of habit?

Do you tend to step in the same footprints you've made before — or are you ready for a new path, a new adventure?

Lessons from nature.

~ ~ ~

Cat Watching Kites

Wednesday 2017-12-6 — If you haven't seen the kites flown by Ray Bethell, you really do need to. I've watched this video (©2004) countless times, and I enjoy it at every single repetition. My cats like it too, as you can see.

And whoever paired up the kites to the Flower Duet from "Lakme" by Leo Delibes was truly inspired.

https://www.youtube.com/embed/nr9KrqN_lIg

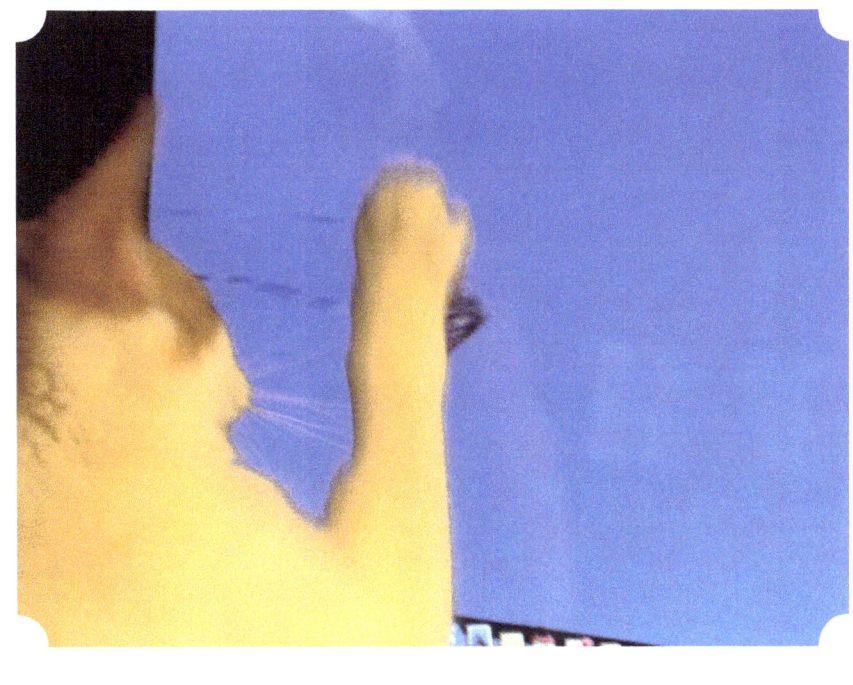

~ ~ ~

Before and After

Thursday 2017-12-7 — Earlier this week, some friends and I went to see "The Man Who Invented Christmas." I thought it was a delightful movie, weaving all the "what-ifs" together in an incredibly well-crafted tale of how Charles Dickens came to write *A Christmas Carol*.

If you've ever wondered even vaguely what we writers go through as we put our stories together, you might want to watch that movie. Now, I'll admit, I never rage around my office throwing books on the floor, but I could completely identify with the pages and pages of scribbled-on, marked-up, and sometimes torn-up pages.

But my characters DO tend to visit me at night or dawn or mid-morning or afternoon, walking into whatever else I'm trying to accomplish and simply deciding to do things their own way regardless of what I (the mere author) think they should be doing.

Rather the way terraces in Thailand turn from mud into green, as shown in these photos my son Eli Reiman took when he lived in that country for a year.

Fran Stewart

~ ~ ~

BLOG #006 Friday December 8, 2017—Ideas

One of the most common questions anyone ever asks a writer is "Where do you get your ideas?"

It's a good question, one for which there doesn't seem to be an answer. "Everywhere" doesn't quite capture it; "They just come out of the woodwork" seems a bit flippant; "I dream them" is true only part of the time; and "I live with my characters long enough that they start telling me what to write" garners funny looks from non-writers who've never experienced such a phenomenon.

You see, getting the idea to begin with isn't the problem. The problem—or, as I prefer to think of it, the adventure—is to take that germ of an idea and turn it into what feels like a living breathing entity.

My ScotShop mysteries came about when my agent said, "Could you craft a three-book series around the idea of someone buying something in Scotland—something that has a ghost attached to it?"

Well, of course I could! The moment he asked me the question, my 14th-century Scottish ghost jumped out of my brain and into my heart.

My Biscuit McKee series started when I heard Harriet Austin speak about how to write a mystery. She said, "Just start writing, and if your characters come alive, you'll know you have a winner." Then she paused and said, "Be sure you put a body somewhere in the first five pages—it's expected."

So I looked down at my notepad and started writing:

There had definitely not been a body on the second floor landing when I had run up to the attic earlier in the evening, but there definitely was a body, and a rather messy one at that, when I sauntered downstairs after a leisurely snack. I have never been very squeamish, but I do admit to pausing a moment before I stepped gingerly over the leg that jutted out on the hardwood floor where the staircase turned down to the left.

I looked at what I'd just written and said (silently of course, for Ms. Austin was still giving her speech) "Who the heck are you?"

I had no idea at that moment that Marmalade, the orange and white library cat, had just stepped, fully alive, from my pen to my paper to my brain. Or maybe she was in my brain to begin with. I don't know. I only know that that exact paragraph became the opening lines of ORANGE AS MARMALADE.

Once the cat was there, the other characters, such as the librarian Biscuit McKee, simply stepped into place.

I'm making it sound awfully easy, which may be something of a disservice to all the writers (such as myself) who struggle at times to get the right words on the paper.

If you'd really like to see this process, I'd suggest you go to see "The Man Who Invented Christmas," a delightful movie about how Charles Dickens wrote "A Christmas Carol." Pay particular attention to the Fezziwigs, who dance on a street in London before they dance in his book. And to Tara, the maidservant who becomes Dickens' treasured beta-reader, one who is brave enough to say, "It just wouldn't happen that way! You can't kill Tiny Tim!"

In writing RED AS A ROOSTER (yes, I promise it will be published sometime in early 2018!), I had an entire family descend on me, from Robert Hastings, an innkeeper, and Jane Elizabeth Benton Hastings, his sturdy wife who becomes something of a town hero, right down through nine generations, complete with a wonderful couple (Grace and Arthur Hastings) to a real scoundrel (Gideon Hastings) who finally—and most satisfactorily—gets what's coming to him. In fact, when I wrote that particular Gideon scene, I ended up cheering.

The next time you feel like cheering (or crying or groaning or yelling or laughing) when you read a scene, will you be able to imagine the author doing the same thing?

~ ~ ~

Wooly Bear with My Tea Cozy

Friday 2017-12-8 — Sigh! Wooly Bear is at it again. I knitted a tea cozy—I know, I know it looks like a hat, but it really is designed to keep my teapot warm—and for the first few months I had it, it sat on my teapot keeping the tea piping hot.

Until Wooly Bear entered my life and discovered the cozy.

I finally took off the little pompom thing and gave it to Wooly Bear. She seems perfectly content. For now.

~ ~ ~

Owl in Flight

Saturday 2017-12-9 — Snow in Georgia! I use an exclamation point because snow here is a rare occurrence. I've lived near the Green Mountains and in the Rocky Mountains. I know what snow—real snow—is supposed to be like. But here? Two or three inches is considered MAJOR. Heck—half an inch is considered major.

My local Wild Birds Unlimited store (where I buy all my birdseed) recently hosted an owl program put on by someone from the Georgia Department of Natural Resources. It put me in mind of the time long ago when I lived in Vermont. A friend of mine struck a sawhet owl with her car, and the owl, still alive, was stuck on the car's grill.

I contacted a friend of mine who was a birder. She took the sawhet to a vet who determined that its wing was shattered, and through a long and tortuous process, my friend got her license to rehabilitate injured raptors. "Fender"—what else were we going to name him?—became the first of the educational birds that she took to schools to teach people about the importance of raptors in the food chain. That one injured bird led her to her life's work, and I was honored to be invited once to witness the release of four raptors back into the wild and another time to hold a great snowy owl while she administered medication to it.

This stunning owl photo, copyrighted by Robert Skreiner, is the 16th of 39 bird photos on the following website: https://uldissprogis.com/2015/04/10/sharing-39-inspiring-beautiful-birds/ (Just keep scrolling down until you find it.)

I spent a VERY long time coursing through the various selections of bird photos on this site and wishing I had a picture of little Fender.

Meanwhile, I'm enjoying the snow.

~ ~ ~

Shadows on Snow

Sunday 2017-12-10 — Did you ever notice how shadows on sand look a lot like shadows on snow?

I took a gorgeous sand photo at Nanny Goat Beach on Sapelo Island, but I can't get it to upload for some reason. You'll have to take my word for it that it's similar to this royalty-free snow shadow image from shutterstock.

p.s. – Here's one I took at Sapelo. Not the one I'd intended to show you, but I like this one as well.

~ ~ ~

Ladder & Bag

Monday 2017-12-11 — Some days I feel on top of the world, the way I did when I climbed the ladder truck during the Gwinnett County Citizen Fire Academy. Other days I feel like hiding somewhere so nobody can see me.

But no matter how I feel, I always try to remember the words of Mike Dooley in his "Notes from the Universe: Perpetual Flip Calendar" when he said:

> "Exactly where you have been
> has made possible
> exactly where you are…"
> © 2010 Mike Dooley

Today, I'm feeling out of the bag and about halfway up the ladder.

All is well.

~ ~ ~

Sapelo Trees from 2012

Tuesday 2017-12-12 — This week will be the height of the Geminid meteor showers.

It's not enough to hope for a power outage and a cloudless night. We have to walk outside and look up.

Amazing what you can see when you do that.

p.s. I know I used this photo last month, but it's so glorious, I'm happy to show it again.

~ ~ ~

Angry People Poster

Wednesday December 13 — What a shame that some people can't seem to get through the holidays without becoming really grumpy. I think a lot of it must come from feeling helpless to accomplish all they want to accomplish. Feeling helpless is never a very happy way to be, so they have to make up for it somehow or other.

The next time you run across someone like that, just remember that we get to choose how we respond to situations in life.

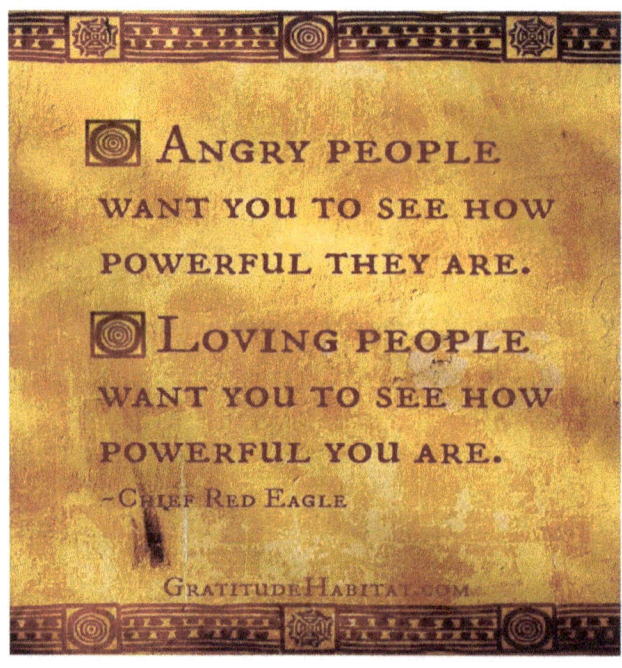

~ ~ ~

Sand Shadows

Thursday 2017-12-14 — Here's the photo I tried to upload a few days ago.

Is this, or is this not, a demonstration of the "if at first you don't succeed..." principle?

~ ~ ~

BLOG #007 - Different kinds of memoirs—Friday December 15, 2017

Whenever my next-door neighbors go on vacation, I cat-sit Cousteau and Picnic. The two cats write daily letters to their mom and dad, telling all about our various adventures. Naturally, they have a lot to say about food.

The letters are a cross between the postcard stories I write for my grandchildren whenever I'm away from home and my own memoirs.

As I tell the folks who take the memoirs classes I teach, memoirs come in a lot of different forms. I take photos of the cat diaries so that—years later—I can remember seeing the sharp-shinned hawk in their back yard or recall the day the tree fell across their fence during the hurricane. Some days are ordinary, some are spectacular, but all are worth writing about.

Have you ever wondered how much of herself a writer puts into her books? Of course, the answer will vary depending on who's doing the writing, but I tend to sprinkle myself around quite liberally in my books, particularly in my Biscuit McKee Mysteries. Of course, the fun of being a writer is that we can revise our personal history somewhat by being very selective about what we tell, just as I select what to tell Cousteau and Picnic's mom and dad about what happens while they're gone.

For some reason this reminds me of a bumper sticker I saw once that said "Don't anger a writer. You'll end up dead in her next book."

Don't tell anybody, but I did that once…

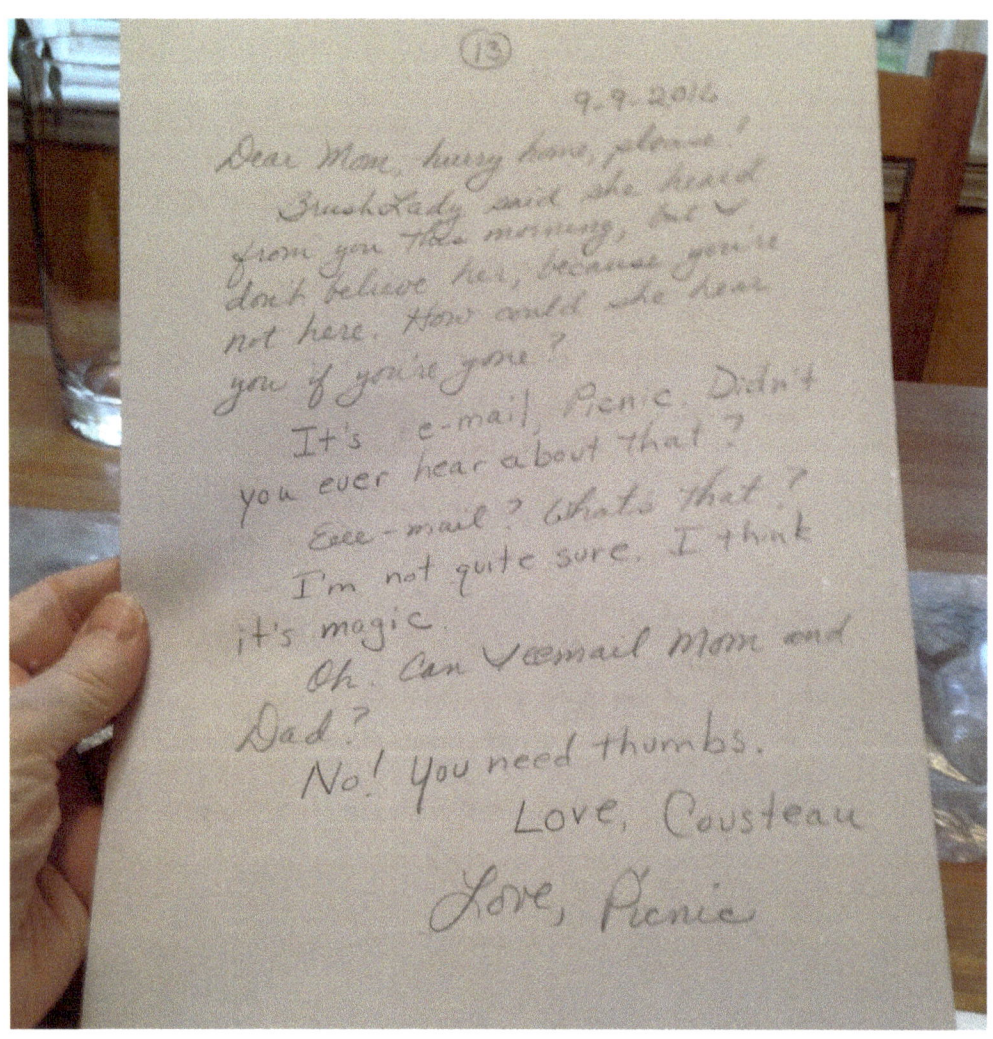

~ ~ ~

Matching Pinks

Friday 2017-12-15 — It's the middle of winter. Despite the cold outside, I can still vividly remember what it was like being beside the azaleas in my front yard at the end of March ten years ago. It was only after my friend Darlene took the picture that we realized my lipstick and turtleneck were color-coordinated with the flowers.

In my Biscuit McKee Mysteries, Biscuit thinks it's the height of fashion when her socks match her turtleneck.

Come to think of it, so do I.

~ ~ ~

Paw

Saturday 2017-12-16 — Bye-bye to this week and hello to the upcoming one.

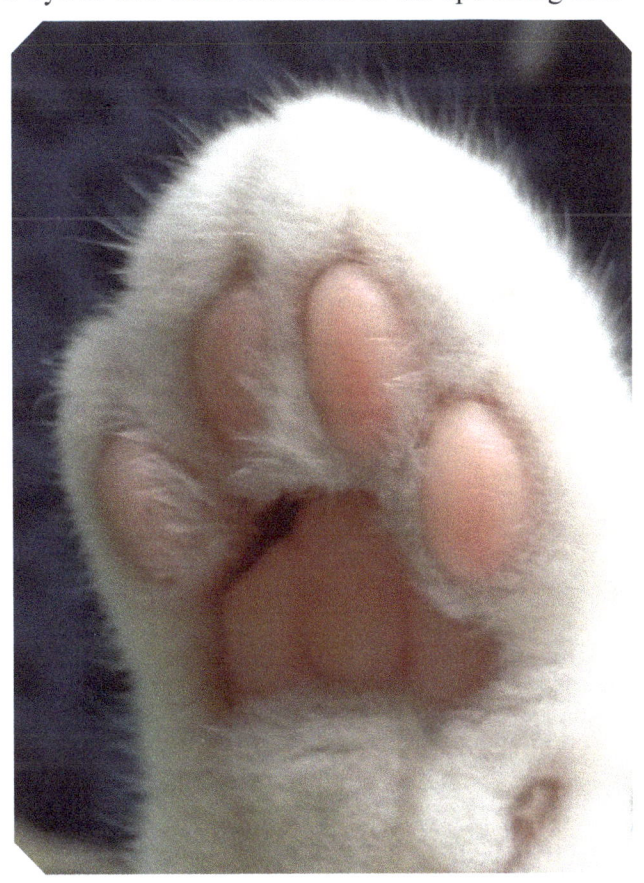

~ ~ ~

Polly and the Piano Cat

Sunday 2017-12-17 — My son's been playing the piano now for several years, dedicating quite a bit of time to practicing, learning, and enjoying it. He sent me a photo recently of his playing in a magnificent deserted hotel ballroom that he found while on a business trip. Since nobody was in there, he preempted the grand piano and played for several hours.

It reminded me of how Miss Polly used to love sitting on my lap when I played. Imagine her delight when I found an internet site showing a cat playing a piano. If I was there to keep playing it over and over, she was willing to listen and watch over and over.

~ ~ ~

Reading Glasses

Monday 2017-12-18 — Since I found more than 24 billion hits when I went to try to find out where this delightful cartoon came from originally, I assume there's a good chance you've already seen it. At least it says Keren in the lower corner, but I was unable to figure out just who this Keren is. At any rate, with 24 billion presences on the Internet, it is assumed that "Keren" is immortal in one way or another.

I use my own reading glasses extensively. I have four different books going at the moment. *Christy*, by Catherine Marshall, the story of a 19-year-old who moved to Appalachia to teach at a Quaker mission school; *My Name is Memory* by Ann Brashares, a CD book about two young people who have lived through many lifetimes together—he remembers all of them, while she doesn't recall any of them; and yet another in a string of Jodi Picoult CD books (this one in my car) about an Amish teenager who is accused of infanticide. My final book is *The Other Einstein* by Marie Benedict, the story of Albert Einstein's brilliant first wife.

How can I keep four stories straight at the same time? Why do you even have to ask? Each one is distinct, and each author has her own unique voice. It's kind of like having four conversations during a day, each with a different friend.

~ ~ ~

2013 Lego Tower

Tuesday 2017-12-19 — Four years ago, when I'd just started to let my hair grow long, my granddaughter and I went to the Gwinnett Environmental and Heritage Center to see an exhibit about architecture. Turned out the Lego company had a corner of the exhibit area dedicated to their oversized blocks. Naturally, we had to play.

More recently, as in the last two months, I've started swimming twice a week for exercise, but since I don't really know how to swim, it's more like playing. I run in place in the 4-foot deep section, and then flutter kick a lot.

What have you played at recently?

~ ~ ~

Tap Dance and Soft Shoe

Wednesday 2017-12-20 — How can anyone not enjoy tap dance and old soft-shoe routines?

Tap dance is so much fun, I had to have Biscuit McKee and her friends begin lessons in GREEN AS A GARDEN HOSE, my third Biscuit McKee Mystery.

Here's one of my favorites. I hope you enjoy it.

[**2020 Note:** The link I included with this post is no longer available. This is why I encourage people who take my memoirs classes to keep printed copies of their life-stories. You never know when your computer may crash, the link may disappear, or the technology may change in such a way as to make things unreachable.]

~ ~ ~

Family with Postcards

Thursday 2017-12-21 — Back on the first of December I wrote about the postcard stories I send my grandkids each time I travel. Then, while I was browsing through photos to share with you (and looking for something to write about other than my dentist visit later today) I came across this five-year-old photo of our gathering to read the story. The only person missing is my son-in-law, Edwin. He has an uncanny ability to avoid pictures, but the single postcard on the front of the coffee table is his, with the address blanked out, of course.

When I was a kid you could believe a photo. Nowadays that truism is no longer true, since there are so many tools that even I can figure out, like the fancy little cover-it-up gadget. I used it on December first to hide every single address on every single postcard pictured there. If I wanted to waste the time figuring out how to do it, I could probably learn how to take one of my other pictures of Edwin and stick him in this one next to his wife.

But a) it's too much trouble, b) it's absolutely unnecessary, and c) I have better things to do. After all, once I finish with the dentist, I'll have the whole rest of the day available to write!

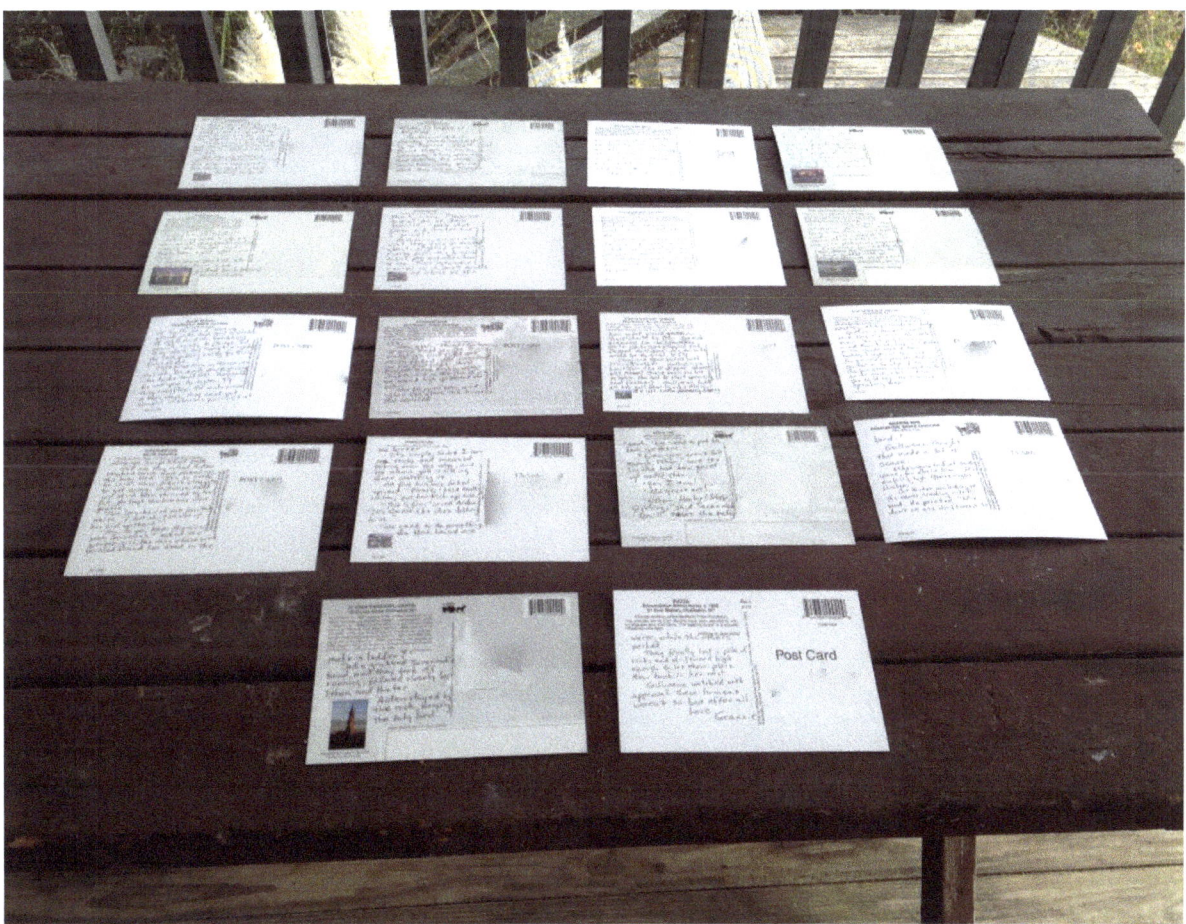

~ ~ ~

Cow in the Field

Friday 2017-12-22 — With so little to do this week (I never decorate for the holidays, nor do I send cards or gifts) I can resonate with this cow I photographed at Rancho Alegre Farm a couple of years ago when I went there to buy goat milk. She lay there chewing her cud, and I stood for the longest time after I snapped the photo, just enjoying the quiet peace of the place.

Then I drove home to my quiet, peaceful house and sat on the porch for a while, enjoying the birdsong that always fills my front yard.

Then I went inside and enjoyed the quiet peaceful presence of my cats (as well as a little catly craziness as they ran around chasing feather toys).

Sometimes peacefulness comes as a gift. Sometimes we have to stop long enough to make it happen.

Where do you find quiet peace?

Monsters Unknown

Friday 2017-12-22 — I've always like praying mantids. Sometimes they're called *preying* mantids, and I'm learning that the second name is more appropriate.

Whatever they're called, one of them showed up on my hummingbird feeder last summer. I welcomed her, remembering fondly the time way back when in Vermont when we ordered a couple of mantis egg cases. When they arrived, we put one in the garden and kept the other one inside so we could watch them hatch.

Naturally, they hatched when we weren't there to see. I don't recall whether it was night or while we were away at work during the day, but we found the baby mantids (or mantises if you prefer) greedily chomping on each other. Naturally, we whisked the terrarium right outdoors and released them all.

Except for one little critter that seemed to like it in the terrarium. I spent hours collecting bugs for her to eat. She got used to walking onto my outstretched finger to take the bugs I offered her, and she grew to a substantial size before I finally let her go.

One day I was weeding a garden patch and a mantid appeared on a nearby flower. Every time I'd seen a mantid that summer, I'd stretched my finger out, but all the mantids reared up on their hind legs and tried to scare me away. With that particular one, though, I stretched out my index finger and she stalked up onto it as if to ask, "So, where's my bug?"

Talk about a moment in nature!

So, when a mantid came to my hummingbird feeder a couple of months ago, I carefully coaxed her onto a stick and transferred her to a plant that had a sizable collection of bugs on it, thinking she'd be happy with such a readily available food source. The next morning she was back on the hummingbird feeder.

This went on for a couple of days, and she finally disappeared. I sighed and went back to writing.

Imagine how appalled I was to find out some weeks later that preying mantids are quite capable of catching and eating a hummingbird. She hadn't been resting on my feeder—she'd been waiting for dinner to come to her.

Phooey on that!

If she shows up again next summer, I plan to evict her.

Victor Borge https://www.youtube.com/watch?v=yCj7OIG1Lrw

Saturday 2017-12-23 — Remember Victor Borge? Oh my gosh, how I've enjoyed laughing along with him for years. Thank goodness he's well-preserved on YouTube. Here's a link to a 1986 Royal Command Performance for the Queen Mother. The show lasts 2 and a half hours. If you want to see only Borge, he starts 10 minutes and 13 seconds into the show.

In this particular skit he talks about Mozart. You know Mozart? "The Danish composer — Hans Christian Mozart."

Love it!

~ ~ ~

Iceland Christmas

Sunday December 24, 2017 — The most literate country in the world. We could learn a thing or two from Iceland.

CBS's Christmas Card

https://www.facebook.com/art.baxter.98/videos/956503831090853/

Monday December 25, 2017 — Does anyone remember this Christmas Card from CBS that first ran in 1966?

It was designed by R.O. Blechman and animated by Willis Pyle. Music arranged by Arnie Black.

It's well worth watching every year.

Whatever holiday you celebrate, I wish you peace and joy.

The Nicest Thing

Tuesday December 26, 2017 — What's one of the nicest things about the holiday? Visits from old friends. I'm looking forward to breakfast in a few hours with a longtime friend who moved away from Georgia a number of years ago. Thanks to FaceTime, we keep in regular touch, but it's just not quite the same as sitting across from each other later this morning at my kitchen table.

'Bye for now. I have breakfast to cook!

Fran Stewart

~ ~ ~

Static

Wednesday December 27, 2017 — When your grandson gets a lounge thing you fill with air, and he lets Grannie try it out and she gets all comfortable for a while and then tries to get up, only her hair has gone all static-crazy, well, this is what you get.

Did anything this interesting happen to you on Christmas day?

~ ~ ~

The Promise

Thursday December 28, 2017 — In my journal one year ago, I wrote that WHITE AS ICE was up to 156,000 words and I was probably going to have to divide it into two books. But now the draft is 383,795 words—four books. I still have the final murder to solve and the last few questions to be answered - but I

PROMISE it will be complete within a few months.

Then, more beta reads and final tweaks and copy-proofing. No date set for the first release yet, but I'll let you know as soon as it's scheduled. In the meantime, be sure you sign up for my newsletter at <u>franstewart.com</u> so you can get a preview chapter every couple of months.

~ ~ ~

Love

Friday December 29, 2017 — This is the time of year when people post all sorts of thoughtful, warm year-end wishes, filled with insight and wisdom, written concisely and with clarity, grammatically correct and logically compelling, gently witty and deeply compassionate.

Then there was this post:

> Why did the run-on sentence think she was pregnant?
>
> >
>
> >
>
> She was missing her period.

~ ~ ~

BLOG #009 How Can an X-ray Help a Writer?

Fran Stewart

Friday December 29, 2017 — Now I ask you, how can an X-ray help a writer? No, this is not the start of a really bad joke, although I could probably spend (waste?) an hour or two thinking up possible punchlines.

An X-ray shows what's going on in the structure of a body. Is this particular disc compressed? Is that particular vertebra out of alignment?

In much the same way, a flow-chart or outline or genealogical table or storyboard or story web delineates what's going on in the structure (the spine) of a novel. Each writer finds what works best — but sometimes what works for one book won't quite work for the next book in that same series, so a writer goes with the flow, just the way a chiropractor may use various methods of treatment depending on how the spine is (or isn't) responding.

For my upcoming final four Biscuit McKee mysteries, which span a timeline from 1692 to the 21st century, what started as a simple chart listing the six major founding families of Martinsville eventually turned into a separate page for each family with notes that told who in which family married into which other family. As I went along, I added birth, marriage, and death dates, notes about which attic "treasure" went with which person, who in the current-day attic descended from which founder, as well as any other pertinent info I needed quick access to.

Just to give you an idea, here's a picture of half of one page showing part of the Hastings family.

Believe me, the completed books will be much easier to understand than my chart!

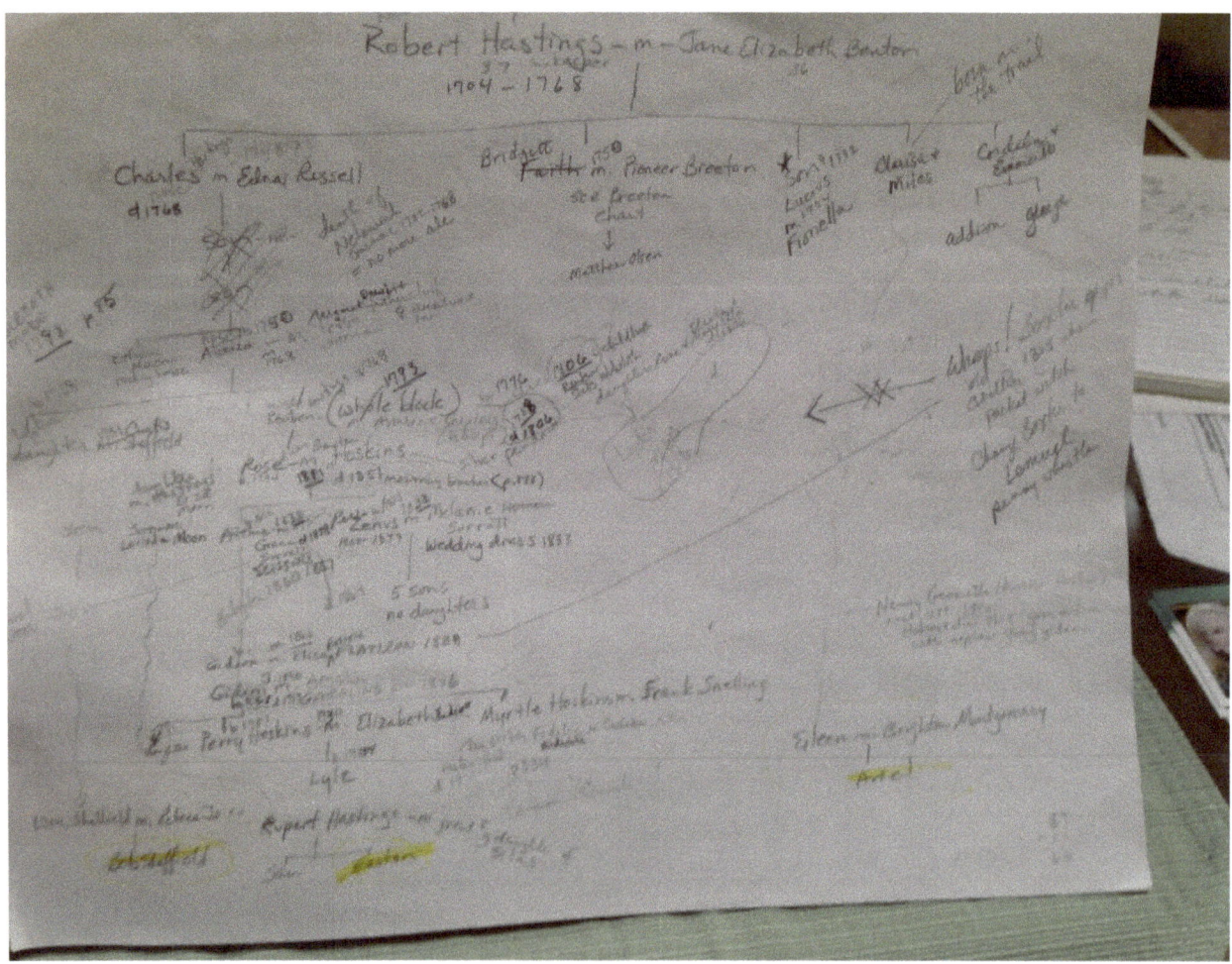

Clear as Mud

~ ~ ~

Bottom to Top Poem

Sunday December 31, 2017— This poem, written by Chani Ghorkin is my wish for you — and for me, too — for the coming year.

<< clearing of throat >> <u>NOT</u> the top to bottom poem. Read it from the bottom to the top to find my wish!

Today was the absolute worst day ever
And don't try to convince me that
There's something good in every day
Because, when you take a closer look,
This world is a pretty evil place.
Even if
Some goodness does shine through once in a while
Satisfaction and happiness don't last.
And it's not true that
It's all in the mind and heart
Because
True happiness can be obtained
Only if one's surroundings are good
It's not true that good exists
I'm sure you can agree that
The reality
Creates
My attitude
It's all beyond my control
And you'll never in a million years hear me say that
Today was a good day

Now read from bottom to top.

2018

January 2018

Monday January 1, 2018 — Happy New Year!

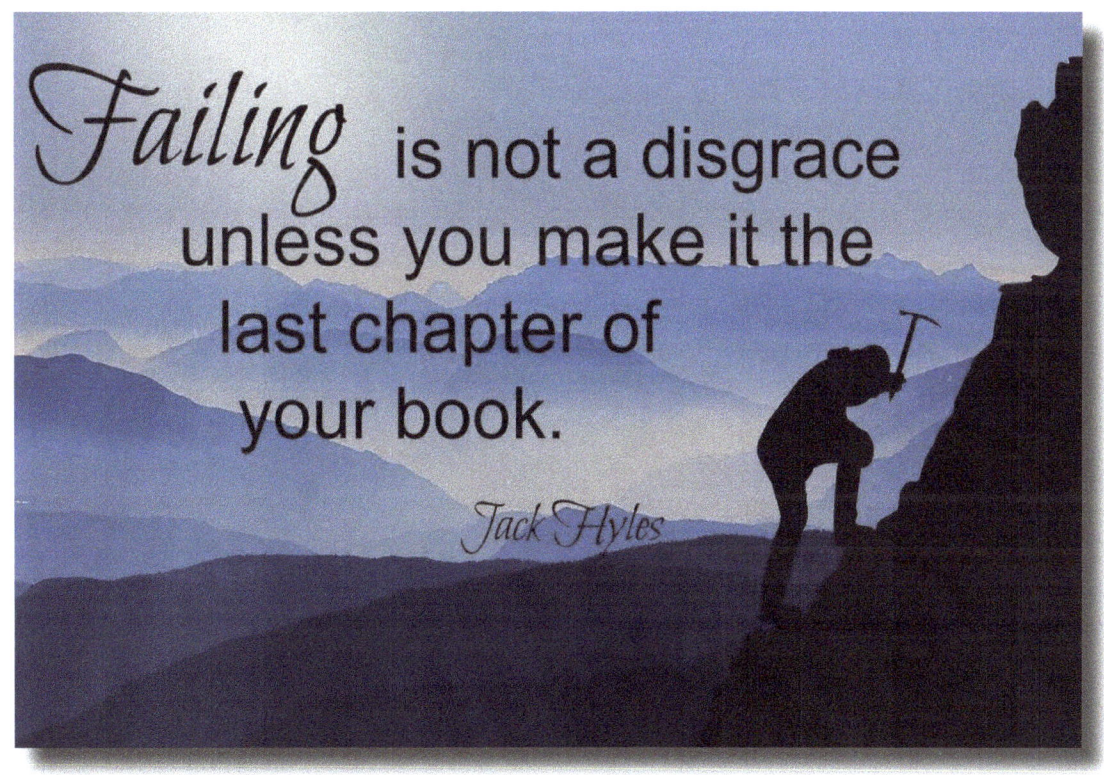

~ ~ ~

Fran's Tongue

Tuesday January 2, 2018 — SPOILER ALERT!
If you haven't yet read all of my first seven Biscuit McKee Mysteries, from *Orange as Marmalade* right through *Gray as Ashes*, you might want to get started. That is, if you like to be completely up on the past stories before you launch into the new ones.

I just finished writing a draft of the Author's note that will be at the beginning of *Red as a Rooster* explaining why I need to say, "SPOILER ALERT." I may change the wording of this around a bit before the publication date, but essentially the idea is this:

> The final four books of the Biscuit McKee Mystery Series were written as one complete book and are meant to be read as such. I make no attempt to "bring the reader up to speed" at the beginning of each of the three later books, for I assume you will read them in order.

> It is not absolutely necessary that you read the first seven books of the Biscuit McKee Series before you begin reading these, but please note this SPOILER ALERT: There are references in these last four books to some of the problems Biscuit and her friends encountered in the preceding seven books, including statements that clearly indicate who the murderer was in those earlier volumes.

These books WILL BE PUBLISHED THIS YEAR!!!! (Note: The caps and exclamation points are more for me than for you.)

~ ~ ~

Cow and Goats

Wednesday January 3, 2018 — One day while I was buying goat milk at a nearby farm, I came out of the milking parlor to find that my car was getting washed by two of the resident cows. The other cow licked one of my yellow polka dots, but she wouldn't stick around long enough (or lick long enough) for me to get a snapshot of her tongue. This lady just wanted to sniff.

I love the curiosity of cows. Just last week I wrote a scene in one of my upcoming books about someone who had an early memory of falling down in a cow pasture and having the cows circle carefully around him, sniffing at his clothes. Sometimes I wonder if everything I write has some sort of connection to a photo I've taken before. The cows in my book look almost exactly like this one. At least, that's the way they look inside my head.

~ ~ ~

I Am Becoming

Thursday January 4, 2018 — I'm a Capricorn, so I figure I get to celebrate my birthday from the 21st of December right through the third week in January. One of the most positive statements about the aging process is in the poem "Finding Her Here" by Jayne Relaford Brown.

I've loved this poem for years, but I finally found a choral arrangement of it that is riveting (https://www.youtube.com/watch?v=7ne60lAKsNc).The first line is repeated over and over again, serving as a "drone" — the underlying note on a bagpipe that infuses the entire piece. It provides a constant reminder that growing is an ongoing process, that change is happening even when we're barely aware of it.

As for me? I AM becoming. Every day, even when everything seems the same, I am becoming something new.

In case you've never read it, here's the text of Brown's poem. If you choose to copy it, please give Ms. Brown the credit she deserves by including her name.

FINDING HER HERE
by Jayne Relaford Brown

"I am becoming the woman I've wanted,
grey at the temples,
soft body, delighted,
cracked up by life
with a laugh that's known bitter,
but, past it, got better,
knows she's a survivor—
that whatever comes,
she can outlast it.
I am becoming a deep
weathered basket.

I am becoming the woman I've longed for,
the motherly lover
with arms strong and tender,
the growing-up daughter
who blushes surprises.
I am becoming full moons
and sunrises.

I find her becoming,
this woman I've wanted,
who knows she'll encompass,
who knows she's sufficient,
knows where she's going
and travels with passion.
Who remembers she's precious,
yet not at all scarce—
who knows she is plenty,
plenty to share."

Fran Stewart

~ ~ ~

Polka Dots

Friday January 5, 2018 — Why the yellow polka dots? (See last Wednesday's post if you wonder where this question came from.) Janice Adams Beene isn't the only one who's asked me that. Whenever I hear that question, I say there are two reasons—the official one and the real one.

Which would you like to hear?

Both?

Sure.

The official reason is that my second Biscuit McKee Mystery, YELLOW AS LEGAL PADS, won not only the GAYA (Georgia Author of the Year Award), but also an IPPY (Independent Publishers Book Award). GAYA was pretty good, but I was ecstatic about the IPPY since it's not only a national competition, but an international one for books put out by smaller, independent presses.

So the polka dots celebrate the award. Right?

Now, for the real reason.

This way, I can find my car in a parking lot.

My car even won a trophy for "the craziest car that showed up" at an antique car rally in 2008, and I have this photo to prove it!

~ ~ ~

BLOG #010: Loving - Brrr - What Is

Brrrrrr!!

Years ago, when I was a junior at Trinity College in Vermont, I took a drama class. The professor, Hugh Cronister, told us on the very first day that the big old drafty gym where this particular class met tended to be hotter than you-know-where on warm days and colder than Dante's version of the same place during the winter.

"I don't want to hear a single complaint from anyone in this class," he said. "There is nothing I can do about it and nothing you can do about it, so we will simply go about our business ignoring the sweat or the goose bumps. Got it?"

We all nodded, but just to prove he really meant it, he continued, "If I hear a single complaint from you, you will lose one point for that day."

The next time we met, the gym was sweltering. Class started, and one student grumped about the temp. Sure to his word, Cronister walked over to his notebook, looked at the student, and made a mark in the book.

Nobody, to the best of my recall, ever complained about the gym environment again throughout that semester. At least, not within hearing range of Hugh Cronister.

Now, here we are in the middle of a Georgia cold spell that I might have laughed about when I lived in Vermont. "You call 15 degrees cold? Ha!"

Well, yes, I do call 15 degrees cold now, particularly since the houses here in the south are built to withstand the heat, but not anything close to frigid.

So, what does this have to do with writing?

A lot of things.

When it's cold, a deadline is still a deadline. Put on another layer and slip on your wrist warmers so your hands don't freeze to the keyboard. Then, write.

There's nothing, short of a complete home remodel, that will prevent the drafts. I've already caulked and done every DIY thing I could think of. So, move the laptop to a different table in a different corner. Then, write.

Nobody's going to give me a demerit if I wait a little later to start my writing on a cold morning, but those characters of mine clamor around in my head, and if I don't get what they're saying written down, I'm liable to forget it. That may not be a demerit, but it feels like one. So, write.

This all sort of reminds me of Byron Katie's book *Loving What Is*. As I understand it, she moved to the windiest town in some state out west. She spent ten years complaining about the wind (like she was going to stop it????) before she woke up, decided to love whatever she couldn't change, and came up with four questions that could change anyone's life.

So, I've decided that Georgia isn't Antarctica, and "cold" is a relative term; that I can change the way I react to the cold, and my writing will progress (or not) depending on those reactions; and that I know, deep inside me, how losing myself in my writing generates an inner fire.

Now, who cares if it's cold?

~ ~ ~

A Diminished Mass

Saturday January 6, 2018 — The final major concert that the Gwinnett Choral Guild presented was the North American Premier of Scottish composer Alan A. Craig's "A Diminished Mass" in October of 2014.

Fran Stewart

Alan flew here from Scotland for the premier. He looked resplendent in his kilt.

We had received our copies of the score the previous June, along with rehearsal track CDs. I started in immediately studying the score, learning my part (alto), and listening, listening, listening. Then I began to sing, sing, sing, going over and over the trickier parts. All this before we even began our rehearsals in August.

It sort of reminded me of the process I use when I'm writing. There are initial drafts, re-reads, revising, tweaking, switching things back and forth. By the time I get around to sending drafts to my beta-readers, I have a pretty good handle on the story.

Of course, beta readers suggest a lot of changes, so I do a lot more tweaking.

Renee Wilson-Wicker, our director, suggested a lot of tweaks I never would have thought of, so I spent three and a half more months working with our group to bring this glorious music alive.

In the process of all of this, I memorized the entire 47 minutes of the piece. Memorized it well enough that I saw no reason to hold music in front of me during the performance, which is why I could keep my eyes on Renee the entire time. I've never before (or since) felt so completely at home in a performance.

There's a lot to be said for memorization. I can't memorize without understanding. I can't memorize without appreciation. I can't memorize without love.

Does it take a lot of work? Yes.

Is it worth it? Yes.

What have you memorized lately?

[**2020 Note**: In the meantime you can watch it here: https://www.youtube.com/watch?v=m10hcTIvwHk

If that link doesn't work, you can Google "A Diminished Mass Gwinnett Choral Guild." I hope it's still available online when you read this.]

Napkin folding

Sunday January 7, 2018 — Okay, are you ready for some fun? Here's a little course on napkin-folding.

https://www.facebook.com/FirstMediaBlossom/videos/10155963410179586/

The only fancy fold I've ever mastered is a sailing ship, which I just put together in both the paper napkin form and the nubby linen form. A fork will easily hold the paper napkin, but I've never found a fork big enough to grasp the folds of the linen.

Hence, the clothespin.

Fran Stewart

~ ~ ~

Messy Tiny House

Monday January 8, 2018 — I went through a phase recently of wondering if I should move into a tiny house. I'm sure you've heard of tiny houses. They run from 100 to 500 square feet or thereabouts. Think Thoreau and Walden Pond — only he didn't have to have a kitchen or a bathroom in his tiny house. And he didn't need room for a computer or cell phone chargers.

With the way my cats like to run around, I couldn't imagine asking them to share such small living quarters, but still … there were times when I longed for something so small, so compact, so tidy.

I cut back on a lot of the "stuff" that used to clutter my house. My closet has more empty shelves than full ones. My cabinets are better organized and less packed. Surely, I thought, I'm ready now for tiny house living.

But then I saw this YouTube video about what life is really like in a tiny house. All those times it's not spruced up for cameras to come in and film. All those times you come home from a necessary shopping trip and can't find a space to put even half what you've bought.

Messy tiny house: http://www.tinyhouseteacher.com/2015/08/28/real-life-tiny-house/ If you don't want to type all this link, just Google "real life in a tiny house."

I think I'll stick to where I am.

~ ~ ~

Finding Photos

Tuesday January 9, 2018 — I finally got it to work. The cat in the bag photos I couldn't show you last month.

I love the way cats like to crawl into bags of any sort. Somebody, I think, should make some really big bags that grownups could fit into. Maybe that's why I love reading nooks so much. Nothing like curling up with a good book in a cozy place.

Nanny Goat Beach

Wednesday January 10, 2018 — I know this is a July photo (from almost five years ago), but somehow the gray of that foggy morning on Nanny Goat Beach on Sapelo Island calls to mind the gray mornings we've been having lately here in this exceptionally cold winter. Well, cold for Georgia.

Just being there on the beach with Mozelle Funderburk and a seagull (and Mikki Dillon who took the picture) and nobody else—it was a treasure of an experience.

Cloudy days, warm or cold, can be thoroughly beautiful.

p.s. In the interest of truth in picturing, there was a ship on the horizon between the two of us, but I blocked it out. Wanted to remember just the sand and the sea and the gorgeous textures.

~ ~ ~

Supper

Thursday January 11, 2018 — Do you ever do popcorn for supper?

I sure do. A lot. My main meal each day is around noon, which means anywhere from 11:00 to 3:00 depending on what my schedule (or lack thereof) is. Also depending on how caught up I am in my writing. If I'm in the middle of untangling a plot element at 11:00 and it takes me 4 hours to follow the various threads, why on earth should I stop to feed?

That means a hefty meal at 3 (or even 4) - so what's the need to eat again until breakfast?

Except maybe a snack. Sometimes it's a hunk of cheese. Sometimes it's that last little leftover bit of soup. But more often than not, it's a bowl of popcorn, popped with coconut oil in a pot on the top of my stove. Then a little salt and a lot of pepper (yes, I put pepper on my popcorn) and I'm good to go.

The fact that I don't put butter on it means I can continue to type without getting the keyboard gooey — a definite plus for a writer!

What's your supper going to be this evening?

~ ~ ~

All About You

Friday January 12, 2018 — "Today, it's all about you." Wouldn't that make you feel good, looking at a plate like this before you slide your scrambled eggs onto it?

Just think about it. A day when every decision you make can be made with your own best interests in mind.

"But, I have kids," you might say. "Don't their interests come first?"

Well, no. Read ATLAS SHRUGGED by Ayn Rand. It's in your best interest to raise children who are responsible, who know there will be consequences to their actions, who learn early on that taking personal responsibility for their decisions is vital to their ongoing success in life. Now, because it's in your best interest, then when you love them to pieces AND expect them to answer for their decisions, you're actually putting yourself first — which is right where you should be.

So, for today, put yourself first. And if anybody questions you, show them this plate!

~ ~ ~

Blog # 011 Friday January 12, 2018

I'm down to the final 25,017 words still to be written in my WHITE AS ICE quartet of books. How do I know that?

I've always wanted to write a book that was longer than *Gone with the Wind*. And although *White as Ice* is going to be published in four separate volumes, with each book coming out one month after the previous one, they still are meant to be read as one big book.

Gone with the Wind has 418,053 words. If I have anything to say about it, WHITE AS ICE is going to have at least 418,054 words. Naturally, the final count will depend on just what else I write in order to wrap up this story that's been evolving slowly over the past number of years.

Did I decide to write that long a book when I first started WHITE AS ICE? Well, no. It's just that as the story evolved, as the women in the attic kept finding more and more artifacts, I simply got drawn into telling the history behind each of those items. The generations of characters began to interweave. The book gradually got longer and longer. And a couple of extra murders that I hadn't planned on originally cropped up.

So here I am now with a spreadsheet that says I can finish the book(s) within about six weeks. Then there will be the final beta-reads, the final tweaks, the final fixes.

Then to my publisher, then check the galleys, approve the cover designs, and set the launch dates.

With the major publishing companies (the big New York Six), it can take a year or more between delivery of the final manuscript and the publication date. With a smaller press, that lead time is shortened greatly.

We're getting closer!

This weekend I'll be sending out another chapter preview to anyone who's signed up for my newsletter (you can do that on the home page of this website).

After that, there may be time for only one more newsletter advance chapter.

I'm getting very excited about this. I hope you are too!

[**2020 Note:** The final word count for the White as Ice quadrilogy turned out to be more than 517,000. The good news is that I wasn't writing simply to fill a word count. I was writing to tell a complete, satisfying story. And I think I accomplished that. Unfortunately, a number of discrepancies (and too many typos) crept into the story. Those were corrected with the revised edition that was published through My Own Ship Press in 2020.]

~ ~ ~

Creek

Saturday January 13, 2018 — And you wonder why I love my little house? A large part of it is because of the tiny creek that runs through the back yard.

Luckily the creek-bed sits well below the level of the house because the last time a hurricane came through here, my peaceful waterway—seldom more than two feet wide—became a raging torrent more than 35 feet wide that swept branches, uprooted plants, and deposited sand bars all along its path.

The river eventually turned back into a creek, and the ferns have all recovered in the years since. I love the way Mother Nature works.

My sister took this photo when she visited in 2013. What you see is the fern bed on the eastern bank of the creek. You can also see the dark west creek bank on the right side of the photo.

~ ~ ~

Hidden Cat

Sunday January 14, 2018 —Is this one of those mornings when you wanted to stay under a fluffy comforter?

I might have this morning, except that Wooly Bear had other ideas, having to do with brushing and feeding and scratching and playing.

Now that I'm up, and all those regular routines are taken care of (as well as a number of cat-hugs), I'm glad of it.

Have a comforting day (even if it's not spent under a comforter).

~ ~ ~

Peggy's Jigsaw Puzzle

Monday January 15, 2018 — Okay, I'll admit it. I'm sort of addicted to jigsaw puzzles. So is my friend Peggy. Every time we go to Sapelo Island for a week-long retreat, one of us (or both us) packs a jigsaw puzzle.

We spread it out on a spare table either in the dining room or out in the solarium, and then everyone is invited to work on it a bit. But we end up being the ones who put the most pieces together. This one we did in the dining room.

And it just about drove us nuts.

What about you? Do jigsaw puzzles float your boat?

Gargling Oil Ad

Tuesday January 16, 2018 — I sent out my January newsletter yesterday, so people could read the story of Young Gideon, the Martinsville vet, and his experience with Merchant's Gargling Oil, an extremely effective liniment.

Yes, there really was such a thing, originally developed to help the aching muscles of the men who worked on the Erie Canal.

I've loved researching these last four Biscuit McKee Mysteries. Oddments like the Gargling Oil just seem to fall into my (virtual) lap, and I have great fun tracking down the details.

What one amazing thing was in your grandmother's attic? Do you think it might need to show up in Biscuit's?

Let me know…

[**2020 Note**: While preparing *Clear as Mud* for printed publication, I realized that I've repeated a lot of photos here and there throughout these posts. Here's a slightly different version of the Gargling Oil label. I can see why the company discontinued this one—that monkey looks downright creepy.]

~ ~ ~

Horsey Ride

Wednesday January 17, 2018 — I've bragged before about my sister—my BIG sister, as she reminds me periodically. The fact that she's older than I means that she gets the final say-so.

Or so she says.

I have no clue when this photo was taken, but it looks like I'm thoroughly enjoying my horsey ride.

Do you have a wonderful sister, too?

~ ~ ~

brand new dinosaur

Thursday January 18, 2018 — I was driving along GA-20 last Sunday and passed by a vet clinic I've never noticed before. They had a sign out front that said:

Fran Stewart

Dinosaurs never went to the vet

And look what happened to them.

Which, of course, reminded me of a book I read recently, called *Why Dinosaurs Matter* by Kenneth Lacovara.

Did you know that dinosaurs never went completely extinct? Every bird you see today is actually a dinosaur. If you don't believe that, just read the book.

And two days ago on CBC News online, I read this article about a newly-discovered Rainbow Dinosaur: http://www.cbc.ca/news/technology/rainbow-dinosaur-1.4487692 Sure looks like a bird to me.

And those starlings who've been raiding my bird feeders? Sure do look like dinosaurs…

Come to think of it, so do the chickadees.

p.s. If you copy the picture to send around, please give photo credit to Velizar Simeonovski/The Field Museum.

~ ~ ~

Hoban Cards

Friday January 19, 2018 — I'm thinking of getting some calling cards.

Not business cards.

Calling cards.

Why? Well, Biscuit and her friends found a set of three calling card cases from the late 1800s, so of course I had to write a story about where they came from, and why they ended up in Martinsville GA.

I love the research part of writing a book, and these final four Biscuit McKee Mysteries are stretching me to the limit — Yippee! Anyway, in looking around for more info about calling cards, I found the Hoban Press https://hobancards.com

Their cards are quite simply stunning. Check out the Hoban products list.

Now, I'm not going to give up on my regular business cards (which were designed by my artist sister Diana Alishouse). After all, they list many of my books (in the correct reading order) on the back.

But these scrumptiously elegant calling cards are hard to resist.

[**2020 Note:** I finally got around to ordering some. My timing was off by a couple of years, since with the COVID-19 isolation, I'm not handing out cards to anyone right now. But they're still simply beautiful!]

~ ~ ~

Blog #012 Lunarbaboon

Friday January 19, 2018 — I almost didn't click on the link when my son posted something about lunarbaboon. I'd never heard of it. Maybe I'm horribly behind the times, but without a TV, I miss a lot of the fad stuff that circulates.

At any rate, because I do happen to respect Eli, I checked out an article about a comic strip that is so completely different than anything I've ever seen, I was astonished.

Fran Stewart

How I wish something like this could have been around when I was growing up.

The sad thing, as I see it, is that one's first reaction to the first one or two frames of each cartoon (at least MY first reaction), is to think of negativity coming out of the dad's mouth.

Guess we all need to clean up our act (if not our actions, then our thoughts).

~ ~ ~

Philosophy of the Day

Saturday January 20, 2018 — "I see you."

I think that was my very favorite line in Avatar, the one that summed up a whole philosophy.

If we all took the time to truly see each other, wouldn't the world be a better place?

~ ~ ~

Waterfall

Monday January 22, 2018 — Have you made a big splash lately, like this waterfall in Hawaii?

Janice Adams Beane commented (on the Avatar posting I did a couple of days ago) that my words brought her joy.

What better splash could anyone make than that? I've helped her see joy, and she certainly brought joy to my life through her comment.

It reminds me of the time, shortly after I'd published *Orange as Marmalade*, my first Biscuit McKee Mystery, when someone from the Depression and Bipolar Support Alliance contacted me to thank me for putting their phone number and website in my author's note. Apparently two people had contacted them as a result of that and got the help they needed.

At the time, I hadn't sold more than a hundred or so books, but I felt like such a success as an author, because I'd made a splash. I'd touched someone's life (two someones).

Of course, depression in one person affects the whole ring of people around that one person, so ultimately a lot more people than two felt that splash.

Hooray!

Fran Stewart

~ ~ ~

Rotary Phone

Tuesday January 23, 2018 — Years ago, I lived in a town that had a small independent phone company. It took us six months to get a phone, and then we were on a ten-phone party line. Talk about a rude awakening.

All those clichés you've heard of people listening in on other folks' conversations? Yep. They were true.

I think there were only three or four towns in that phone company's coverage area, and each town had a different 3-digit beginning to the 7-digit phone number. If I was dialing somebody in the same town, all I had to dial was the last 5 digits of the 7-digit number. If it was the next town over, 5 digits would get me to there as well, since the 3-digit prefix of each number was different.

Does this make any sense at all? Probably not, so here are some examples:

Let's say my number was 123-4567. Every phone in my town started with 123.

The next town's numbers all started with 234 (such as 234-5678).

If I dialed 3-7654, I'd get my next-door neighbor.

3-8765 was the town clerk's office.

But 4-7654 was a house in the town down the road,

and 4-8765 was liable to be that town's grocery store.

See?

Nowadays with cell phones, everybody's used to dialing 10 digits — or just hitting the name on a contact list and then selecting which one of that person's 8 or 9 phone numbers you want to call.

The other thing was that you could only get six feet away from any phone in the old days, because that's how long the cord was.

I still remember the first time I got a 15-foot phone cord. Freedom ! ! ! !

Then there was the time I lived in Central City, where the phone numbers were—if I remember correctly—four digits long, and one of those digits was a letter. But that's a whole nother story…

~ ~ ~

Books?

Wednesday January 24, 2018 — Lesson #1 for the day: When volunteering at your grandchildren's school library, if a fully loaded cart of books begins to tip over, DO NOT try to stop it from tipping.

Lesson #2: Go immediately to the chiropractor - do not cross "Go," and do not stop at any station along the line.

~ ~ ~

Balancing a Pole

Thursday January 25, 2018 — My dad used to be able to balance a kitchen chair on his chin. During the Depression, he worked for a time with a traveling circus.

Now, all these years later, his grandson (who looks a great deal like him) has followed in the tradition, without even having known that he was carrying on his grandpa's legacy. Eli does acrobatics, silk climbing, fire spinning. All of it is for fun. I love this photo of him balancing a pole on his chin.

Just like his Grandpa Stewart.

~ ~ ~

Inside the Roller Tube

Friday January 26, 2018 — Back in 2013, my grandkids received a big plastic roller-thingie (no, I don't know what it's called). I just know that once it was blown up, they took turns climbing inside and rolling down the hill beside their house. Luckily nobody got dumped in the creek.

"You wanna try it, Grannie?"

Let's see — all the reasons not to try it cropped up in an instant.

I'm claustrophobic

I get motion sickness

It looks scary as heck

I'm terrified

AAAARGH!

But then, all the reasons to go ahead took their places

It's open on both ends, for heaven's sake.

It's not too far down the hill - surely I can stand that much roly-poly.

So what if it looks scary?

I can overcome any fear I have.

WHEEEEE!

I'm glad I tried it.

Will I ever do it again?

Nope.

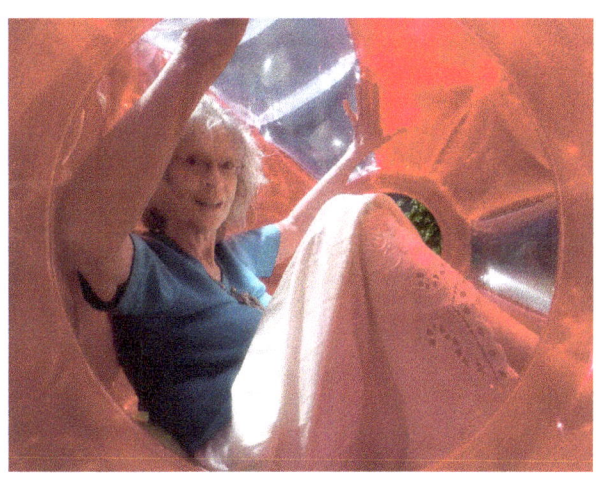

~ ~ ~

Blog #013 - Making a Mark in this World

Friday January 26, 2018 — How very anonymous this woman is.

We all (most likely) want to make our mark in the world, leave a legacy of some sort, know that we've made a difference.

The truth is, we all DO make a difference in someone's life, whether it's someone we know well or someone who is simply passing through our life. That difference is no less important even if nobody puts it on our tombstone. But a stone without an epitaph is kind of sad.

This woman may have been an angel or a harridan — we don't know. All we know is that she lived and died as someone's wife.

This is where writers can let their fancy roam free. Who was she? What did she do? Who did she know? Who did she influence? Was she angry, happy, sad, content? Did she have fourteen children, or two, or none? Was she educated or illiterate? Was she married for ten years or fifty? Did she die peacefully or in pain? Was it a natural death, or was she pushed on her way before her time?

Just what sort of story can I come up with about her?

She just might show up in my next book.

Fran Stewart

Oh, it boggles the mind…

[**2020 Note:** It's taken me a long time, but I found out that "His Wife" is a placeholder on gravestones in national cemeteries where the husband has died, but the wife is still alive. After she dies and is buried in the same grave with him, her name and dates are added to that second side of the marker. I assume that now, with so many servicewomen serving and dying in wars overseas, there will be a lot of stones that say "Her Husband" on the reverse side.]

~ ~ ~

Limerick's Tongue

Saturday January 27, 2018 — I thought you might want a laugh today.

My grand-dog Limerick is always ready to supply one.

Sandcastle

Sunday January 28, 2018 — How long has it been since you built a sandcastle?

For me, it's been two and a half years. Dawn over Nanny Goat Beach on Sapelo Island in July of 2015.

And yet, come to think of it, I've built plenty of castles since then. Just not ones made of sand.

Every time I sit down to write, I'm building a castle.

The circumstances around a particular scene form the wall, that either contains the scene or, if there are plenty of crenellations on that wall, that allows a broad vista.

There needs to be a road, an approach to the problem in the scene (there's always a problem lurking somewhere, which is what keeps you reading more and more). And of course, there needs to be a gate — what's keeping the character in the scene from getting where she wants to get? How do we get the dang thing open? Or is it already open? Who opened it? Uh-oh—does danger lurk within?

Is there a dungeon under the castle (cue the scary music)? Are there rings of walls to get through? Is there a flag waving on the topmost tower?

The various structures inside the castle walls are most often the other characters, the ones your lead person needs to interact with, roam around, explore. There may also be a challenging setting — like the ice storm in my current Biscuit McKee quadrilogy (is that a word?). I finished RED AS A ROOSTER and BLACK AS SOOT and PINK AS A PEONY, only to have a situation (knights attacking the castle!!) in WHITE AS ICE that made me go back and do extensive rewrites on the first three books.

Yep. I guess I build a sandcastle almost every day.

And a big deadline is looming, so I'd better get busy! Bring on the sand!

Woman in Muff

Monday January 29, 2018 — It's amazing where ideas come from.

I was at a FedEx one day last June to make some copies (dead printer at home) and happened to notice a stack of large photographs the woman next to me was making copies of. "A family reunion," she told me. "I'm making copies for all my brothers and sisters and cousins."

Her grandmother, the woman wearing the muff, was so stunning, I had to ask permission to describe the muff—and the hat—in my upcoming book.

Now, I'm about frantic, because I can't find the piece of paper that contains the name of the woman in the hat—and her granddaughter as well. I always acknowledge the people who help me. That's a little heard to do if I misplace the paper.

<<SIGH>>

I'll keep looking.

~ ~ ~

SuperMoon Lunar Eclipse

Tuesday January 30, 2018 — Looks like we're out of luck here in Georgia as far as seeing anything noticeable on the super moon eclipse tomorrow, but it's nice to know so much of the Pacific Ocean will experience it.

Did you ever wonder what whales must think when an eclipse happens? I wonder if the songs of the humpback whale will reflect the event?

Thanks to NASA for this photo.

~ ~ ~

Eli in red

Wednesday January 31, 2018 — Just thought you might like to see one of the happiest smiles ever. This is my son, Eli. You may recall that last week I shared the photo of him balancing a pole on his chin.

This picture always brings out a smile in me. Do you have a photo like that - maybe one you keep on your desktop so you can just check it out once in a while?

Fran Stewart

~ ~ ~

February 2018

My Empty Bin

Thursday February 1, 2018 — Earlier this week, as I turned into my neighborhood after a visit to my chiropractor, I saw a garbage can stuffed (as many of them were along the street) almost to overflowing.

I seriously considered pulling over to the curb to take a photo of it, but the owners of the house were standing there in their driveway, and the garbage truck was half a block behind me, so I went looking for a stock photo (credit: Brett Lamb).

This reminded me of a story I read years ago (probably in Reader's Digest) about a well-known woman from India who visited this country. As she prepared to get onto the plane at Idlewild, a reporter asked, "What is the most vivid memory of America you will take home with you?"

Without missing a beat, the woman said, "The size of your garbage cans."

The other picture is my blue garbage bin as of yesterday. It's been just like that for the past two weeks. By next Thursday or Friday, I'll probably have one bag to put in there. Our county requires that garbage be bagged, but I haven't bought a box of plastic bags in the past dozen years or so. The birdseed I buy (in large quantity) from Wild Birds Unlimited comes in 20-lb. bags. They work just fine to contain what little garbage I produce.

I truly believe in the "Reduce, Reuse, Recycle" maxim.

Would you like to join me in my campaign to put out a half-filled bin of garbage once a month (rather than an overflowing bin once a week)?

 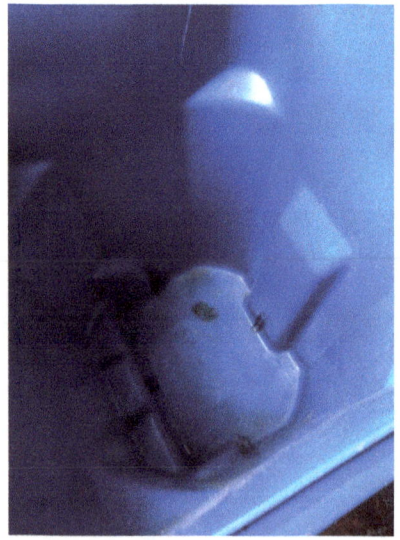

Photo credit: Brett Lamb

Word Counts

Friday February 2, 2018 — Head over to my website blog today to see how I keep track of all the scenes in my quadrilogy. I swear that's not a dictionary word, but it sure is a handy one for the upcoming four books that will end the Biscuit McKee Mystery Series.

Quadrilogy. I like that word. It's better for a book, since Quadrille brings Renaissance dancers to mind, and Quartet reminds me of Mozart—or barbershops!

As these four books of mine (all of them really truly just one big book) grew longer and longer, I decided I might as well fulfill a longtime ambition to write a book that was longer than *Gone with the Wind* (418,053 words). So I set up my daily word count spreadsheet to reflect that my final goal is 418,054 words.

Will I meet the goal? Absolutely. Will I exceed it? Who knows?

Will I get to the length of *War and Peace*? 587,287 words? Probably not.

But then again, W&P isn't my goal. GWTW is.

On the other hand, if you figure that the whole Biscuit McKee series is one very long story, then Tolstoy can step aside, because I've already beaten *War & Peace* hands down.

p.s. Why did I include this particular picture of my daily word count chart? Because on January 29th, when I got ready to shut down my computer for the day, I plugged in the numbers and found that on that day, I had added precisely 4,000 words to my manuscript. Notice how I used my handy photo-fixer thingie to highlight it.

It was just as satisfying as seeing the odometer roll over to 88,888 or 121,212.

Date	Start of Day	End of Day	# added	
				Deadline Table
01/17/18	395,780	395,780	0	
01/18/18	395,780	397,310	1,530	brc
01/19/18	397,310	397,310	0	
01/20/18	397,310	397,310	0	
01/21/18	397,310	399,300	1,990	
01/22/18	399,300	401,286	1,986	
01/23/18	401,286	401,286	0	
01/24/18	401,286	401,319	33	wok
01/25/18	401,319	401,714	395	
01/26/18	401,714	402,736	1,022	
01/27/18	402,736	402,736	0	
01/28/18	402,736	403,444	708	
01/29/18	403,444	407,444	4,000	
01/30/18	407,444	407,992		
01/31/18	407,992	409,127	1,135	
02/01/18	409,127	410,190	1,063	chan
02/02/18	410,190	412,873	2,683	

Fran Stewart

~ ~ ~

blog #014 Keeping Track

Friday February 2, 2018 — Yeah, yeah, yeah. When you're writing a book, the information needs to be organized. Scenes need to be in some sort of order. Characters who are dead should not show up four chapters later just because the author forgot who lived when.

So, what to do about keeping it all straight?

I'm glad you asked.

I head for my spreadsheet program.

This particular one shows a little bit of how I have everything listed.

I have columns for:

1. which of the four books this scene occurs in (color codes for Red, Black, Pink, and White)

2. whether it's from a letter, a diary, and who it's referring to (Silas, Hubbard, Mary Frances, Charlotte, Miss Julia, Homer), whether it's a mealtime at Biscuit's house (day 3 supper / day 4 breakfast / day 4 lunch). It's amazing what you can cram into one little column just by color-coding.

3. page # in the current manuscript

4. the first sentence or two copied and pasted from the manuscript (so when the page numbers don't match up—they never seem to, since I'm always going back and adding or deleting something—I can do a search for those words).

5. year the scene takes place

6. month and day ditto

7. day of the week if it's necessary to know that—the "time and date" website has proven invaluable for days back in the 1700s

8. various other columns about who found a particular artifact in the attic, whether or not the scene has been sent to my beta readers, and the ubiquitous "NOTES" column where I put everything else I want to include.

I'm getting closer to the end of the book(s) and beginning to be able to visualize the actual publication of them. Bear with me, please! I'm writing (and entering stuff in my spreadsheet) as fast as I can.

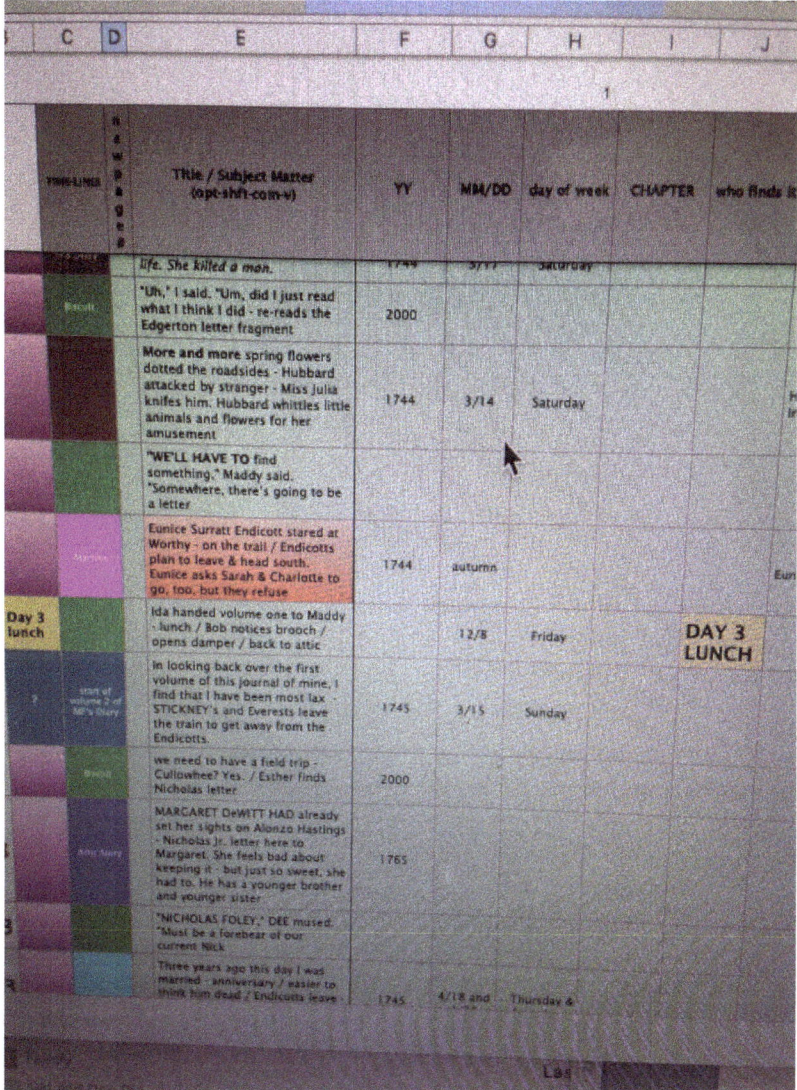

~ ~ ~

Yellow-Rumped Warbler

Saturday February 3, 2018 — There's a new bird coming around to my feeders - one that I thought somebody had flung paint at because of the bright yellow splotch just north of its tail.

Turns out she's a yellow-rumped warbler, a species that's often called a "butter-butt" by experienced birders. Funny the little tidbits of wisdom you can pick up searching the Internet.

She likes insects. She seems to be enamored of my suet. She's cuter than one of my grandmother's buttons.

And in the almost 25 years I've been feeding birds here in Georgia, she's the first one I've ever seen.

I hope she brings some friends around to my front-yard bird restaurant. (The beautifully clear picture is from ebird.org. The fuzzy one is from my phone camera.)

~ ~ ~

Purple Plastic Hand

Sunday February 4, 2018 — Did you ever want to make a huge difference in someone's life? Lend a helping hand?

Two Canadian teenagers did just that when—just for the fun of it—they 3D printed a hand.

Turns out, the hand made a big difference.

I loved this story from CBC News. Hope it brightens your day.

I couldn't copy the picture(s), so to see it yourself, Google "Alberta girl's printed plastic hand."

~ ~ ~

So Much in Common

Monday February 5, 2018 — I have so much fun when I'm meeting new people at a bookstore.

Yesterday I did a book signing at Another Chapter Bookstore in Buford. The parking lot was full. It was busy there all day, but one of the many fun conversations I had happened just shortly after the store opened at ten.

Jim, it turns out, is 86. He retired at 65 and began keeping a list of every book he's ever read since then. "Yesterday," he told me, "I finished reading book #1,260."

He said he rates every book, from 1 to 10, and most of them are around a 5 or 6. "I've rated only three with a ten."

Of course, I had to ask him which those three were, and it turns out two of them are 10s on my list as well — *Atlas Shrugged* by Ayn Rand and *Gift From the Sea* by Anne Morrow Lindbergh. I told him I loved Lindbergh's idea that there was no need to collect a hundred seashells when one was easier to appreciate and to learn from.

You know how you feel when you suddenly meet someone who treasures the same things you do? Well, Jim and I felt that connection.

Katie Anderson, who owns Another Chapter, wouldn't let me pay for a book I tried to buy just before I left at 4pm. Thank you, Katie! It was the collected letters of Rachel Carson and Dorothy Freeman, and I'm finding that the friendship these two women shared had that same quality of connection, deepened by more than a decade of close communication. The book, in case you're interested, is called *Always, Rachel*.

Daisy's Footprint

Tuesday February 6, 2018 — Years ago, when I bought this house, there was a LOT of repair and remodeling work to be done. Roof, floors, A/C, fridge, range, windows. Had to have all the carpet ripped out, only to find nothing but sub flooring beneath them. With all the other stuff that took precedence, replacing the linoleum in the kitchen and dining room was low on my to-do list.

So I left the crummy linoleum and put up with it for a number of years while I did all that other stuff.

One of the first things I did was clean those ratty floors (the plywood ones), seal them, and paint them. For the living room, I chose a dark blue. I painted it in sections that I cordoned off so my cats (I had nine of them at the time) wouldn't walk through the wet mess.

Daisy jumped the partition, though, and then trailed across the dining room before I could catch her, leaving little paw prints, most of them smudged as she slipped and slid on the slick floor. I began cleaning them up immediately, but when I got to this last tiny print, I just couldn't make myself wipe it off.

Instead, I let it dry and I lived with a daily reminder of sweet Daisy (she died in 2009).

The print is still there, although it's buried now beneath fancy new flooring.

I'd like to think that someday, somebody's going to tear off the top layer and find that one little print. I hope they get a chuckle out of it.

Come to think of it, I hope you do, too.

p.s. It's official now, and I wanted you to be the first to know. My WHITE AS ICE Quadrilogy is—as of yesterday at 5:45 pm—464 words longer than *Gone with the Wind*. And I still have the final murder to wrap up. War & Peace, here we come.

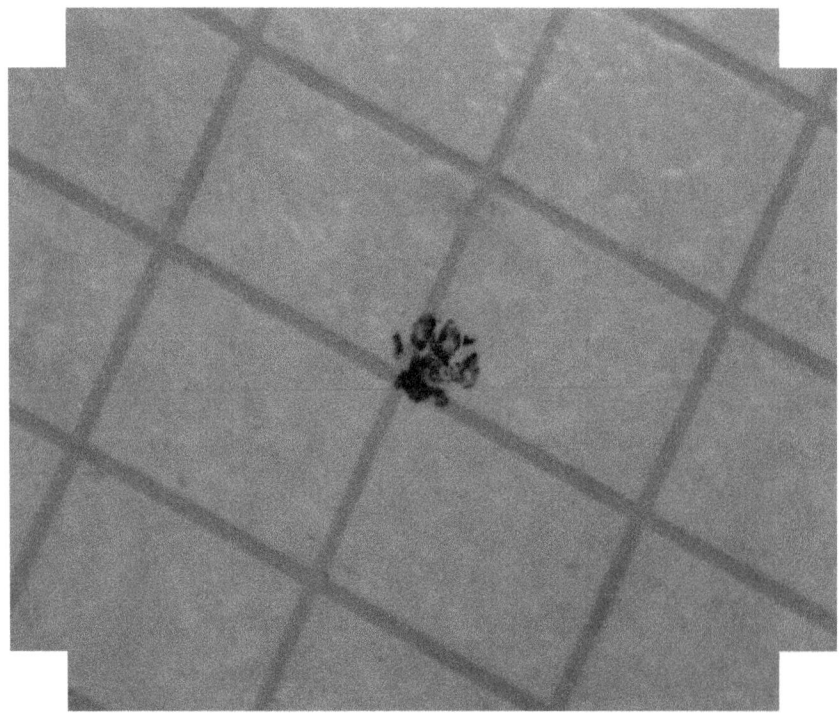

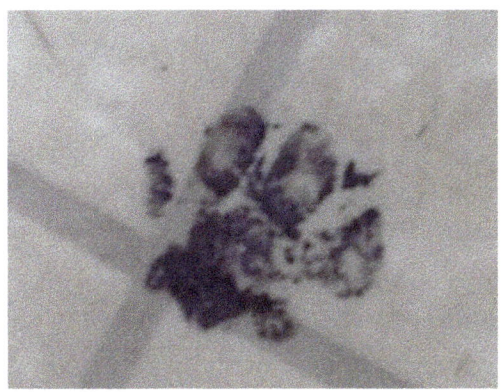

~ ~ ~

Miss Polly's Nose

Wednesday February 7, 2018 — I'm teaching a series of memoirs classes at the Collins Hill Branch of the Gwinnett County Library System. One of the things I talk about is the importance of instilling our memoirs with the five senses. How did the wind in your hair feel when you took that bike ride? What did your grandma's spaghetti sauce smell like? What about the siren of the fire engine as it approached your burning house? Or the time your friend got you to try artichokes for the first time—do you remember that taste? Can you describe it?

Then there are the other senses — emotion, anger, distrust, elation. Let's work a few of those into our stories as well.

Even if you're writing simply for your own growth, never expecting anyone else to read what you've written, won't it be more fun for you to go back a decade from now and be able to see, smell, feel, hear, and practically taste whatever you're writing about?

I keep this picture of Miss Polly's nose nearby so it can remind me every day as I write that evoking senses can make a story come alive.

~ ~ ~

Warbler

Thursday February 8, 2018 — Yesterday I a heard a thump against the glass in my front door. On the porch just outside lay the twitching body of a tiny Yellow-rumped Warbler (see the photo on my February 3rd post). I gathered her into my cupped hands and breathed on her gently to warm her up. It took a couple of minutes for her to right herself (just long enough for me to snap these two photos), and then she simply flew away.

~ ~ ~

Grans 'n Grads Teapots

Friday February 9, 2018 — I love speaking to book clubs. Wish I had the time/energy/money/whatever to travel all over the country meeting book lovers.

But then, I'd miss my cats.

The compromise?

Skype or FaceTime. It makes the travel a moot point, since I can be in anyone's living room so easily without ever having to leave my desk.

The problem with this?

I wouldn't get to see the special arrangements some of my book club hostesses have arranged for me, like this teapot collection the Grans to Grads Book Club set up to show me ten years ago when I attended one of their meetings to talk about my (at that time) newest book.

Then there was the group that read A SLAYING SONG TONIGHT. It was a dinner meeting, and the table was decorated with a most clever arrangement of murder weapons (all of which I'd used in the book). I wish I had a photo of it to share with you. I should say, there were REPLICAS of the weapons. No, there was not a jar of poisoned tomatoes in the centerpiece!

~ ~ ~

Blog #015 No Voracious Reading – February 9, 2018

You know me … or maybe you don't, but you feel like you do because you know and love the characters in my books — it's almost the same thing since I put so much of myself into the writing.

So, you'll know I'm a voracious reader.

You'll also know I don't make New Year's resolutions. I've never seen much sense in them.

But you may also realize that when I make up my mind to do something, I do it.

I've made up my mind. I swear I'm NOT going to read as many books this year as I did last year.

GASP ! ! ! ! ! !

Not read as many books? Why ever not?

Here's a thoroughly enlightening article about <u>why memory works better</u> when we read more slowly. The idea is that when we race through a book, we retain the plot, characters, and maybe even the name of the book, in our short-term memory queue. As soon as we go on to the next book, that queue erases and another one takes over.

https://www.theatlantic.com/science/archive/2018/01/what-was-this-article-about-again/551603/?utm_source=twb

That means that three months from now—or three weeks—I won't recall much about the book, even though I stayed up late reading it. You know the scenario: "Just one more page. Just one more. Gotta find out what happens."

It turns out that when teachers had us read three pages of a book at a time, they had the right idea, because then we were more likely to be able to recall it later.

So, no more of this racing to finish a book. If I like it well enough to be reading it in the first place, I'm going to limit myself. That way the reading of the book will last longer, and hopefully the memory of it will last as well.

Do you want to join me in my slow-reading campaign?

~ ~ ~

Chewing My Cud

Saturday February 10, 2018 — Do you ever have days when what you feel like doing is sitting in the sunshine and chewing your cud?

Instead, I suppose I should ask, how often do you have days like this?

I'm feeling that way this morning, but I'm also headed out to speak at a daylong seminar on book-writing sponsored by Sisters in Crime. Guess I'll have to chew my cud in the car and wait 'til afternoon to enjoy the sun (if the rainclouds will cooperate).

p.s. I think I've already used this photo—but since I like it, I might as well use it again.

~ ~ ~

What to Sense

Sunday February 11, 2018 — Good Morning!

I hope you see something wonderful today, and taste something new and delicious, and hear something marvelous, and smell something mouth-watering, and feel something soothing.

Let your senses come alive.

Fran Stewart

~ ~ ~

Learning to Walk in the Dark

Monday February 12, 2018 — In preparation for the Memoirs class I'll be teaching beginning tomorrow (a brand-new class, similar to the ones I've taught before but with lots of new material), I've been reading memoirs, memoirs, and more memoirs.

Some of them have been frankly awful, but many of them give fascinating glimpses into situations that I'll never encounter personally—some of which I desperately hope I won't encounter. Others show me alternate ways of dealing with life events I've experienced myself but may (or may not) have handled quite as well as the writer.

I'd like to recommend one book in particular. *Learning to Walk in the Dark* recounts author Barbara Brown Taylor's exploration of blindness — in its physical, metaphorical, and spiritual manifestations.

I'm careful about which books I buy. I'll usually try a new author at the library. Taylor's book is one I bought, one I'll re-read periodically, and certainly one I'm using in my Memoirs class, which incidentally, is called "Walk a Mile in My Shoes."

~ ~ ~

Dr. Seuss Quote

Tuesday February 13, 2018 — I used to think this way. Do I believe it anymore, though?

No.

Over the past few years I've divested myself of hundreds—thousands?—of books. The ones in my house now are books I truly love, books I plan to re-read, books I use on a regular basis.

Then there are the stacks of library books from three different libraries. These books fall into six different categories.

1. Some of them are ones I've been asked to read and rate for suitability for 6th, 7th, or 8th-graders by the librarian at the school library where I volunteer.

2. Books that have been recommended by people I trust.

3. Book club books (I belong to three book clubs).

4. Books I'll use in teaching my Memoirs classes or as research for my mystery writing.

5. Ones that satisfy my curiosity.

6. And those few books that fall off the library shelf as I walk past (yes—that does happen, and I figure if a book wants to be read badly enough to fall at my feet, I'd better listen!)

If I don't love it or need it, I either return it, throw it out (only the TRULY awful ones), give it away, or take it to a used bookstore.

How about you? Are you ready to free up space in your life?

Fran Stewart

~ ~ ~

Crawl inside Books

Wednesday February 14, 2018 — As long as we're talking Valentine's Day (we were, weren't we?), how about remembering that a love affair with books can fill immeasurable longings?

How many times have I read *Pride and Prejudice* or *Atlas Shrugged* or *Gift from the Sea* or Diana Gabaldon's entire Outlander series or Louise Penny's Inspector Gamache series? Too many times? No such thing!

I saw Romeo and Juliet at the Atlanta Shakespeare Tavern Sunday night, and was struck again by the way a timeless story (whether book or well-produced play) can transport me to new places and fill me with new ideas or rekindle ones I'd somehow lost along the way.

How many times have I seen R&J? Twenty-nine, I think. Is that too many times? No.

Any time I open a new book, I have an unquenchable hope that this may be one more treasure that will truly enrich my life.

I hope my WHITE AS ICE "quadrilogy" will prove to be one my readers want to crawl into. I'm getting closer to completing it, and I can't wait to see it in print.

What books do you want to crawl into?

~ ~ ~

Around the Corner

Thursday February 15, 2018 — Spring is just around the corner!

~ ~ ~

Blog #016 Facing Fears with a One-Eyed Horse

Friday February 16, 2018 — I've talked a lot in these weekly blogs and my daily FB author page posts about my plans for the future, and about what's going on now, with my writing, with my life. But I'd like to back up a little bit for this edition of Friday Fare.

A few years ago, I launched myself on an intensive journey to face my fears — chickens (yes, I was afraid of chickens), enclosed spaces (claustrophobia can truly paralyze someone), and a number of others that were lesser, but no less scary.

One of the things I was afraid of was horses.

Until I met Daisy, a one-eyed therapy horse, whose owner assured me that Daisy was the gentlest horse she'd ever had. "She'll help you get over that fear."

So, I signed up for a two-hour session.

First, I watched Daisy for a while.

Next, I fed her some carrots, standing well back away from her.

Then I graduated to patting her nose.

After that, I stepped about six inches inside her stall, with the owner and therapist right beside me.

Another foot or so, and Daisy's person put a brush into my hand. "She loves to have her coat brushed." She stepped nearer to Daisy. "Why don't you start with this side? Just go in the direction the hair grows."

I'd never known a horse could have such intricate swirls and patterns in her coat. I got caught up in the

Fran Stewart

brushing, not noticing that Daisy kept sidestepping nearer and nearer to me. Each time she moved, I took a step back but kept on brushing. Eventually, my back went clunk against the side of the stall. Daisy had pushed me (so gently I hadn't even noticed) into a corner.

All my fear of being pinned down flew up into my face. I couldn't get past that huge leg and foot of hers—not in either direction. Short of screaming, what was I supposed to do?

When I asked (with a certain amount of panic in my voice—okay a lot of panic) the therapist said, "Place the palm of your hand flat against her side and show her gently what you want her to do."

"What do I want her to do?"

Dumb question. I wanted her to let me out of the corner, but to do that, she'd have to move.

Low and behold, I placed my hand and gave the gentlest push—not even a push, really. I just applied some pressure. Daisy took one step away from me. I pushed again and she took another step.

"Try using just one finger."

I did, and Daisy moved again, enough for me to step around her. But the funny thing was, by that point I didn't need to escape the stall, so I kept on brushing. Until it was time to feed Daisy some more carrots.

Have you faced up to a fear lately?

p.s. Another fear—a small one, but still there—has been trying to figure out what I'll do once my Biscuit McKee Mystery Series is completed. Writing has been my life for so long now, I've felt somewhat unnerved about the prospect of not having a daily deadline. Don't worry. I'll put out one finger and push and see what happens!

Helping Beak

Friday February 16, 2018 — I laugh every time I see this photo. It's been around the internet a few billion times probably, but it still has a message to impart.

We never know where our friends are going to come from, right?

~ ~ ~

Half-Staff

Saturday February 17, 2018 — This flag at half-staff, beside several spring-blossoming trees, looked particularly poignant yesterday.

Although life does go on, my heart goes out to the parents who lost children in Florida.

Expressing Your Happiness

Sunday February 18, 2018 — Back when I had two beehives on my back deck and was so delighted with the first batch of honey from their hives, I took this picture of three of the jars, along with one of my all-time favorite sayings.

Searching for happiness never works. It took me a lot of years to figure that anytime I said, "I'll be happy once I can …" I was unconsciously pushing happiness away from me.

Now I can BE happy and FEEL happy, and I don't have to wait for anything external to happen. Happiness bubbles up regardless of outer circumstances.

~ ~ ~

Reading Glasses

Monday February 19, 2018 — This morning, as I groped around, trying to find my glasses, I remembered seeing this depiction of what keeps reading glasses busy when they're not on my nose.

Thought you'd enjoy it…

[**2020 Note**: This is another one of those instances where I used a photo I'd already posted some time ago. Sorry about that …]

~ ~ ~

Snow Dog

Tuesday February 20, 2018 — You'd think, with the days getting warmer, I'd be dressing in lighter clothing, but doggone it, it's still cold enough for a turtleneck and sweatshirt.

Reminds me of Vermont.

Which reminds me of the snow dog my kids and I created one winter. The dog, patterned after Tubelo (shown here posing alongside), was big enough for the kids to sit on. Wish I'd put some black stones in for eyes to give it more character.

Fran Stewart

~ ~ ~

Puzzle

Wednesday February 21, 2018 — I'll be missing the trip to Sapelo Island this year. It's happening during a week when I'm already committed to give a speech, lead a workshop, and conduct a class.

This picture, from three years ago shows what I did when I rested between stints of writing. Putting together a jigsaw puzzle is rather like working on the book I'm currently completing. All those little pieces that will eventually fit together. They will. They will! If I can just write them the right way.

~ ~ ~

Grandma's Hair

Thursday February 22, 2018 — Did I already share this photo with you? Somehow I think I did, but then again, maybe I didn't…

How's that for decisiveness?

At any rate, I love this picture enough to share it several times. When my grandmother was in her thirties (a few years after this photo was taken), she had scarlet fever, and they cut off her hair. When I knew her, her hair was long enough for her to sit on.

In this picture, though, if her hair hadn't been rolled up so tightly down the side of her head and at her neck, it would have been long enough for her to stand on.

As you may have noticed, I'm in the process of growing my hair longer and longer.

The downside of this? My dust-bunnies now consist of shed hair that is LONGER THAN TWO FEET. That's long enough to jam up a vacuum cleaner.

Anybody know of a solution?

Fran Stewart

~ ~ ~

Blog #017 - **Firefighter's Shoes**

Friday February 23, 2018 — When I was in the research phase of writing *Gray as Ashes*, my 7th Biscuit McKee Mystery, I took part in the Gwinnett County Citizen Fire Academy. During the course of the classes, which stretched over a number of Thursday evenings, we had a chance to visit several fire stations.

At one of them, as we were busily asking questions of the firefighters, they got a call. Within less than a minute they had donned their bunker gear—pants, jackets, boots—and were out of the station, leaving behind this evidence of their having been with us just a moment before.

Two lonely pairs of shoes.

I'm so fortunate to be able to do work I love, for the research portion of my book-writing has been fun, exciting, informative, and sometimes distressing, such as when I sat with a fire investigator looking through photographs from closed arson cases in order to glean the details I'd need to show the results of arson in *Gray as Ashes*.

Then there was the time I spent with a nurse discussing the results of gunshot wounds to the abdomen. Discussing it over lunch, which didn't bother either one of us one bit. The people at the next table turned a little green, though.

Do you have to do research for your line of work?

Is it as interesting as mine?

~ ~ ~

Jail-like Retreat

Friday February 23, 2018 — In the final four books of my Biscuit McKee Mysteries (which WILL be published sometime this year, I promise) Biscuit and her friends who're stranded by an ice storm go up to Biscuit's attic and begin investigating the contents of old steamer trunks and armoires and hat boxes.

Each item they find dissolves into the story of why it ended up in Biscuit's attic—her house is more than 200 years old, and the attic is jam-packed. Who put the item there? Why? What happened to those people?

Biscuit and her friends can't go anywhere because of the storm. They can't do any of their usual jobs. It's kind of like a retreat.

Imagine my surprise at seeing a story in the CBC News Digest a few days ago. This is another type of retreat. I'm appalled at the necessity of it. I'm delighted that it's available to people who so desperately need it. If you search for "In a land of workaholics," you'll find the report of how overworked people in Japan pay to spend their vacation in a tiny room with nothing but water, a small table with a blank diary, a yoga mat, and a chamber pot. They wear a loose-fitting uniform, sit on the heated wooden floor and sleep on the yoga mat.

This retreat center is called *Prison Inside Me*.

I can always sit on my front porch and watch the birds chittering around my feeders. That's like a mini vacation, a retreat. Afterwards, I step back into my routine refreshed and invigorated.

Do you have a way of retreating when the pressures of your life seem to expand?

Fran Stewart

~ ~ ~

Treasures

Saturday February 24, 2018 — Good morning!

Spring always amazes me. Where do these treasures come from?

Thank you, Mother Nature.

~ ~ ~

Polly Claire's Tea Shop

Sunday February 25, 2018 — Yesterday Linda Bell and I went to Chattanooga to have a cup of tea at Polly Claire's.

https://www.pollyclaires.com/main-lunch-menu/

Of course, by the time we got there (from Atlanta) it was time for lunch, so we indulged ourselves with the Afternoon Tea. I didn't think to take a photo until we'd already removed half of the goodies from the 3-tiered china serving tray, but despite that, I think you can see how very elegant it was.

Then we proceeded to spend three and a half HOURS eating, chatting, drinking two fat pots of tea (one was Chocolate Rooibos with Calendula Flowers — the other was Caramel and something or other with a spot of fresh cream).

When we arrived at 1:00, the place was completely packed as they always are on Fridays and Saturdays. They were turning away walk-ins. Be sure you make reservations! By 2pm people had begun to leave and, except for one other group, we had the place pretty much to ourselves.

The service was impeccable, the food was beyond delicious, and the company was delightful—I enjoyed our time together, Linda!

~ ~ ~

Collie on Board

Monday February 26, 2018 — Last November, my chiropractor suggested that I start swimming for exercise. "I can't," I told him. "I don't know how to swim, plus I'm afraid of the water."

He looked me square in the eyes and said, "Get over it."

So I went to a nearby county aquatic center and signed up for a year-long senior weekday pass. No excuse. I'm trying to go twice a week every week. And I've almost met that goal.

Still haven't learned to swim. Still haven't gotten my head under the water. But I run in place (hard) in the shallow end (water up to my neck), I flap my flippers (I mean my feet), and I do arm-things. I feel like I'm getting a good workout.

When I left the center one day last week, I saw a Collie peeking out of the back of a car in the parking lot, its white paws lapping over the window. Hoping it (how do you tell the difference between a male and a female collie???) wouldn't jump out, I walked closer, only to find … (see attached photo).

I sure got a laugh out of that.

~ ~ ~

You Need Thumbs

Tuesday February 27, 2018 — I've always had such fun dog sitting my grand-dogs or cat-sitting Picnic and Cousteau, my next-door neighbors' cats. As I think I've shared before, I always write a dog (or cat) daily diary so the mom and dad will know what's been going on. I was looking through some old pictures and found this three-year-old note — one of my favorites.

p.s. Picnic loves being brushed, so naturally, she calls me BrushLady.

p.p.s I already showed you this letter on one of my blog posts last December, but if you didn't happen to read it, now you have another chance!

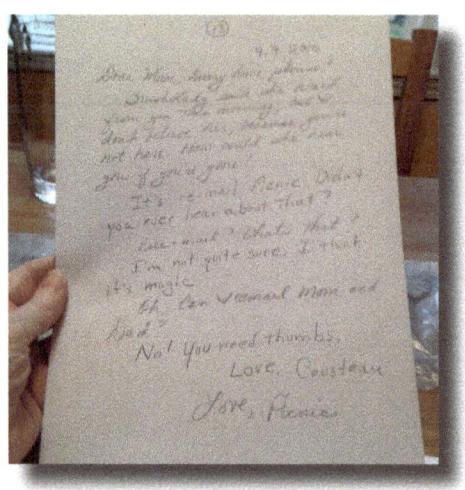

~ ~ ~

Sea Oats

Wednesday February 28, 2018 — It's been too rainy for the past few days here to see any shadows. Everything's a uniform diffuse light. I love cloudy days, though. With my vitiligo, I avoid direct sun as much as possible, at least during the mid-day hours.

That's why, when I'm at Sapelo Island for the art and writing retreat, I go to the beach before dawn, stay until just a bit after the sun appears, and then head back to the shady house. I love this photo of the early morning outline of sea oats on Nanny Goat Beach.

March 2018

Callie Behind the Lace Curtain

Thursday March 1, 2018 — I know lace curtains are horridly passé, but they keep the birds from trying to fly through my windows.

Callie loves them because she can hide behind them (or so she thinks), just like this.

How often, I wonder, have I thought I was hiding, when all that shielded me was naught but lace…

The poet Anne Sexton wrote:

> "As it has been said:
>
> Love and a cough
>
> cannot be concealed.
>
> Even a small cough.

Even a small love."

Especially not with lace curtains.

~ ~ ~

blog #018 -- Tin whistle

Friday March 2, 2018 — In the next few days, I'm going to be sending the "Tin Whistle" story to those of you who've signed up for my newsletter. I promised you a story every month or two up until the WHITE AS ICE quadrilogy (yes - that's a word. I made it up, but it's definitely a word) is published.

Here's the opening to the story, just to wet your whistle. (I admit it. I love puns.) The story comes near the beginning of *Red as a Rooster*, the first of the four books, and the women have just walked up into the cavernous attic. Biscuit McKee—she's the main character in these mysteries—looks around the space, wondering if, even with the help of her women friends, she'll ever manage to organize all that stuff.

A couple of card tables, their spindly legs folded in as if they'd been relegated to "time out," leaned against the wall off to the right of the stairs, and I saw another three farther down the way. Why would anyone need five card tables? Maybe a bridge club? "Feel free to poke around," I said as the women spread out, weaving among the old trunks and dressers and stacks of miscellaneous items.

Glaze crossed her arms. "There doesn't seem to be much organization here."

"Humph!" Ida drew her fingers across the top of an old trunk, leaving a trail in the dust. "There isn't *any* organization here."

The sight of all that … that stuff was a bit daunting, I had to admit. Not only were there numerous trunks and boxes, but a lot of items weren't packed up in any way. The tops of several rickety-looking dressers were piled high with unidentifiable jumbles. I walked over to one of them and brushed aside a hodgepodge of costume jewelry. An old penny whistle caught my eye, so I picked it up and blew into it. Of course, it let out a piercing shriek, which brought all conversation behind me to a stop.

"Sorry," I said. "Couldn't resist it."

Maddy stepped closer to me. "Could I see it?"

"Sure."

She lifted it to her lips and played a merry little tune.

Naturally, we all applauded.

At this point, the story goes into November of 1866, where we meet Josh Hawley.

Josh Hawley's mare was not quite lame, but she had slowed down so much, Josh thought perhaps the nag was on her last legs. He wished he could have stolen a better animal …

If you'd like to find out what happens, be sure to go to my home page, scroll down a bit, and sign up for the newsletter.

[**2010 Note:** Even though the website has changed, you can still sign up for my newsletter on the home page. You just have to scroll all the way to the bottom to do it.]

~ ~ ~

A Gift from Wooly Bear

Friday March 2, 2018 — Guess what greeted me when I came home last night from a marvelous school concert?

It sort of reminded me of what my manuscripts look like after my eagle-eyed beta readers get through with them. There are always scenes that need to be jumbled up and put together in a different way (although that's kind of hard to do with toilet paper).

~ ~ ~

Feet

Saturday March 3, 2018 — A whole lot of years ago, my son took this photo of his niece and nephew. It's another one of those day-brighteners that I thought you might enjoy seeing.

~ ~ ~

Sunday March 4, 2018 — I love March Fourth. It's the only day of the year that gives us a positive instruction.

So, let's do just that.

March Forth!

And, while we're marching, let's plan for the change to daylight savings time next weekend. I do this by setting my alarm fifteen minutes earlier every other day for a week.

This morning, instead of the alarm going off at 4:50, I'd set it for 4:35. That's for today and tomorrow. Then for Tuesday and Wednesday, I'll set it for 4:20. Thursday and Friday will be 4:05, and Saturday will be 3:50. YAWN!!!!! For next Sunday, I'll set the alarm back to the usual 4:50, but my body will (hopefully) be acclimated by then to having lost an hour.

It works better than anything else I've tried over the years. If you want to try it, be my guest!

The Monday after DST kicks in always sees a lot more accidents during commuting time. I'd like you to stay safe this year!

[**2020 Note**: To find out why those accidents occur, read *Why We Sleep* by Matthew Walker. If everybody read it and paid attention, we'd ban daylight savings time in a heartbeat.]

~ ~ ~

Look for Rainbows

Monday March 5, 2018 — If you've ever had one of those days, it's time to concentrate on the goodness.

Fran Stewart

This isn't "airy nothings" either. It makes darn good sense.

~ ~ ~

Seahorse

Tuesday March 6, 2018 — When was the last time you held a miracle in your hand?

This picture was taken in January of 2015 at the Ocean Rider Seahorse Farm and Research Center in Kailua-Kona on the Big Island in Hawaii. The biologist/tour guide told us to form our hands to look like an enclosing coral reef. I did the best I could, and this very pregnant daddy seahorse swam over to investigate. He wrapped his tail around my pinkie finger.

Truly a miracle.

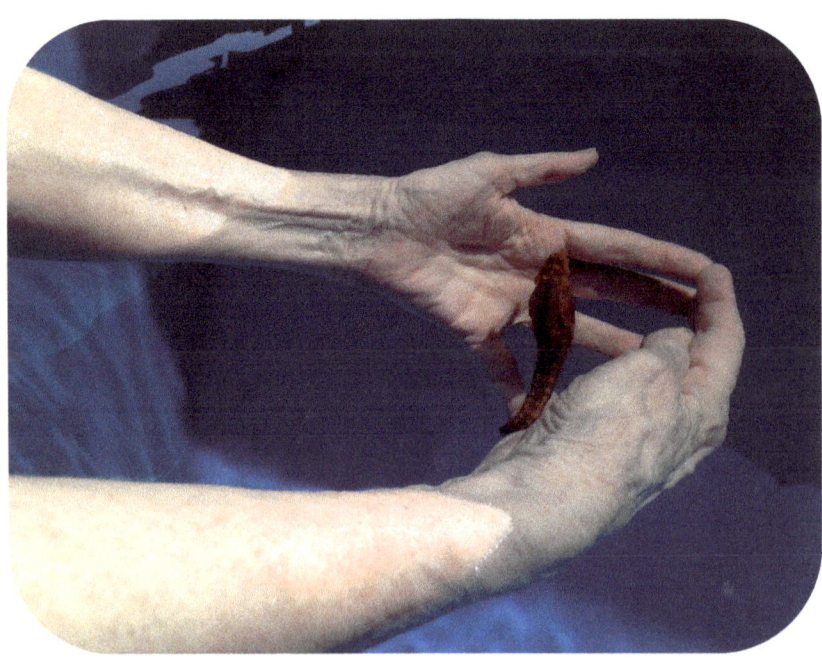

~ ~ ~

Barrymore

Wednesday March 7, 2018 — If you're anywhere near the Atlanta area this weekend, you might want to check out the Atlanta Shakespeare Tavern. shakespearetavern.com

They do Shakespeare 10 or 11 months out of the year, but then they always produce some non-Shakespeare plays in the other months that usually knock my socks off.

This month, I'm looking forward to seeing **Barrymore**, a one-man show about John Barrymore, who was arguably the greatest Shakespearean actor of his generation.

Hope to see you at one of the shows (at least one). I've been known to attend a play twice if I really enjoyed it the first time around, and I think this one is going to be a real winner.

~ ~ ~

Lion in the Circus Room

Thursday March 8, 2018 — My artist friends are at Sapelo Island this week, and I'm not. Each time I've gone there on the weeklong retreat I've gotten so much writing done, usually in the third-floor circus room, decorated by the famous painter, Athos Menaboni. I especially like to set up my laptop underneath this painting of a lion. He seems so sad, looking out from behind the bars, and I can get lost in those eyes of his.

Mystery writers are always looking for a good place to write murder scenes.

But I'll have to do that here at home this week, since I'm lined up to speak to the Alpharetta Chapter of the Georgia Power Ambassadors (wonderful folks who retired from GA Power) on Thursday.

This means that, instead of Menaboni's lion, I'll have Callie sitting on the desk with me and Fuzzy Britches curled up in my lap. My miniature lions, who are considerably happier than the one at Sapelo Island.

~ ~ ~

Will it Last?

Friday March 9, 2018 — Another cat in the bag picture?

Yes.

I happen to like cat-in-the-bag stuff like this.

That particular bag lasted only a couple of months, and then a small rent turned into a major rip as I left the grocery store. No major harm done, but it made me appreciate the old canvas tote bags I got about 35 years ago in Vermont. They're stained as can be, but I'm still using them—for groceries, books, library runs (and cat play places).

Some books are like that. I read them once and that's it. Like a cheap tote, they won't stand the strain. But then there are the books that are still around year after year—the ones I love to re-read because they give such good value.

I sure do hope people feel about my books the way I feel about my good old canvas totes. Those four final books in the Biscuit McKee Series, for instance, the ones that will be released later on this year, I'm hoping they'll stand the test of time, so much so that people will still be reading them thirty, forty, fifty years from now.

Is that too much to expect?

I don't think so. Those four books are turning out to be the best writing I've ever done.

I can hardly wait for you to read them.

p.s. I know I already used this photo once before, but—come on—isn't it cute enough to see again?

~ ~ ~

Boot Hill

Saturday March 10, 2018 — Nine years ago, when I visited my sister in Colorado, she showed me the "cemetery plot" behind one of their outbuildings. Her husband is a retired wheat farmer who has worn jeans and cowboy boots pretty much his entire life.

Now, I ask you, what else do you do with worn-out boots?

The High Cost of Cat Toys

Sunday March 11, 2018 — I spent a fair amount of time recently with friends who have every cat toy imaginable.

Their cat spent most of the time I was there curled up on my lap or stretched out on the carpet of whatever room we were in.

I think cats get bored with the same old toys day after day (even though there may be 300 of them littered around the house).

The advantage of my kind of cat toy is that it is easily replaceable (every time I get a new shipment of books), easily remodeled (every time I cut a new hole in the box), and easily moveable (how much muscle power does it take to move a cardboard box from room to room?)

Yawn

Monday March 12, 2018 — Remember on March 4th when I said I was going to condition my inner clock to readjust, so I'd be ready for daylight savings time?

It didn't quite work.

YAWN!

So, next year, I'll start two weeks early.

 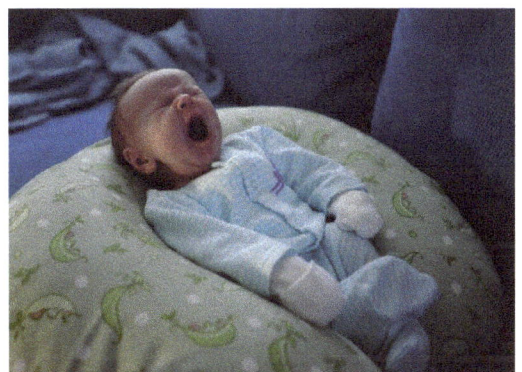

~ ~ ~

yellow iris

Tuesday March 13, 2018 — I had an email from an old friend yesterday, someone I haven't heard from in quite a while. He said he and his wife had five inches of snow and were expecting more.

I told him it had been cold and rainy here.

What I didn't say was that the daffodils are almost bloomed out and we're expecting things to look like this pretty soon—it's a photo taken in my back yard a few Aprils ago.

Treetop Experiences

Wednesday March 14, 2018 — Did you ever try one of these treetop adventures?

I did, five years ago.

Haven't tried another since then.

You see, I got stuck on this one, trying to advance from a teeny platform onto a wiggly walkway made of dangling wooden poles. Try as hard as I could, I simply could not get my feet to cooperate with what my head was trying to tell them to do.

A very kind young employee came up and rescued me, holding the first bouncy wooden stepping pole still enough that I could get my feet in place. He waited to make sure I made it all the way across the chasm, and then he zipped down to the ground with the insouciance of the young.

Good for him.

The rest of my family was finished a LONG time before I got through.

Sort of reminded me of the time I went cross-country skiing in Vermont with a group of friends, all of whom raced ahead, waited for me to catch up, and then immediately headed out for the next stop along the way. I was so busy trying to catch up with them, I never took the time to stop and catch my breath.

Have I mentioned I'm not particularly athletic?

At least I have this one photo of the part of the treetop excursion that I managed just fine.

I'm going to forget about the rest.

~ ~ ~

Is That Your Granddaughter?

Thursday March 15, 2018 — A whole bunch of years ago, I was looking at the huge photograph I have of my grandmother and thinking, wouldn't it be nice to have a big photo like this of myself so I can pass it on to my granddaughter someday. (She was an infant at the time).

So I arranged for a sitting with professional photographer Nancy Welsheimer. This portrait of me is almost three feet tall.

I know my hair's different now (white instead of brown). I know I have a few more wrinkles (all right, already, a lot more wrinkles). I know my skin's gotten crepe-y instead of smooth. But it's still me in there, right?

A month or two ago someone came to my house, took a look at the photo, and said, "Oh! Is that your granddaughter?"

<<sigh>> I guess that's *not* me in there anymore.

~ ~ ~

blog #020 We Can't Unchoose

Friday ~~March 14~~ **March 16, 2018** — Do you ever wonder what writers go through to keep all the details right in their WIP (work in progress)?

I thought I'd share this photo of a page that covers the genealogy of the Hastings family. I have five other charts like this, one for each major family in these last four Biscuit McKee mysteries.

I don't know how clear this will be on your computer or phone or tablet, but there's a note on the right-hand side of this page that says, "Whoops! Baxter only 4 years old in 1865!" I've had other mix-ups where someone was twelve the year he was supposed to be getting married. Or somebody else had already died five years before I show her interacting with her grandchild.

So far, I've managed to correct each of these problems, but no matter how much charts help — they help only if the author pays attention to them.

In teaching the Memoirs class last Tuesday, I read something to my students from *Learning to Walk in the Dark* by Barbara Brown Taylor. She talked about people reaching a certain stage of their lives when they "live with the consequences of choices they cannot unchoose." I've had many of those moments in my life when I realized the path I was on was one I'd plotted out for myself by the numerous choices I'd made throughout my life. I haven't always been happy with where those paths led me.

"What I'm asking you to do," I told the memoirs class, "is to pick one of those choices you can *not* now unchoose. Then go deeper." You see, there's no need to dwell on the anguish that might have resulted or on what appears to be a dead end you've gotten yourself into. "Tell us about what you learned from the experience," I told them. "Tell us the rich lesson that awaited you there at the end of that path."

Just like my genealogy chart, though, we may not see the lesson unless we look for it.

Who was it who said, "The unexamined life is not worth living"? Socrates, you say? Thank you. I thought so.

Now, for a writer who simply writes the wrong character at the wrong age or the wrong place in the story, it's a simple job of editing out the mistakes or correcting the timeline. I take that back. It may not be a simple process at all. But at least it can be done.

The "choices we can't unchoose," though, the ones we make in life (as opposed to those in a book draft) need a different approach. Perhaps we could embrace them, so that they no longer frighten us. Perhaps we can welcome these lessons, hard as they may seem.

It's worth thinking about, wouldn't you say?

[**2020 Note**: See the last paragraph of my post on 3/20/18 to find out why today's date and the next few as well have been corrected.]

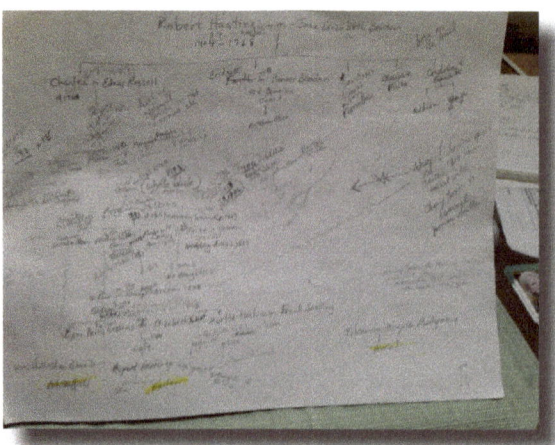

p.s. I know I've shared this photo with you already, but maybe you've forgotten about it?

~ ~ ~

Sapelo Sea Oats

~~Friday March 15~~, **Saturday March 17, 2018** — My artist friends are back from Sapelo Island, and I'm sitting here wishing I'd been able to go with them. I've had a busy, busy two weeks, and I really feel like I could have used some Sapelo time, away from meetings, chores, phone calls, emails. Time to get some solid writing done.

You see, I've been promising you that these last four Biscuit McKee Mysteries WILL be released this year. Since they're coming out one month apart, that means the first of the four (RED AS A ROOSTER) has to be out by September at the very latest, so the fourth one will be available no later than December.

AARGH! I don't have the final murder(s) wrapped up yet. On my blog today, I show an example of the genealogy chart I use for one of the six major families in the books. My gosh, but it's confusing, even for me (and I'm supposed to know what it's all about).

Since I haven't had Sapelo time, I have a built-in excuse. But I will not make excuses for myself. I will not. I will NOT.

"Sit your butt in your seat and write." That's the advice I gave the memoirs class I'm teaching.

Maybe I need to follow my own advice… Ya think?

[**2020 Note:** This rushed deadline is the reason a number of errors weren't caught in those final four books. If I had it to do over again, I would have pushed the deadline out three or four months. Instead, what I've done is to put out a revised edition of ALL my Biscuit McKee books. You can find those better editions at my website franstewart.com]

Fran Stewart

~ ~ ~

Sun on His Tongue

~~Saturday March 16,~~ **Sunday March 18, 2018** — I like Nordic runes. Years ago, my son made a set for me. He took an old cedar root, cut it into sections, and carved the runes onto them. Yesterday I drew the one called Sowelu, which is a rune that represents the sun's energy.

This is certainly the time of year for it, as the earth begins to warm up for the coming springtime. (My apologies to my fans in Australia and New Zealand — I know you're headed into the winter season now.)

Credit for this sun photo goes to Steve Reiman. He took it eleven years ago, and Aiden's mom (Aiden is the one balancing the sun on his tongue) shared it with me.

So today, I wish you a taste of the sun. Even though it might be cloudy, the sun IS shining up there!

~ ~ ~

Sticking Out Her Tongue

~~Sunday March 17~~ **Monday March 19, 2018** — Yesterday it was the sun on my grandson's tongue. Today it's my big sister's tongue—for what reason I have no idea, but the two of us obviously thought it was funny all those years ago.

So, here's your laugh for the day.

Go ahead. Stand in front of a mirror and stick your tongue out just the way Diana is doing. Bet you'll have to laugh!

~ ~ ~

Grandma's Photo

~~Monday March 18~~ **Tuesday March 20, 2018** — A couple of days ago, Lollie Beck said she wanted to see the "grandmother photo" I mentioned in my post. Grandma was seventeen when this photo was taken. It always hung in the bedroom where my parents and I stayed when we visited. I loved the nights when rain pounded on the tin roof. The house had been built in the mid 1800s, and you could still see places where pegs (rather than nails) had been used.

Anyway, one day I heard Grandma telling my mother that her daughters and daughters-in-law all wanted the picture. "What they really want is the frame," she said, and I could hear the bitterness in her voice.

Fran Stewart

I piped up in my five-year-old voice and said, "If they get the frame, could I have the picture?" My mother told me to hush.

When my grandmother died twenty-some-odd years later, she willed me the photograph, including the frame.

~ ~ ~

The Other Photo of Grandma

~~Tuesday~~ **Wednesday, March 21, 2018** — While we're talking about grandmothers, here's another photo of my grandma (Mary Frances) with her mother (Geonette). When you read my WHITE AS ICE quadrilogy — once I get it finished and published — you'll notice I used both those names for historical characters. Mary Frances is something of a star in the saga, while Geonette is more of a minor character.

In fact, I've used a lot of names from my family tree — Morgan, Tobe, Surratt. They were just too good to pass up. Tobe, by the way, is one syllable, with a long O sound.

I'm getting closer to the end of the writing. One more beta-read cycle after that, and then, to the publisher!!

Blessings, by the way, on my patient beta-readers, Darlene, Diana, and Millie. This book in four volumes is way longer than *Gone with the Wind*, and they've read multiple versions of it.

Can't wait to see these books in print.

And thank you, to my old college roommate, Kay Eatmon, for pointing out that I've had the dates mixed up on these posts for the past five days. That could be because I've been sicker than the proverbial dog since late Thursday. I thought I was doing pretty well just to get something posted each day. About the only other thing I've done is sleep 18 hours each day. Fortunately, my granddaughter came over and forced me to eat something. Bless her!

Another Post for Today – Starburst

Wednesday March 21, 2018 —Do you leave love notes in odd places? School lunch bags, for instance?

Thought this note from my daughter to her daughter would brighten your day.

~ ~ ~

Jump for Joy

Thursday March 22, 2018 — Celebrating springtime.

This is my daughter of the heart expressing the joy that abounds in her.

Go ahead. Jump for joy today.

~ ~ ~

Blog #021 Not Ready to Flower Yet

Friday March 23, 2018 — If you've read this blog (all 20 previous Friday Fare posts on it) or any of my other blogs over the years, you may have noticed that I tend not to be political in my writings. It's always been a conscious choice.

But with the shootings in the schools and with so many students protesting against guns, I think it's time to speak out.

Please understand, I will not discuss the Second Amendment here. This is not what the problem is about.

Instead, I offer an open letter to America's students.

> Dear future leaders of this country:
>
> I understand your anger, for my generation felt similar anger. We marched, we protested, but ultimately, this country is still involved in unnecessary wars because the protests did not change the power structure that fed those wars.
>
> If you want to make a true difference, run for office. As soon as you're old enough, start locally. It will take not hundreds of you, but thousands of you. But you have the numbers; you have the passion. What you need is the vote and the chance to make changes from the bottom up. School board,

zoning commission. Attend their meetings, starting now if you can. Learn everything you can about how government works in this country so you will be fully prepared when it's time to run for those offices.

How many of our current senators and representatives, particularly on a state level, started out as county commissioners or school board members? That's a good starting place for you.

A plant needs to start as a seed before it can ever reach the level of leaf or flower. As your age increases, and your knowledge about government deepens, and your political base widens, you will be able to work at the state level. Once you're there, if there are enough of you voting together, you can make real change.

For one, introduce the concept of term limits. We have far too many professional politicians in office whose sight is always on the next election rather than on how they can make a real difference.

A second idea: Eliminate gerrymandering as much as possible. With the changing demographics of this country, skewed political regions no longer make sense — not that they ever did.

A third idea: Rearrange the seating in our houses and senates. Wouldn't it be easier to work together if there weren't an aisle separating the Democrats from the Republicans? There's nothing wrong with strictly alphabetical seating.

You will have many more ideas about what will improve this country.

I applaud your desire for change.

I agree that things have gone desperately wrong in many ways.

And let me know when you run for office. I'd love to support you.

Most sincerely,

  —Fran Stewart

~ ~ ~

My Rant

Friday March 23, 2018 — I'm on a rant against Facebook, folks. For some time I've been trying to shift my personal page to show only posts of and by family and closest friends. That hasn't worked, since any friend requests by my book fans get shunted to THAT personal page rather than to my author page. I've been trying to delete my personal page and keep only my FranStewartAuthor page. I even announced publicly that that was my intention.

It turns out, I can't do that.

The only way to get rid of the "personal" page is to delete my account completely, which will wipe out ALL of my FB presence, including this author page. Then I'd have to start over again and re-create my author page, the one I post on every single morning.

Now the questions are:

    1. Do I want to do this? Or will it turn out to be more trouble than I want to tackle?

    2. Do I just continue to ignore the personal page? I've bookmarked the pages of my family and dear friends—those are almost the only FB things I ever look at.

    3. Do I continue to put up with the stupid spam friend requests? You'd be surprised how many military colonels there are (HA!) who want to be friends with me. Or maybe you wouldn't be surprised, since you've probably been inundated with those fakes yourself.

    4. Does someone know of a miracle cure for this—a way of getting rid of FranStewart and saving FranStewartAuthor? If so, I'd love to hear from you.

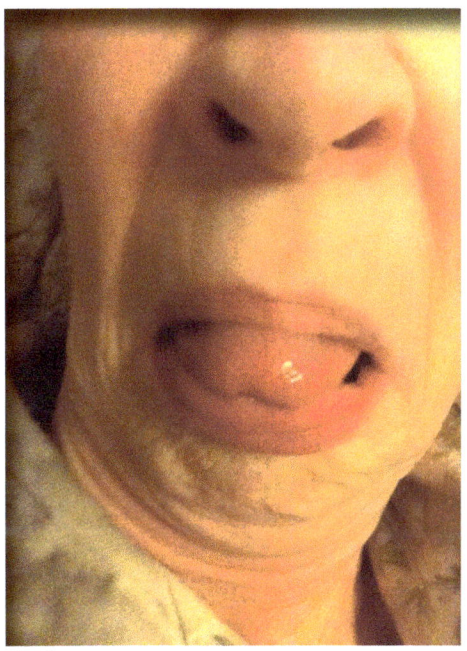

Cat Hair in the Suet Feeder

Saturday March 24, 2018 — It's nest-building time. The little Carolina Wrens have been dead set on emptying the mealworm feeder, and the cat hair I've been saving all winter long is going fast, as countless birds gather the fuzzy clumps to line their nests.

Every time I brush the cats, which means every single day year-round, I pull the hair out of their brushes and stick it in an old suet feeder hanging under the eaves of my front porch.

A couple of weeks ago, this "fur feeder" was packed full. Now there are all sorts of empty spots. I'd better get to brushing more vigorously.

I used to include the contents of my own hairbrush as well, but the last bunch of years my hair has been too long, and the birds couldn't unwind it from the wire. Three or four inches was easy for them, but two-foot-long silver strands are more than they can handle!

What do you do to get ready for spring?

~ ~ ~

rain on leaves

Sunday March 25, 2018 — What was that old song about rainy days and Sundays?

They don't get me down. I love rainy days—or, in this case, a rainy night. Five years ago, I took this photo of raindrops in my yard. Each little drop seems to be a world unto its own.

Sort of like people in a crowd.

I plan to think about that this evening when I'm walking through the rain. All those little worlds pelting down around me. Hard to feel lonely with that much company.

On the Fence

Monday March 26, 2018 — Ah! Memory Lane.

How I wish I knew where that particular fence was. My sister said she doesn't know either. That's the trouble with not labeling photos…

p.s. I love that hat I'm wearing. Wish I still had it. And the hand-knit sweater with the bumpy little pocket? Wonderful.

~ ~ ~

Poem

Tuesday March 27, 2018 — Imagine walking into a building (the art department at the University of Texas Austin) and seeing a big square column with only the left-hand side of this picture showing. Read that diatribe. Now change your perspective by walking a little farther so you can see the whole picture (both sides of the column at once).

I enjoy the cleverness of this sort of poetic construction, but the thought it expresses is even more impressive. Especially now, when so many events seem to be conspiring to drain our very souls, we need to take back our power—our ability to determine how we will respond rather than simply reacting to the world around us.

Have yourself an absolutely good day. You *can* change the world.

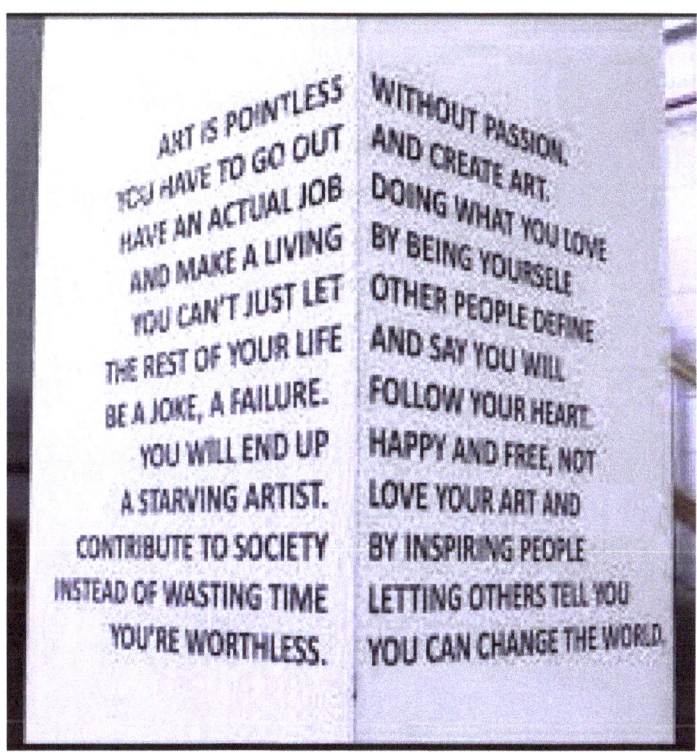

Photo credit: Jasmine Kay. Used with her permission

~ ~ ~

Pile of Leaves

Wednesday March 28, 2018 — The leaves are just beginning to bud out on the trees (at least they are here in Georgia). And here I am remembering the piles of autumn leaves that will need to be raked off the deck six or seven months from now.

Jumping into a pile of leaves is one of those things that's a lot more fun to think about than it is to actually do. The leaves look like they're going to be all cushy and soft — and then you jump and crash right to the hard deck (or the hard ground) at the bottom.

Did that ever happen to you?

Do you wish it could have ended up differently?

~ ~ ~

Everything We Do

Thursday March 29, 2018 — Did you ever have one of those days when you had a kazillion things to do and only about sixteen waking hours in which to do them?

Yeah. Me too.

So, I can choose to be frantic about it, or I can choose to be peaceful about it.

I choose peace. What are you going to choose today?

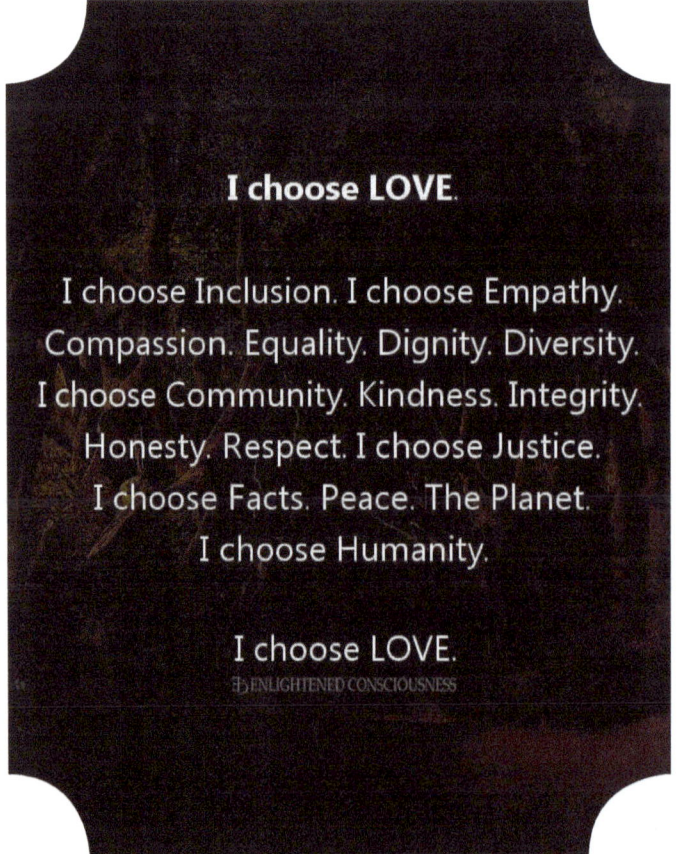

~ ~ ~

blog #022 When People Walk Away from You

Friday March 30, 2018 — I've had a lot of people ask me why I'm choosing to end my Biscuit McKee Mystery Series after the final "quadrilogy" is published later this year.

The question reminds me of this quotation about "their part in your story." There simply came a time when I knew without a doubt that it was time to let Biscuit and Marmalade go.

For I've told a story, over the course of these eleven books, that encompasses a whole town and a whole lot of lives and a number of issues. This is a story that only I could tell. It's one I'm proud of. It's one I hope people will read and re-read over the years to come, the way I periodically re-read every book Louise Penny wrote, simply because I love the way her characters evolve and interweave.

My characters are going to be around a long time, after all. Every book or e-book is a part of my ongoing legacy.

I'm getting close to the end of the writing process for these four final books, by the way. Just a few more loose ends to tie up.

So, if you want to read all the books in order, you might want to start now with ORANGE AS MARMALADE. That way, by the time RED AS A ROOSTER comes out, you'll have the first seven books fresh in mind.

In case you're wondering about the correct order of the books:

Orange as Marmalade
Yellow as Legal Pads
Green as a Garden Hose
Blue as Blue Jeans
Indigo as an Iris
Violet as an Amethyst
Gray as Ashes
Red as a Rooster
Black as Soot
Pink as a Peony, and
White as Ice.

"When people walk away from you...
Let them go.....
Your destiny is never tied to anyone who leaves you, and it doesn't mean they are bad people.

It just means that their part in your story is over."

Fran Stewart

~ ~ ~

The Things You Want / The Things You Have

Friday March 30, 2018 — Something to think about.

Gratitude is one of my guiding principles, so when I saw this reminder on the website for The Miracles Store, I identified with it completely.

Today, on my Friday Fare blog, I talked about the legacy I'll be leaving when my Biscuit McKee Mystery Series ends. I hope you'll head over there and check it out.

~ ~ ~

Fear has Two Meanings

Saturday March 31, 2018 — For years I've heard that F.E.A.R. stands for "False Events Appearing Real," and that interpretation has a lot to say for it.

But I like this idea better. I found it at The Miracles Store website. Two meanings to choose from — not just to philosophize about, but to give us a choice of what sort of action to take. React or respond.

What about it? Are you picking the first meaning or the second one today?

Bet you can guess which one I'll choose…

April 2018

The light is in you

Sunday April 1, 2018 — The start to a new month - the start to a new week - April Fool's Day - and, for some people, the Easter holiday (holy day).

No matter how we approach today, let's remember that light always overcomes darkness.

As Bobby McFerrin said in his musical version of the 23rd psalm,

"Even though I walk

through a dark and dreary land,

there is nothing that can shake me,

She has said She won't forsake me,

I am in Her hand."

Today—and every day—walk in the light.

~ ~ ~

Mirror

Monday 2 April 2018 — Here's another one of those mirror photos by my dad. I'm constantly intrigued with the idea of mirrors. After all, everything we see in them is backwards. I still remember seeing a photograph of myself once and wondering why my hair was parted on the wrong side.

It's something to keep in mind. No need to gaze into a mirror too long or too often, because what we see there isn't how the world sees us.

Instead of looking into a mirror today, I plan to look into my heart.

~ ~ ~

I don't want to just read books …

Tuesday 3 April 2018 — This explains how I feel about books by a lot of my favorite authors. But it's also how I'm feeling about the WHITE AS ICE quadrilogy I'm getting close to finishing.

Fran Stewart

The characters over many generations interweave so beautifully, I find myself wishing I had an attic just like Biscuit's that I could explore with a number of good women friends. Since I don't have an attic, the next best thing for me to do is infuse my life (and my books) with these people's stories.

Yeah, okay, I know—I really do know—that I've made all this up, but the people in these books are so very real to me. I'm hoping you're going to love them as much as I do. That you'll want to spend lots of time with them (remember the post I did about s-l-o-w reading, to make the story last longer and to remember it better?)

To date, the manuscript (all four books in one enormous file) adds up to 439,886 words. And they're 439,000+ good words. Best mystery I've ever written.

~ ~ ~

My To-Do List for Today

Wednesday 4 April 2018 — A to-do list like this sure beats the one I put together last night.

~ ~ ~

Six Years Ago

Thursday 5 April 2018 — Exactly six years ago, these Dianthus blooms greeted me when I walked outside.

I have a tendency to think that I shouldn't need the furnace on in April in Georgia. So I generally turn the doggone thing off somewhere around April 1st. That's what I did this year. And opened my upstairs windows a few inches. Last night I didn't think to read a weather report. During the night, I pulled the extra blanket over me (after wrestling it away from under Woolly Bear).

This morning, the outside temp is 35 degrees and the inside temp is 56. Brrr!

Needless to say, I closed the windows and turned the furnace back on. Equally needless to report is that the Dianthus blooms haven't appeared yet this year.

~ ~ ~

Genie Guthrie's gift flowers

Friday 6 April 2018 — Did you ever get a package decorated with real live flowers?

I did last summer, from Genie Guthrie. It was almost too pretty to open—although open it I did after appropriate oohs and aahs. I've often wondered whether Genie realized that I appreciated the wrapping almost as much as the wonderful handcrafted gift inside.

I saved this photo of the package to remind me how much little touches can mean.

~ ~ ~

blog #023 – blue & gray ribbon hat

Friday April 6, 2018 — One of my favorite bloggers, Heidi Wilson from ThursdayNightWrites, asked last week if there is ever such a thing as too much research for writers. Although many critics warn writers against becoming so caught up in the research that they stop writing, Heidi contends (as do I) that research is one of the fun things about writing, so why should we limit ourselves?

One of the byproducts of research is that it can lead us into new story twists that we might not have devised otherwise.

She quotes Christopher de Hamel's 2017 blockbuster, *Meetings with Remarkable Manuscripts*. "Okay," she says, "it may not have been on the bestseller lists. But it's 632 pages long and weighs three pounds." That must count for a lot.

De Hamel writes about medieval manuscripts, and Wilson was fascinated by his description of the numerous drawings in the margins of these manuscripts. The marginalia, she writes, are:

…calculated to appeal to a child. One of them shows a cat playing a rebec, a sort of early fiddle. This image occurs in many illuminated manuscripts and harks back, de Hamel believes, to whatever tale or folk belief gave us "Hey diddle, diddle, the cat and the fiddle." He adds that when a dinner guest of his own, a master of medieval music, arrived with a rebec, an experiment became possible. The musician played, and de Hamel's cat "rushed in as if drawn by a magnet, rolling on the floor in ecstasy, as punch drunk as a dervish."

Now, I ask you, can you imagine what Wilson might have missed if she'd stopped after just a page or two into de Hamel's book?

If you want to read the whole blog post, here's the link to it: https://thursdaynightwrites.com/2018/04/02/remarkable-manuscripts/

I've gotten sidetracked myself in researching the numerous subjects and time periods covered in my WHITE AS ICE quadrilogy. I researched the first World's Fair of 1876, which was put on in honor of America's first centennial celebration; I looked up "woolgathering" which came from the aimless appearance of people who roamed around meadows gathering tufts of wool caught on shrubs after sheep had passed by; and the powerful solar storm of 1859, which set telegraph offices on fire. I looked into the gas-rationing program of 1942, the origin of the straw boater, and women's hats in the 1800s, which is how I found this photo of a "hat" made of ribbons"

I didn't think to look up "hey diddle, diddle," but I did do quite a bit of reading about nursery rhymes in general and about jump-roping chants. Great fun.

Can't wait for these four books to be released so you can share in the fun!

~ ~ ~

One Day

Saturday 7 April 2018 — Zen in a cartoon.

It's a good way to live.

I was thinking about writing a long, involved essay about this idea, but now that I'm here at the computer, I realize I don't need to add a thing.

Mount Vernon Songbird Sanctuary

Sunday April 8, 2018 — As long as we're talking about the weather (as we were a few days ago), I couldn't resist this little bit of bird humor from the Mount Vernon Songbird Sanctuary.

Go ahead, start your day with a laugh.

It can't hurt.

It might help.

~ ~ ~

"Idiot" daffodil bulb

Monday April 9, 2018 — And then here's a bit of garden humor, from the same FB page as yesterday.

Sometimes, writers get into a quandary like this — the way I've done with WHITE AS ICE. I wrote myself into a corner with a character who (I've assumed for the entire time I've been writing this) was going one way, and I just figured out that particular character has been headed in a different direction all along. I thought spring was coming, and I wrote in that direction, and now I have to backtrack and do a heck of a lot of tweaking along the way to make this work out right in the end.

At least I have the luxury of a publisher who's willing to let me extend my deadline. Otherwise I'd be fighting the bitter winds of panic just like these daffodils.

Fran Stewart

~ ~ ~

Ready to Open

Tuesday April 10, 2018 — Yesterday when I walked out to put a letter in the mailbox—I send the big Sunday newspaper crossword to my sister every week—this iris (along with a whole slew of its sister flowers) was ready to burst open. I love my Grandma's irises.

About twenty years ago I'd visited my Aunt Mary Nell in Tennessee and she gave me a whole box of iris corms. This dark indigo/purple. A bunch of lavender/white combinations.

The original irises had come from her mother's (my grandmother's) garden. Grandma was the one with the long, long hair that I wrote about a number of months ago here on this FB page.

I planted the corms at the house I lived in at that time. When I moved here onto the other side of Hog Mountain 14 years ago—has it really been that long?—I divided the irises, leaving plenty behind for the new owners, and transplanted them here.

This particular bunch served as inspiration for some of the action in *Indigo As An Iris*, my fifth Biscuit McKee mystery. And the name of the book as well.

It's hard to kill an iris. As delicately beautiful as they are, they're also pretty darn tough. This morning I woke up around one o'clock with an iris type of idea that I could incorporate into my WHITE AS ICE quadrilogy. Just in the same way these iris buds are ready to burst open at any minute the way the one on top of this stalk is doing, these ideas of mine swell and grow and finally burst forth at any and all times of day or night until I have to get up and write them down.

This particular "one a.m. idea" was a letter from Nicholas. Remember that - so when you come across it in the book, you'll be able to say, "I know where she got the idea for this one!"

And then send me a message about it. I'd love to hear from you.

~ ~ ~

On Her Lap

Wednesday April 11, 2018 — I think this is the last of the "walk down memory lane" photos of my sister and me.

Unless I find some others.

Sort of like the "attic stories" in WHITE AS ICE. Two days ago, I thought I'd completed all of these tales of where the various items in Biscuit's attic came from. But then Biscuit and her friends found a few more things that needed inclusion and explanation.

Such an adventure!

Fran Stewart

~ ~ ~

Blue Iris

Thursday April 12, 2018 — I'm feeling a little out of focus this morning, sort of like this photo of Grandma's iris. It may have something to do with the fact that I stayed up WAY too late last night. I was reading; Fuzzy Britches was comfortably ensconced in my lap; I had a big mug of licorice root herbal tea at hand; and I wasn't wearing my watch, so I had no sense of the passage of time.

As to this photo, I was actually taking a picture of a newly planted viburnum, off to the left of this one, and this iris showed up in the lower right-hand corner. When I finally decided the iris was more interesting, I cropped the photo. A lot. So the greatly enlarged iris shows up as a bit grainy.

As I said, it's sort of the way I'm feeling right now.

Maybe a cup of tea would help.

blog #024—Miss Polly's White Whiskers

Friday April 13, 2018 – A writer, particularly a mystery writer, has to pick up tiny clues from all around, kind of the way cat whiskers do. The tiniest vibration transmits its way to a cat's brain, even from far out on the tip of the longest whiskers, giving the cat a clear picture of just where that cat is in its environment.

When I'm immersed in writing, I feel like my whisker messages are coming at me at full speed. Until, all of a sudden, they aren't.

Like the past two days.

I'd been writing up a storm and then, the way it sometimes happens, life kind of got in the way. As if my virtual whiskers had been shaved off. My total increase in word count for the past two days? Zero.

That's right. Zero. It's a little hard to meet a deadline when that happens.

So, what can I do to change this picture?

Well, in the Memoirs class I'm teaching, I talk about prompts — those words or phrases that tickle your memory about something that needs writing.

So, just a few minutes ago I went through the basket I have here beside my computer, pulling out stray scraps of paper. "Square spectacles," one of them says. "Moose fat candles," "strangely unnerved," "Johnny Cakes," "S tells MF to be careful."

Will any of these help get me re-started?

How the heck do I know? But I can feel the whiskers beginning to tickle, so there's hope. There's always hope.

Fran Stewart

~ ~ ~

"Just when the caterpillar …"

Friday April 13, 2018 — A number of years ago, I was at a crossroads in my life, without knowing which way to turn.

A squirrel or a passing bird or maybe it was just the wind ferried a maypop seed into my front yard, and I ended up with maypop vines growing higgledy-piggledy all over the place.

I let them grow.

Which was a good thing, because the maypop is the host plant for the Gulf Fritillary Butterfly, an enchanting little orange creature with silver underneath its wings. Unbeknownst to me, the mama fritillaries laid their eggs on the maypop vines, which meant that scads of caterpillars munched on the vines repeatedly. Thank goodness so many had grown up there. It was like a banquet hall.

And then the caterpillars began to attach themselves to vines, trees, house siding, wherever, and spin their cocoons. I counted more than twenty chrysalises hanging on the side of my house at one point.

And I was fortunate enough to be able to watch one caterpillar work (it's really hard work) to change itself into the chrysalis form right beside my front door. A scant few weeks later (can't recall the exact time sequence), I walked outside one Saturday morning and saw that the cocoon looked—somehow—different. I stood there for hours and watched the complete hatching process.

Throughout that summer I was, somehow, revising myself. It wasn't as obvious as the transformation from egg to caterpillar to chrysalis to butterfly, but it was ultimately as life-changing.

My butterfly life as a writer was beginning, even though I wasn't quite aware yet that my chrysalis was beginning to crack open.

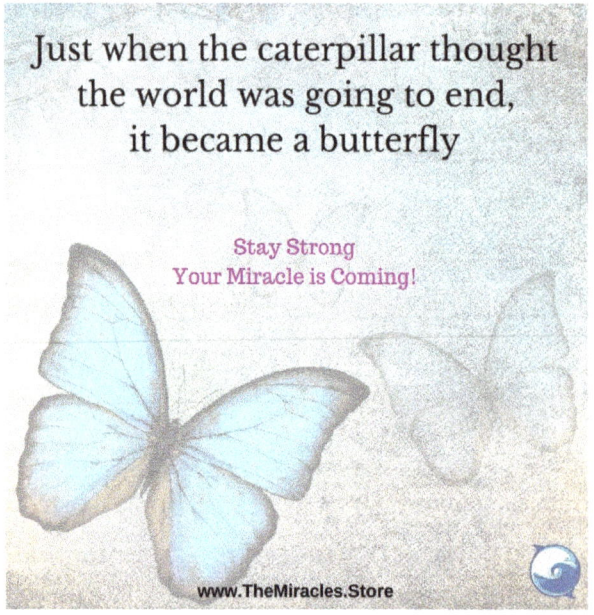

~ ~ ~

My Backyard

Saturday April 14, 2018 — Sometimes, if you don't get what you want, maybe you're not reaching high enough.

Fourteen years ago, while I was looking for a house to buy, I gave my realtor a list of what I wanted. Mainly it was just a bay window. And a skylight.

After weeks of fruitless searches, we had an appointment to go on a Saturday to look at houses. The evening before, I sent my realtor a new list:

1. bay window

2. skylight

3. wood burning stove (or a fireplace inset)

4. a creek in the back yard

5. a back deck and

6. a front porch.

When he picked me up, he was not happy. The first house we looked at had 2 of the 6 items. The second one had a different set of two. The third house had only one. The fourth house had 4 of the 6. The fifth house is the one I bought. It had everything I asked for.

This photo, taken in April of 2013, shows part of my back yard—the part with the creek in it. Looking out from my deck now, this is pretty much what I'm seeing, although the ferns aren't quite as unfurled as these. Another two weeks, and they'll be fully open.

I'm so glad I extended my list.

Cat Paw and Tail

Sunday April 15, 2018 — A paw and a tail.

Quite a lesson there.

Do I want to move forward or trail behind?

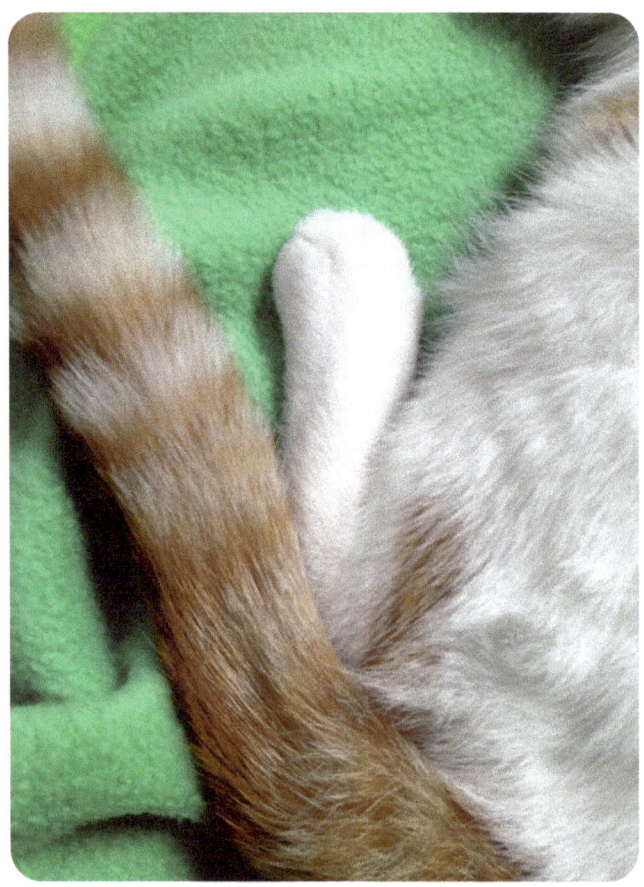

White Flower

Monday April 16, 2018 — I loved finding out that there were flowers that bloomed from December to February here in Georgia. Back in Vermont, even the winter-blooming witch hazel sometimes didn't make it quite that early.

Some of the people I know are like that. You never know when they're going to bloom…

~ ~ ~

Rain on the Skylight

Tuesday April 17, 2018 — Two days ago it rained all day long. I love the way the rain on the skylight makes it look all out of focus. When a day is out of focus like that, it's amazing how much I can get accomplished.

What, you may ask, did I accomplish that day?

Drum roll, please.

I sent the manuscript for RED AS A ROOSTER to my publisher.

YES ! ! ! ! ! The first of these last four books of mine is complete ! ! !

How many exclamation points can I work in here?

Now—as a reality check—there still are a number of steps before any of us will see the actual book, but it's on its way, and all I need to do is tweak the other three.

Celebrate with me, please!

Fran Stewart

~ ~ ~

Dandelions and Golden Iris

Wednesday April 18, 2018 — Guess what else is blooming in my yard? Not just the gorgeous irises, but the humble sturdy dandelions as well.

Why do I let the dandelions grow? Aren't they just weeds? What possible good are they?

Every once in a while, I come across a dandelion kind of person, and I find myself wondering why on earth that person has come into my life.

Dandelions:

    1. They're bright and beautiful

    2. They produce a lot of pollen and nectar that the bees just love

    3. Their tender spring leaves make a great addition to salads

    4. Dandelion wine, anyone?

Dandelion People:

    1. They help me appreciate my bright and beautiful life

2. They produce those kinds of feelings in me that make me think

3. They may do a pretty good job of masking their tender insides, but I know that they're carrying a heavy load. I may not know what it is, but I know it's there.

4. A new friend, perhaps?

~ ~ ~

If speaking kindly to plants…

Thursday April 19, 2018 — In one of the scenes from PINK AS A PEONY, Biscuit recalls having been told once that if she's upset with someone, she can light a candle and imagine all the anger being consumed by the candle flame.

If we'd all just hold our tongues a bit longer. After all, not everything that we think necessarily needs to be spoken.

I'm going to try little extra kindness today.

Won't you join me?

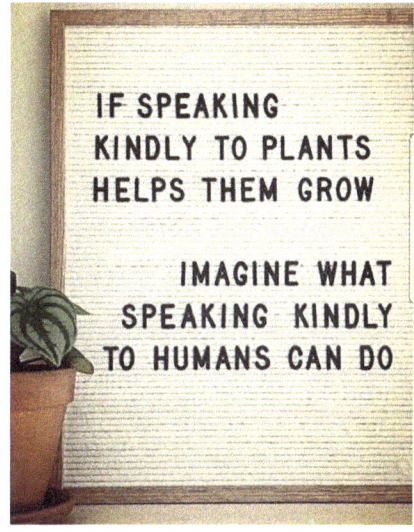

Fran Stewart

~ ~ ~

blog #025—Mozelle's Frog

Friday April 20, 2018 — Imagine for a moment that I'd cropped this photo until the only thing showing was the frog itself. Unless you're a frog specialist who could identify this tiny tree frog, you'd probably believe me if I warned you that the frog was a giant invasive species, at least a foot and a half long.

But with somebody's index finger in the shot, you have a better sense of perspective.

Writing is sort of like that. We authors can choose what to emphasize in our scenes, what to discount. We can crop the picture any way we want to tell whatever story we're focusing on.

This is particularly true when we write mysteries — how to put the murderer in the story without bringing too much attention to that particular character. You have to be sure he or she is there so the reader won't feel cheated at the end—but you really don't want people guessing who it is too soon.

I got to thinking, though, since I'm teaching a series of classes on how to write memoirs, that what we choose to emphasize or crop out almost completely comes into play when we're writing the stories of our lives. There are episodes in every life that could do with some cropping, right? Or the ones where we wish our rather minor role had been considerably more heroic.

So, think about it. Those frogs in your life? Are you going to blow them all out of proportion or will you Photoshop in a great big index finger so the frog seems minuscule by comparison?

Really, it'll be up to you.

Imagine the feeling of power!

On the other hand, if you publish the book, you're going to have to take responsibility when somebody says, "Hey! That frog of yours is completely the wrong size!"

Lion in the Tree

Friday April 20, 2018 — Come on, admit it. Wouldn't you love sometime to be able to climb up in a big old tree and relax as completely as this lion is doing?

I used to love climbing trees when I was a kid, but somewhere along the line I got out of the habit. I've tried thinking back, but I can't remember the last time I climbed a tree. Maybe it was the time Phillip Van Stavern, the little neighborhood boy I was climbing a great big ole pine tree with, fell on his way down and broke his arm. Was that it? I was only five or six, and I honestly can't remember any more trees after that. I found out later that Phillip had never climbed a tree before, but he wasn't going to be outdone by the new girl on the block. He shoulda known better.

My daughter used to love climbing trees, too. Once, when she was five or six, she climbed almost to the top of a 30-foot white birch. She called out a cheery hello as I stood next door talking to a neighbor. The first thing the neighbor said was: (to me) "Oh my God!" and (to Veronica in a loud voice) "You're going to fall!!!"

I could have willingly strangled that woman. How often do we do exciting, happy, adventuresome things, only to have some well-meaning but clueless person preach to us about the dangers involved?

Veronica knew perfectly well how to be careful in a tree. She'd learned on little trees and then gradually stretched herself to take on more challenging ones. I don't know for sure, but I wonder if she ever climbed another tree after that neighbor prophesied doom to her.

Did you climb trees when you were a kid?

Ever take a nap in one of them?

Keep Calm

Saturday April 21, 2018 — Have you met a new author lately? No telling how much fun you'll have if you give it a try.

My friend Doug Dahlgren hosts a monthly "Evening with Authors You Should Know" at the Georgia Center for the Book, which is in the Decatur (Georgia) Library auditorium the first Friday of each month at 7:15 pm.

This free event is always a fascinating round table discussion with four authors at a time. The next one (May 4th), the four guest authors will be Dr. William Rawlings, Tori Bailey, Duncan Dobie, and my writer friend Sharon Marchisello.

If you're anywhere near Decatur, I hope you can make it.

In the meantime, do what feels good – read a book!

~ ~ ~

Give 100%—Except When You're Giving Blood

Sunday April 22, 2018 — Yesterday, I donated blood at the Red Cross. Why do I do it?

A number of years ago, while I still lived in Vermont, the daughter of some friends of ours spent her 12th birthday in the hospital, dealing with aplastic anemia. For months, she was kept alive with blood and platelet transfusions. That was when I began donating my blood on a regular basis.

One day, when I was sitting with her (so her parents could go home and get a shower and some rest) someone knocked on her hospital door. In walked an unassuming fellow carrying a white package of some sort. He said his name was Jerry and he'd heard Susannah liked ice cream. "Our company's developing some new flavors," he said, "and we wondered if you'd give them a try and let us know what you think."

She agreed, so he opened the well-insulated package to reveal six little containers of ice cream. He handed her a couple of tiny wooden spoons and a postage paid postcard where she could write in which flavors she liked and which she didn't.

Then he left.

She let me taste them, too.

The one we both liked the most was the brand-new Cherry Garcia.

It was only later that we found out her visitor was THE Jerry of Ben & Jerry's.

Today, Susannah's not only alive, but she thrives. And I'm still giving blood every other month.

~ ~ ~

bird nest with cat hair

Monday April 23, 2018 — I have a bird house out in my front yard that nobody's used for three years. Last week I decided just to take it down. Fortunately, before I lifted it off the pole, I thought to look inside.

Here's what I found.

Note the fluffy white layer (from a cotton bird-nesting ball I bought at Wild Birds Unlimited), topped with clumps of cat hair. The birds — all the birds, not just the ones who've built this nest—have been emptying the cat hair basket (see my post from March 24th) every two days. I couldn't brush Fuzzy Bear fast enough (or she wasn't shedding enough) to keep it full. The birds prefer light-colored hair, so they left the black Wooly Bear and Callie fur until they were desperate).

Luckily I remembered that in my garage I had an old bag filled with cat hair.

Don't ask me why I kept it.

Fran Stewart

People save the strangest things.

Anyway, I've been going out every other morning and replenishing the hair basket with hair from Chaucer and Agatha and Rimski and Dexter and … all the light-haired cats I've had over the years. As well as the daily brushings from Fuzzy Britches.

So the question for today is: What useless things do you have piled up in your garage? Maybe they're not as useless as you think.

~ ~ ~

red clover

Tuesday April 24, 2018 — When the red clover begins to bloom, I usually expect to see the honeybees. They love red clover.

This year, I haven't seen any honeybees out yet. Maybe it's because of all the rain, or maybe I just haven't been outside at the right time, or maybe it's because my red clover patches are more sparse this year than last.

I'm praying nobody within a five-mile radius of my house has used bee-killers, often referred to as herbicides, but I realize that's probably a futile wish.

I'll let you know when the honeybees arrive. It won't be long till the *Koelreuteria paniculata* (golden rain tree) will be blooming. That should bring the bees a-running … er, a-flying.

In the meantime, if you'd like to know a lot more about honeybees, you can check out http://beeskneesbeekeeping.blogspot.com [**2020 note**: Better yet, take a look at the 6 volumes of my beekeeping memoirs – BeesKnees #1, BeesKnees #2, and so on.]

~ ~ ~

Iris Veins

Wednesday April 25, 2018 — While I was looking at this iris a day or two ago, I realized that it's a lot like these last four books of my Biscuit McKee Mysteries. See how the veins branch out? See how the petals seem to interweave? See how the colors meld and blend and yet somehow stay distinct?

All the stories in the WHITE AS ICE quadrilogy are like that. People that come into the story in the 1700s or 1800s are connected, and as the story (stories) unfold, we see the family connections that branch out.

Of course, Marmalade is there, too, like the yellow center of this iris.

This is a saga I hope people will return to again and again. I love to re-read the Gamache books by Louise Penny, because I see new threads and connections in them each time I re-visit those books. I hope you'll do the same with mine.

Of course, I have to finish writing them first!

~ ~ ~

What to Marvel At

Thursday April 26, 2018 — When my friend Jackie White dropped by for a visit a couple of days ago, she stood by her car and waved to me on the porch. "You have to come see this!"

"This" turned out to be leaf fragment lying on my driveway with these crystal-clear water droplets beaded up on it.

Worth stopping a moment or two to look at and marvel. Even the little fleck of dirt in the big droplet is perfect.

What have you marveled at lately?

~ ~ ~

Start Where You Are

Friday April 27, 2018 — Last night was another Memoirs class at the library. Leading these classes is fun and challenging at the same time. The experience also is getting me closer to writing my own memoirs (once I get the last four Biscuit books out there).

They're teaching me to go about the process differently than I would have done if I'd started on this project a year ago. Why? Because in reading dozens of memoirs as background for these classes, I've discovered a lot about what works and what doesn't work with such material.

Take this quotation from Arthur Ashe. A disconcertingly large number of the memoirs I've read have been merely a bunch of whining. These people may be starting where they are, but they don't seem to be doing anything about it.

The classes I'm teaching are about writing family stories, the ones you want to pass along to children and grandchildren, so there are a lot of tales of "the good times." Some of the stories that are coming up, though, are about difficult issues.

How do you write about those?

I think at the next class, I'm going to relay this Ashe quotation. It applies not only to life, but to writing about that life.

What are you ready to start?

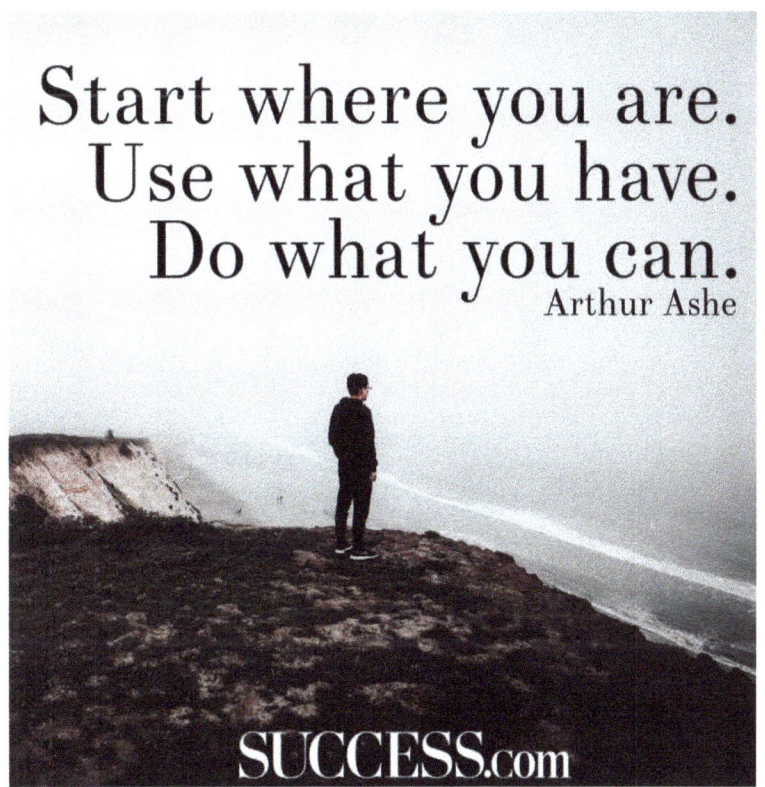

I am not what you think I am

Saturday 28 April 2018 — You may need to think about this one a bit. I know I did. Just as the picture says, "You are what you think I am."

I can remember reacting negatively to someone I'd just met, based only on the fact that she reminded me so much of someone I'd had a great deal of difficulty with when I was a child. This new person was not who/what I thought she was. Instead, my response said more about me than it did about her.

Do that ever happen to you? Or (since it happens to all of us) perhaps I should ask, how often does that happen to you?

Today, I plan to see the people I run into as they are.

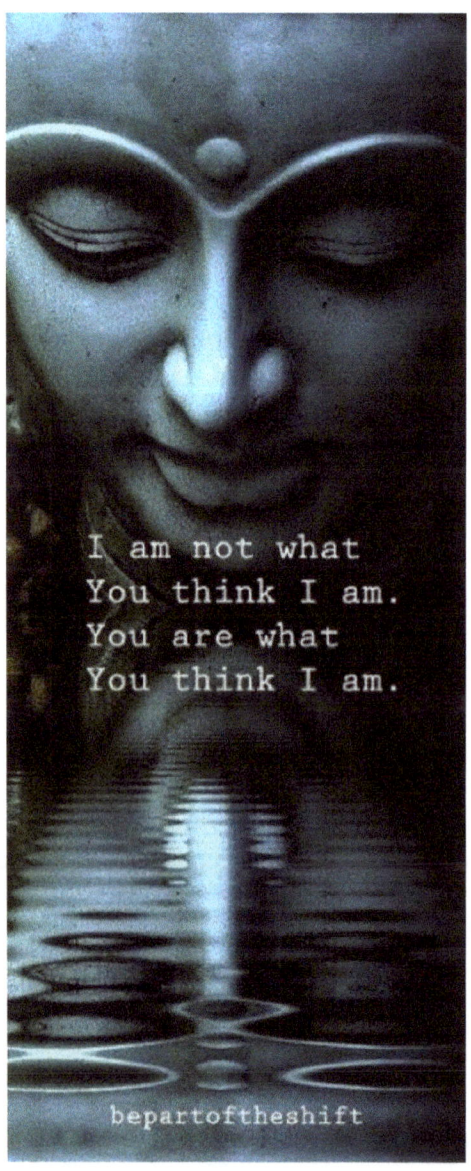

~ ~ ~

Sailboat napkins

Sunday April 29, 2018 — Do you ever want an easy way to spruce up a meal? I have a feeling I've already used this photo in an earlier post, but today I have something different to say about it, so here goes.

To spruce up a meal, try folding the napkins. Even paper napkins can look spectacular. I have a favorite sailboat fold that I learned years ago. It's designed so the tines of the fork hold the "boat" in place, but I found recently that my nubby linen napkins are too bulky, so the folds don't fit between the fork tines. The solution? Clothespins.

After all, my brunch guests were good friends and we all got a laugh about the elegance of the napkin fold versus the homey quality of the holder.

Anyway, the importance was the conversation, which took us places even a sailboat couldn't go.

Where have your conversations travelled recently?

~ ~ ~

No Anachronism

Monday, 30 April 2018 — Every once in a while, just for the fun it, I browse through the dictionary. I have an old copy of Merriam Webster. Inside there's a note that says, *"Presented to W. E. Schulenberg Aug. 23, 1986."* The cover, as you can see, is badly stained, but the inside still works just fine.

Fran Stewart

On a whim I decided to look up some of the words in an online dictionary. Not a single word in this photo was included online. Really? I can see never having to use the word "anabasis." But "anachronistic" wasn't there? How can anybody go through life without using "anachronistic" at least two or three times?

I thought of anachronisms just last week, when I came across one of those "fabulous quotation on top of a really cool picture" things you see almost constantly on Facebook (including occasionally on this FB page). It attributed something or other to Buddha, which was so blatantly not true, I almost gagged.

The Buddha had a lot going for him, but throwing his label onto truly anachronistic sayings is — well — it's cheating.

So, stop it!

May 2018

Some Don't Have Wings

Tuesday May 1, 2018 — I've been so fortunate over the years to have had a number of angels gracing my life. I'm sure you have as well.

Clear as Mud

Some angels don't have wings. They have four paws, hairy bodies, round noses, and unconditional love.

~ ~ ~

Birthday breakfasts

Wednesday May 2, 2018 — There's something so reassuring about good family traditions. One of ours is the birthday breakfast. This photo was from a few years ago while we were waiting for our orders to arrive at the table. I'm still waiting for my daughter to send me the photo of the whole group from this morning.

I've written several scenes in the WHITE AS ICE quadrilogy that deal with family traditions, although so far not a single character has mentioned birthday breakfasts. I wonder why not? Maybe because they don't have an Einstein's Bagels in Martinsville. Avocado Toast and hot chocolate. Yum!

Did I mention that we're getting a lot closer to publication time? Late summer, maybe? Early fall?

For now, though, what are the great traditions you remember? Do you still carry through on them?

~ ~ ~

Cat Paw (1/20/2018)

Thursday May 3, 2018 — Did you ever really look at how a cat walks? A front foot moves forward, and then the back foot on that same side steps in exactly the same place where the front foot was a moment before. This way, they don't have to worry that the back foot might be stepping on something unsafe.

It's something we could all learn.

Cats teach us to step softly.

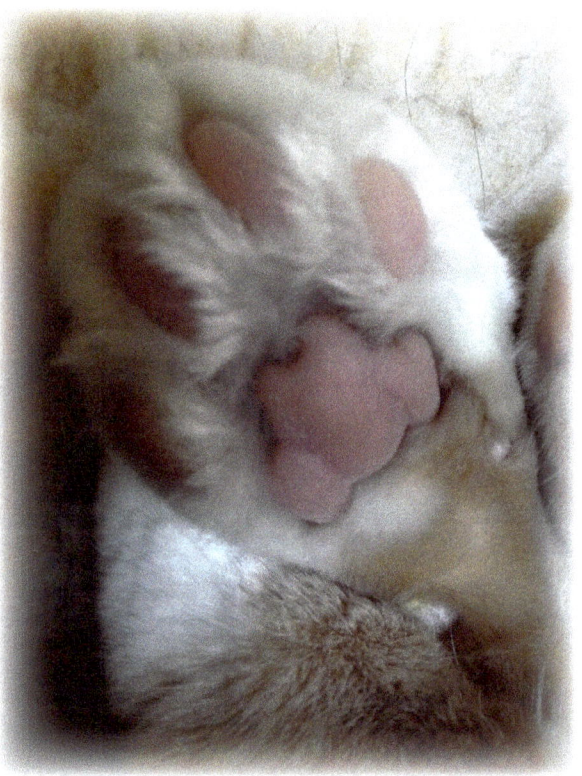

~ ~ ~

All Booked

Friday May 4, 2018 — My weekend truly is all booked. I'd planned to be in California at this time, but a funeral in my extended family rearranged everything. This is just an explanation of why I won't be posting anything here until next Tuesday.

If you're anywhere in the Atlanta area, be sure to head to the Decatur Library this evening to see Doug Dahlgren's literary guests. I'll be appearing there the first Friday in November, talking about my four new Biscuit McKee mysteries.

~~~

Eggplant

Tuesday May 8, 2018 — Why no posts for the last three days? I spent a good deal of time this weekend with my son and daughter-of-the-heart. The event was a funeral, but I felt a great deal of joy simply being with the two of them.

After the service, we gathered at Rumi's Kitchen in Roswell. My daughter and I ate and ate and ate, and never felt stuffed. I'd never had a chance to try such a variety of Persian food. One of the staple foods of that culture is aubergine, better known in this country as eggplant.

I've always liked eggplant but have really eaten it only as eggplant parmesan.

You'd be amazed what a good chef can do with this purple fruit. [Yes — I understand it's considered a fruit, not a vegetable.]

I have an eggplant sort of character in these upcoming four books of mine. I'd been considering the person just like I've always seen the eggplant—only from one viewpoint. But once I came home from the funeral, I found that this particular character has blossomed into all sorts of manifestations I hadn't known about.

Only in the last week or so did I finally figure out what the character looked like (and I'm sure you've noticed that I'm deliberately not telling you whether this figure is a male or a female), but the description came from a friend of mine who asked me to include so-and-so in my book.

You're welcome. (You know who you are.)

Photo credit: John Lambeth [Pexels.com]

Asparagus

Wednesday May 9, 2018 — Did you know that May is National Asparagus Month?

I've been trying to figure out how I could possibly use that fact in one of my upcoming Biscuit McKee books —but, you know what? I decided I couldn't.

Thank goodness.

Someday I'll tell you why July 1st is my own personal Asparagus Day.

When you're in a dark place

Thursday May 10, 2018 — Bloom! What a great time of year to think about that. Actually, any time of year is good for blooming, but particularly now, since today is the birthday of a dear, long-time friend of mine, a sister of my heart, who was planted there (in my heart) more than thirty years ago, when we were both going through a "buried" time.

So, Happy Birthday, Shar. I love blooming with you.

When you're in a dark
place, you sometimes
tend to think
you've been buried.

Perhaps you've
been planted.

Bloom.

~ ~ ~

Carpet Rose

Friday May 11, 2018 — Old fashioned roses have a lot going for them, but the most important, as far as I'm concerned, is the fact that their blooms are open, making it very easy for the pollinators to access them.

Unlike the overbred varieties that are way too full of petals. You can't even see the nectar-bearing middle of those blossoms, and bumblebees have a heck of a time getting in to where the pollen is.

Those newfangled hybrids may look gorgeous in the catalogs, but your yard will be a desert where the honeybees and bumblebees are concerned.

My old roses are blooming now—each flat blossom is only a few inches across—and the bees are happy.

Fran Stewart

~ ~ ~

Walnut litter

Saturday May 12, 2018 — You wouldn't think cat litter is an appropriate subject for a Facebook page about writing. Not that I always deal with writing here, but every few days I do try to work in something about the book(s) I'm working on.

Early on, when I was writing ORANGE AS MARMALADE, my first Biscuit McKee mystery, I wrote a scene where Biscuit was pondering something as she cleaned the litter box. Fortunately, one of my beta readers at the time was NOT a cat person. TMI she wrote in huge letter across that page. So I left it out, and have never put any such matter in my books since then.

But—let's face it—if you're owned by a cat, you've probably dealt with heavy, smelly clay litter. Or pine litter that turns into sawdust and floats through the house. Or litter made of corn or wheat that seems to attract flying insects (at least, they did around here). I finally got fed up with the whole thing and went to the PetSmart a few miles from my house. One of the people there, who turned out to be a manager, although I was unaware of that at the time, listened to my tales of woe and suggested a litter made of ground-up walnut shells.

It's dark brown; it clumps, but not disgustingly so; it doesn't have that "litter smell"—and best of all, it's easy to scoop without getting all sticky. No insects, either!

If you're revolted by talk of cat litter, you probably quit reading after the first paragraph. Tomorrow I'll write about the pink old-fashioned roses in my yard. I promise.

~ ~ ~

Open-petal Rose

Sunday May 13, 2018 — Today is the day everyone seems to be writing about their wonderful mothers. I'm going to do that only peripherally, simply because for a long time in my life I couldn't celebrate Mother's Day in my heart, a heart that was filled with too much pain and anger and fear and resentment.

It took a lot of work to get to the point where I could acknowledge the gifts my mother gave me, and by that point she had sunk so far into dementia, she was a different woman. Dementia allowed her to forget everybody she'd ever been angry at. Yes, she forgot my name, but she also forgot that she hadn't spoken my name for the seven years before her dementia took over. And she forgot why she hadn't.

To the best of my knowledge, my mother never forgave anybody.

Five years before she died, I woke up to the fact that I had a choice. Follow in her footsteps or embark on a new path. It was one of those "I-took-the-road-less-traveled" moments.

At the time she died, around 1a.m. on the day after Mother's Day, I was with her. The lovely thing was that it was just my mother and me in that room. Neither one of us was carrying along excess baggage— the garbage of anger, of fear, of resentment. She was free of anger because her mind had forgotten so much. I was free of it because I had learned to forgive.

Today, whether you're where I was twenty years ago or whether you're at the more peaceable place I'd arrived at by fifteen years ago, I wish you a day filled with old-fashioned roses. The kind that have wide open petals to welcome the pollinators.

Closed petals, like closed hearts, have no place in my life now. What about yours?

No Grievances

Monday May 14, 2018 — As I said yesterday, there's no room for grievances around here. In the WHITE AS ICE quadrilogy I'm writing—and getting SO close to finishing!—one of the ongoing characters in my Biscuit McKee Mysteries comes up against the need to forgive.

To forgive herself.

If you've read the first seven books in the series, you'll know Sadie Masters, the woman who wears nothing but yellow. She's in her eighties, but I wasn't fair to her in *Orange as Marmalade*, the first book. In there, I showed her as a ditzy, almost stereotypical "little old lady" who couldn't remember names, couldn't drive worth a darn.

Oh, I made it up to her later in the series by letting her explain to Biscuit (the librarian) that she'd gone through a time when she'd been taking a number of medications and they'd muddied up her mind. As I mentioned yesterday, she'd been letting her history define her. Now that she'd gotten all that straightened out, she became a role model to every woman in the town.

In the WHITE AS ICE books, I promise you'll finally find out why Sadie always wears yellow. Her yellow house, yellow car, yellow shoelaces, yellow everything will make sense. I can hardly wait for you to read it.

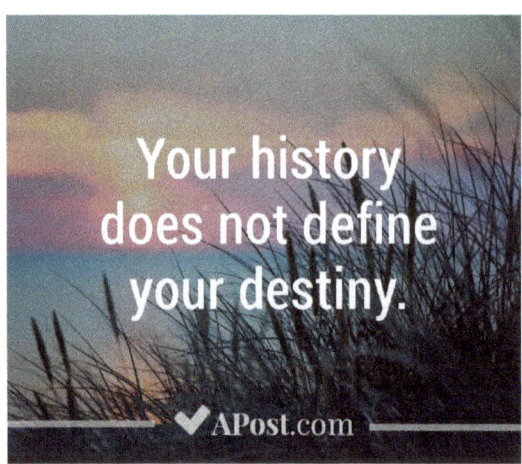

Let the Light Shine Through

Tuesday May 15, 2018 — My irises are pretty much all bloomed out now. Instead of intricate light-filled miracles, they're nothing but shriveled brown lumps.

I was looking through an old photo album the other day and found a picture of myself in my twenties wearing a bikini. Looked like an iris back then. Not so much anymore. In fact, not at all anymore.

And you know what? I'm okay with that.

But I'm not going to show you that photo…

~ ~ ~

Fifth Reflection

Wednesday May 16, 2018 — Last night I had the delightful opportunity to interview Ellen Kirschman, who is an award-winning police psychologist, non-fiction writer, and mystery writer. The event? An online book club sponsored by our Atlanta Chapter of Sisters in Crime.

Ellen's the author of *I Love a Cop: What Police Families Need to Know* and *I Love a Firefighter*, as well as the Dot Meyerhoff Mystery Series. In preparing for the interview, I read all three of her mysteries and thoroughly enjoyed each one. Dot, her main character is—guess what?—a police psychologist, and Ellen manages to infuse a great deal of information about the stresses faced by cops AND by psychologists into each of her novels.

Fabulous characters, great dialogue, and a darn good story. That's what you'll find in Ellen's books. If you haven't read them yet, I'd suggest starting with book #1, *Burying Ben*, followed by *The Right Wrong Thing*, and *The Fifth Reflection*. I'm looking forward to book number four.

~ ~ ~

Blow Your Mind—the Perfect Prescription

Thursday May 17, 2018 — I found this drug commercial on Ellen Kirschman's FB page, and I'd say it's a drug that's just about right for everybody. All you have to do is Google "this drug commercial is gonna blow your mind."

Here's the link if you feel like copying it.

https://www.youtube.com/watch?v=g_3BWqy9l0c

Enjoy!

~ ~ ~

Book Hangover

Friday May 18, 2018 — What I love about reading a series by a favorite author is that the "book hangover" lasts for 8 or 9 or 10 books. I don't have to go on to someone else's writing while I'm so caught up in the evolving world of the one I'm immersed in.

I feel that way about Louise Penny's Inspector Gamache mystery series. This is the third time I've re-read all her books in order, beginning with "Still Life," set in the fictional town of Three Pines, Quebec. Yesterday I began book #8, *The Beautiful Mystery*, which means I'll have five more to read before *Kingdom of the Blind* is released in November.

Believe me, her books are worth multiple readings.

In writing my WHITE AS ICE quadrilogy, I've had to re-read my own words multiple times as the story evolved, getting deeper and richer each time. My hope is that when all four books are available, people will want to read them once to get the overall story, a second time to begin to see the developing connections between founding families in the 1700s and the ones now in my fictional town of Martinsville, a third time to appreciate the way the stories interweave, and maybe even a fourth time simply to say, "Ah, yes."

Of course, you're quite welcome to go back to the very beginning, to *Orange as Marmalade*, so you can read the seven books up through *Gray as Ashes* before you begin *Red as a Rooster, Black as Soot, Pink as a Peony,* and finally *White as Ice.*

They're getting closer!

Book Hangover:

Inability to start a new book because you're still living in the last book's world.

Butterfly Bush

Saturday May 19, 2018 — The first few butterfly bush blooms popped open a couple of days ago. I haven't seen any butterflies yet, but by golly, the *buddleia* blossoms are open for business whenever the butterflies get around to finding them.

~ ~ ~

Mint Closeup

Sunday May 20, 2018 — When a friend stopped by to see me a few days ago, I happened to be sitting on my front porch with my laptop in hand … that is, in my lap. Usually I'm working inside, so I don't always see a friend until she's right at the door. This time, though, I watched as she maneuvered her way along the walkway.

I'm not a terribly unobservant person, but each time I skirt the front porch, I just blithely push my way through the knee-high lemon balm mint that's grown up along the walk, enjoying the scent of the fuzzy leaves as I brush against them.

I never noticed how the mint has quietly taken over, and how it does a good job of deterring casual visitors. Somebody who walks to my front door really has to want to get there.

I've had a few characters do that in my books. They started out as minor characters — I'll just plant this one little bunch of mint right over here — and before I knew it, by the third book in the series they'd become major players.

The mint? I'll need to do some judicious cutting. But Sadie and Ida? They're here to stay.

~ ~ ~

Procrastinator

Monday May 21, 2018 — Ignore this sign. I'm not a procrastinator. Not much, anyway. Well, hardly ever. Okay occasionally. But not about writing. In fact, my idea of procrastinating is more a matter of leaving the breakfast dishes in the sink ("they can soak while I finish writing this one little section") where they are eventually joined by a lunch dish or two ("I still need to re-work this part about Biscuit and Marmalade"), and then I skip the evening meal altogether ("I can always pop up a bowl of popcorn later").

The sink's been getting fuller lately because the deadline is looming, folks. I spoke with my publisher yesterday, and we've set the release dates for August, September, October, and November. The first one, *Red as a Rooster*, is already at my publisher's office, but that means I must, must, must complete the other three: *Black as Soot*, *Pink as a Peony*, and *White as Ice*, the last of my Biscuit McKee mysteries.

Please send me good writing vibes!

Won't change if you don't vote

Tuesday May 22, 2018 — If you've taken the time to research the candidates, please vote.

If you haven't — or you've listened only to TV ads and sound bites (where you DO NOT get the best information), please don't.

~ ~ ~

Oak Leaf Hydrangea

Wednesday May 23, 2018 — Rain, rain, rain. Here we are in another series of rainy days. If you live in a super-dry area, I apologize. Don't mean to rub it in. In fact, there are many people around here who would love to send you some of our rain.

I just keep thinking that, come August, those same people are going to be begging for rain.

Meanwhile, regardless of the weather, the *hydrangea quercifolia* (oakleaf hydrangea) is having a good time shading one whole corner of my front yard. Love to sit out there with a cup of tea and just soak up the green.

Except when it's raining.

~ ~ ~

Where to Sit

Thursday May 24, 2018 — Why do so many of the inspiring photos you see running around on the internet involve people perched on mountains or cliffs?

Luckily, I'm not afraid of heights, but even I get the willies sometimes looking at the precipitous falloffs in these photos. Years ago, I visited the Black Canyon of the Gunnison and stood with a park ranger on the edge of a cliff. He pointed to a white area in the river far below. "That's a waterfall down there," he said. "Care to guess how far it falls?"

"Ten feet?" I guessed, since the thing didn't even look like a waterfall from this high up.

Turns out the fall was closer to a hundred feet, which gave me a pretty good idea of just how high that cliff was. The one I was standing near the edge of.

When I visited my friends Jan and Matt in Hawaii in early 2015, she took me to see the lava cliffs close to her home on the Big Island (near where the volcano's erupting now), but we couldn't go anywhere near the edge. "The surf undercuts the rock," she explained. "There's no telling when big chunks may collapse."

Sort of undermines one's confidence in exploring.

So what's all this about? Last month (I think) I used the Arthur Ashe quotation: Start where you are; Use what you have; Do what you can. But I don't intend to start, use, or do anywhere near a drop-off, whether it's ten feet or two thousand.

If you want to climb a mountain and sit on the edge, I wish you well, and I hope you enjoy it. My front porch is good enough for me.

~ ~ ~

Old and Wise

Friday May 25, 2018 — Yesterday during the memoirs class I'm teaching at my local library branch, one of the students shared a moving story about a particularly painful lesson she didn't learn soon enough.

Everyone else in the class could identify.

Probably everyone on earth who is beyond a certain age could identify.

And then, this morning, I remembered this "To be old and wise" comment I came across a number of months ago.

How true. Of course, some of our best stories come from recalling our earlier stupidities. What would we do without them?

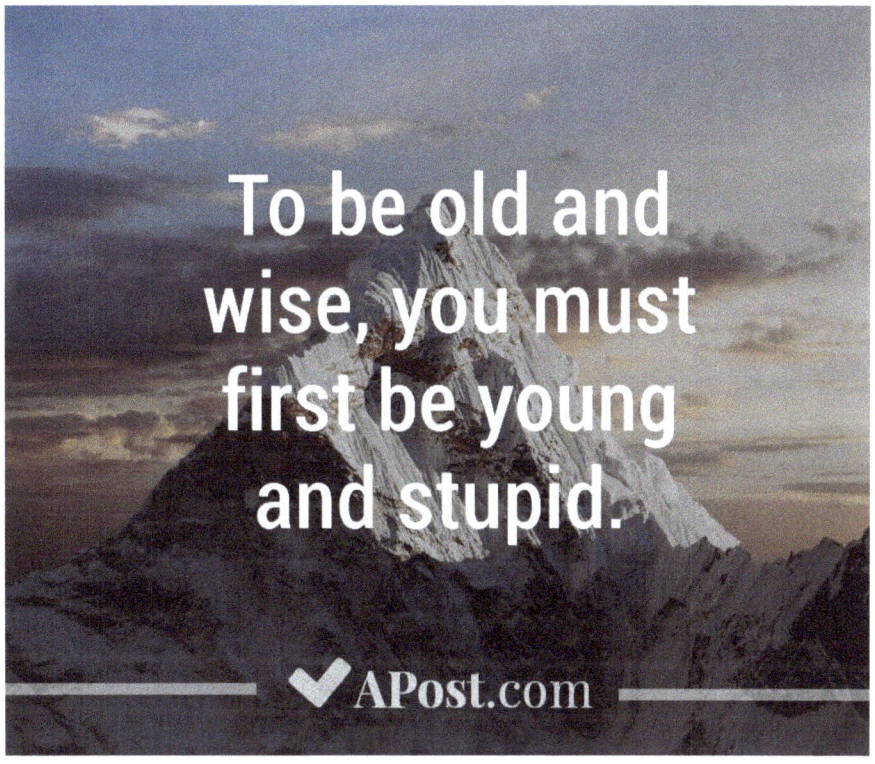

~ ~ ~

When I Get Old

Saturday May 26, 2018 — I think this just about sums it up.

Shortchanging Our Children?

Sunday May 27, 2018 — I was fascinated by this research that shows how reading a picture book to children helps them learn to integrate knowledge and make the connections necessary for processing information.

If you want to read the article from NPR, do a search for "what's going on in your child's brain when you read." It's truly eye-opening.

If you read to your children now or you did in the past, pat yourself on the back!

And the snuggle, in my opinion, is as important as the book.

Credit: Andrea Piacquadio (pexels.com)

Credit: Andy Kuzma (pexels.com)

~ ~ ~

Peaceful Statue

Monday May 28, 2018 — Wishing you a peaceful day.

~ ~ ~

Last of the Lilies

Tuesday May 29, 2018 — The last tiger lily may have finished with its blooms, but the gardenia has begun to blossom. I'm always taken by surprise when I notice that there aren't any more flowers on a particular plant. When did that happen? I'm not like the gardener I read about years ago who kept elaborate charts showing not only the first bloom date for each of the hundreds of varieties of flowering plants in her extensive yard, but also the last bloom date.

I just let it creep up on me, so the first and last are unknown dates.

Fran Stewart

It's the same way with my writing. Some authors I know plot out their books carefully ahead of time, so they know the complete story arc well before they write even the first sentence.

I, on the other hand (and a lot of other author friends of mine), wake up with a book idea in mind and then watch the bud swell and the flower open. Somebody asked me the other day, "When will you know when you've finished these four books you're writing?"

Good question. When the last blossom falls off, I guess.

RED AS A ROOSTER is already at my publisher, awaiting the magic of transformation from manuscript to printed book. BLACK AS SOOT is almost at that point — just one or two blooms left to enjoy. PINK AS A PEONY? I'm pretty happy with it as is. And WHITE AS ICE? There's still a bud or two waiting to open. Have to get the bad guy arrested and the loose ends tied up.

Since my deadline is June 30th, I think I'll stop this post and go get some writing done!

~ ~ ~

Getting Through

Wednesday May 30, 2018 — Yesterday I wrote one of those perfect scenes that caught my breath.

I didn't quite trust it.

So, I called my friend Peggy and read it to her.

It caught her breath, too.

This is one of those "book moments" that I hope will get into your bloodstream.

It's in BLACK AS SOOT. Can't wait till the release date in September.

~ ~ ~

play in the puddles

Thursday May 31, 2018 — Another Chapter Bookstore in Cumming GA has a FB page that I check each morning. I'll be doing launches there as my next four books are released (August, September, October, and December). I'll let you know the exact dates once they're set. [**2020 note:** Another Chapter closed its doors last year <<sigh>>]

Fran Stewart

Meanwhile, if you're having a rainy day, play in some puddles; and then I hope you have a chance to curl up with a good book, even it's only for a little while.

If you're enjoying a sunny day, take a sunny walk, and then I hope you have a chance to curl up with a good book, even it's only for a little while.

June 2018

lightning bug

Friday June 1, 2018 — Last night I went out onto my front porch at dusk and simply sat there, watching several dozen lightning bugs.

As a child I was entranced by the hundreds (thousands?) that filled the front yard of my grandparents' farm-house. My yard has nowhere near that many, but the ones that are here, I treasure.

Mine is the only yard along this street that has fireflies. Mine is the only yard that looks like a jungle. Mine is the only yard that's never had an application of bug sprays or herbicides. Mine is the only yard that's safe.

I'm on the side of the bugs.

photo credit: Wikipedia

~ ~ ~

Not All Classrooms

Saturday June 2, 2018 — My daughter and granddaughter are in Greece as I write this. My son and his love recently spent an extended time in India.

I've thoroughly enjoyed their trips vicariously. Here I sit writing and writing—and thoroughly enjoying that process—yet there is a piece of me that would like to jump in my polka-dotted car and head up the road with no particular destination in mind.

Thoreau said he could see the whole world while staying at Walden Pond.

Yes.

I get that.

Still …

Fran Stewart

~ ~ ~

What I'd Rather Do

Sunday June 3, 2018 — Good morning. Happy start of the first full week in June.

I'm not sure why the swift passage of time seems to surprise me some mornings more than others, but as I turned over to the next page of my *Thoughts From the Universe* perpetual calendar a few minutes ago, I marveled that we could have come so far into the year without my having noticed it.

Of course, I've been writing.

I have a DVD from Netflix that was shipped to me on March 19th. There it sits, and I haven't taken the time to watch it.

I'd rather write. Or have lunch with friends. Or watch lightning bugs. Or read. Or do Sudoku.

Or enjoy the dianthus. Aren't these blossoms amazing?

~ ~ ~

Be You

Monday June 4, 2018 — I plan to enjoy a quiet day.

I hope you enjoy your day as well.

~ ~ ~

Enjoy What You Have

Tuesday June 5, 2018 — Other than writing, I didn't accomplish much last week,

No, wait. That's wrong. I accomplished quite a lot, but most of it wasn't what I had planned on accomplishing.

The good news is – I enjoyed the week thoroughly. I had a number of good talks with good friends. I laughed a lot. I had a good book with me while I sat for four hours at the car service place.

What more could I ask?

Fran Stewart

~ ~ ~

cat teeth in pencil

Wednesday June 6, 2018 — I once wrote an essay for the Atlanta Writers Club about the uses of a good old-fashioned pencil. My publisher later included that essay in my non-fiction book *From the Tip of My Pen: a Workbook for Writers*.

I should have mentioned that one of the valuable uses of a pencil is that it serves as a good cat toy.

Ready for a round of Sudoku the other evening, I retrieved my big fat #2 Ticonderoga from the middle of the living room floor where Fuzzy Britches had been tossing it around. Here's the evidence of her enthusiasm.

Why bother to buy cat toys when cardboard boxes and pencils serve the same purpose?

p.s. Did you notice how fat this pencil is? I buy "My First Ticonderoga" pencils because I like the feel of them in my hand. They're easier to grip than a regular skinny pencil.

~ ~ ~

Jury summons

Thursday June 7, 2018 — Look what I received in the mail yesterday.

Have you ever served on a jury? I did, about thirty years ago. It was a bank robbery case. The evidence was pretty straightforward, I thought, but I must admit that I truly wanted to find the fellow guilty simply because (and I'm ashamed to admit this) his defense attorney was such an obnoxious sleaze bag.

Apparently ten of the other jurors felt the same way, and one of them said so. One woman held out, though. "I don't like that lawyer any more than you," she said, "but if I were a defendant, I'd want a jury that voted based on the evidence."

Okay. So we went over every piece of evidence. And then we found him guilty.

I have to admit, I felt a lot better about the verdict after that.

The trouble is, now I'll never be selected for another jury. Why not?

I'm glad you asked.

Since that time I served as a juror, my daughter was robbed at gunpoint at an ATM, my son was knifed as he tried to defend a young woman who was a stranger to him, I worked as an underwriter for worker's comp insurance, my credit card info was stolen, I was the passenger in a car that was t-boned, and—oh, a couple of other interesting things like that.

Of course the defense attorneys will strike my name.

I like the British system, where the next 12 people in line are the jury. Period.

~ ~ ~

Iris

Friday June 8, 2018 — When the irises have completed their bloom time, I can remember them by looking at photos of when they were full and beautiful.

Just so, I've been encouraging people to call back the memories of other days as they write their memoirs. The class last night, the last of a four-class series, had some pretty special "iris moments" as the folks who attended shared a number of their memories.

Fran Stewart

I'll be teaching another round of Memoirs classes in September and October. Hope you can join us!

~ ~ ~

Fuzzy Britches in the Cat Tree

Saturday June 9, 2018 — Good morning!

Sorry this photo of Fuzzy Britches is a bit, well, ... fuzzy, but I love the way the light from the skylight above plays through the hole in the top of the cat tree.

Peacefulness comes in all sorts of forms, doesn't it?

~ ~ ~

Limerick in the Mud

Sunday June 10, 2018 — One reason why I'm a cat person.

Don't get me wrong. I love Limerick and Max, my granddogs. They're great fun to play tug-o-war with. They give great big doggie kisses (especially Limmie). They're unfailingly enthusiastic about EVERYTHING.

Including sand and mud.

I'm glad my daughter is the one who gets to clean them up.

~ ~ ~

Red Cloak Photos

Monday June 11, 2018 — Three pictures hang in my upstairs hall. I can barely remember the woman who is in them. Even though that woman was Fran Stewart. A friend of mine who was a portrait photographer wanted to work with draped fabric, and my woolen Irish cloak was perfect for her experiments.

I had great fun being her guinea pig, and now I have these photos.

Someday I may show you my one and only "glamour shot," taken about four years after these three. But, for now, I'm content to leave the glamour in the photos and just keep on writing.

~ ~ ~

Sapelo's Sunrise

Tuesday June 12, 2018 — One of the things I enjoy the most when I visit Sapelo Island is hiking down to the beach before dawn so I can watch the sun come up over the ocean.

Sunrises have always been a favorite time of day for me, ever since I lived in Colorado Springs for five marvelous years when I was a kid. We lived on the easternmost street in town—beyond us was nothing but prairie, so every day at dawn I'd head for the big windows on the west side of the house. Yes. That's right. The WEST. The sun touched the tip top of Pike's Peak, setting the snowcap to glowing a bright pink — about the color peeking through the clouds in this Sapelo Island photo.

We'd watch the sun inch down the mountain. By the time it reached half-way down, it was time to leave the breakfast table and look out the eastern windows to see the sun's edge peek up over the sand and prairie grasses.

Now, that house we lived in on the edge of the town (which held around 35,000 people) is practically in the middle of the city, which numbers more than 416,000. The prairie where my sister and I played is long gone. But the sun still comes down the mountain the same way every morning.

~ ~ ~

Scheherazade

Wednesday June 13, 2018 — I've often thought back to the time I was in seventh grade, and the school orchestra played "Scheherazade" by Rimski-Korsakov. I think it was just the second movement, with that lovely violin solo. We were inordinately lucky that year, to have had a student who had been studying violin since he was three and whose skills were up to the challenge.

That was my introduction to the music of Rimski-Korsakov. To say I was entranced is like saying lava is hot.

As I'm completing *White as Ice*, there are several scenes with Korsi, Doc Nathan's office cat. Korsi first showed up in the Biscuit McKee mysteries when Biscuit found him as a stray while she and Bob were on their honeymoon in *Yellow as Legal Pads*.

She brought him home and named him Tank because of the way he was built. Marmalade lost no time in ushering the sturdy kitten to the local doctor's office, where he was renamed Korsi because of his propensity to cuddle up to the stereo as it played Rimski-Korsakov.

Naturally, as I'm writing, I'm also listening to that magnificent music. Here's a rendition I hope you'll enjoy (if you want to copy all these letters and numbers): https://www.youtube.com/watch?v=KOEX-8GhicU

~ ~ ~

Curling Up

Thursday June 14, 2018 — When I find myself wide awake at 2am, I wish I could curl up like one of my granddogs and zonk out.

"Zonk," by the way is a word I have to be sure not to use in the WHITE AS ICE scenes set any time before the 1940s. I've been looking up words right and left throughout this writing process, just so I'm absolutely certain I haven't used a word that didn't exist at that time.

Sure hope I haven't missed any.

The other day I wrote something about a man (in 1764) admiring his wife for her feisty attitude. Had to change it to "I courted you because you were a woman of such valor, so unlike the insipid other women of this town." If he'd called her feisty, she wouldn't have known what he meant.

"Valor" has been around for eons; "insipid" came into use in the early 1600s; while "feisty" never showed up before 1896.

When you're reading a good book, do you ever think about all the things the author had to figure out before the story ever made it to print?

Fran Stewart

~ ~ ~

XX

Friday June 15, 2018 — Hip-hip-hurray! The first launch date for RED AS A ROOSTER is set for Sunday, August 19, 2018.

Another Chapter Bookstore in Cumming GA will be hosting me from 1:00 to 5:00. If you're there, you can be among the first to pick up the first volume of the last four Biscuit McKee Mysteries.

The coolest thing, though, is that Katie, the owner, is conducting a drawing. When you visit Another Chapter between now and August 19th, you can sign up for a chance to have your name used as a character in WHITE AS ICE, the final book of that quadrilogy.

The character is a woman. And she's not the murderer. That's all I'm gonna say about her.

We'll hold the drawing at 3pm on 3/19/18 at the launch party.

This picture shows you an example of how I write scenes where I don't even know the name of the character yet. I just type in some big red XX's so I can easily go in later (the day after the drawing) and fill in the winning name. Don't mind the mess — I had to white out some of the words so I wouldn't give away any major plot points.

Hoping to see you at Another Chapter in August! And I hope you win.

p.s. I'll announce the other bookstore signings as they're arranged.

~ ~ ~

Doug's Radio Show

Saturday June 16, 2018 — Yesterday Doug Dahlgren interviewed me for his weekly radio show on Artist First Radio.

We had a great conversation, with subjects ranging from editing, to my upcoming books, to the memoirs classes I'm teaching — and classes I'll eventually be developing webinars about. Doug's an excellent interviewer, and it's always a joy to be his guest.

I can appreciate him as an interviewer because back in 2009 I took on a year-long project. Every Friday morning at 10:00 for that entire year, I interviewed a mystery writer for a full hour on internet radio. I called my show "Mystery Matters."

When I first chose to take on this responsibility, I decided that I would read every single book that every one of my guests had written. And I did it (except that I missed reading one book by somebody who'd already written more than 20 of them).

Obviously, I got NO writing of my own done that entire year. But by golly, I sure did ask some great questions of those other authors—and we had marvelous discussions about how their characters developed, how they interwove themes that were important to them, and what they hoped to accomplish with their writing.

~ ~ ~

Gardenia

Sunday June 17, 2018 — Today may be the last day I manage without the air conditioner. While most of the people I know have had their A/C's running for months, I've made do with open windows. There's a great advantage to living in a house that has a deciduous forest on the west side. That afternoon shade makes a huge difference in the inside temps. Then there's the sassafras tree outside the living room on the east side of the house. It keeps the morning sun from warming up that room too much.

Ceiling fans help, too.

But there comes a time each year when the humidity levels become unbearable. The gardenias love it, as you can see from this picture. But I begin to wilt.

Oh well. It won't be long until the autumn, when the windows can fly open again, and I'll be able to hear my neighbor's rooster at 5:30 or so. Love it!

~ ~ ~

Anything that Costs You Peace

Monday June 18, 2018 — It's time for me to send out another preview of one of the stories in the WHITE AS ICE quadrilogy (maybe this coming weekend?) and I haven't been able to decide which one to send. Actually, I probably should have sent out my newsletter a month ago, but I've been procrastinating.

Clear as Mud

Why such a quandary? I'm procrastinating about a lot of things lately. On the one hand, I'm so excited about the books' release dates in August, September, October, and November (or possibly December). On the other hand, I'm reluctant to see my mystery-writing days end.

I need to pay more attention to the messages I put up here on my daily FB post. Anything that costs me peace truly is too expensive.

Quit worrying, Frannie. It'll all work out.

Fuzzy Britches Sleeping

Tuesday June 19, 2018 — Have you ever wished you had a nice round scratching pad to curl up on for your naps?

No?

Guess you're not a cat.

~ ~ ~

A Diminished Mass

Wednesday 20 June 2018 — I know I've mentioned this before here on my FB posts, but the other day somebody asked if I was singing with any sort of group now that the Gwinnett Choral Guild has been disbanded.

Well, no.

The North American premier of "A Diminished Mass" by Scottish composer Alan A. Craig was the high point of my singing experiences.

The piece is 47 minutes long, and I had the entire thing memorized. That's what comes of studying the magnificent score a kazillion times and practicing the singing several hundred times. Ending my choral singing with the best I've ever sung is sort of like ending my Biscuit McKee series with the best four books I've ever written.

Does this mean I'll never sing again? Of course not. I pull up this YouTube site frequently and sing along (I still remember all the words!). I sing in the shower. I sing at the kitchen sink. I sing on my front porch. I sing to my cats. I just don't sing with a group anymore.

[To listen to our recording on YouTube, just search for "Diminished Mass" and "Gwinnett" – Those two terms together will get you to the right place.]

And the writing? As I've mentioned, I'll be concentrating on my memoirs once these four books are released. Writing like crazy—just possibly not for publication.

Unless I change my mind.

[**2020 Note**: As you can see, I changed my mind. First, I released my 6-volume beekeeping memoirs, and now, with *Clear as Mud,* I'm releasing those parts of my memoirs that I'm willing to make public. The others, the stories that are only for my immediate family and closest friends—well, those won't be put out for anybody else to read, but I am most definitely writing them. If any of them are okay for the world to read, I'll be posting them on my Facebook author page anyway, so you'll see them in the next volume, *Clearly Me.*]

~ ~ ~

Forget All Those Reasons

Thursday June 21, 2018 — I just finished reading *Thru* by Richard Judy. It's a novel about thru-hiking the Appalachian Trail from Springer Mountain in Georgia to Mount Katahdin in Maine. I'm also watching YouTube videos (Champ Hikes) posted semi-regularly by a neighbor of mine (trail name Champ) as he hikes the Trail. Champ is a NOBO - a thru hiker going northbound (as opposed to the SOBOs, who trek southbound, beginning at Katahdin).

Most everybody who hikes the Trail chooses a trail name. The names range from cute to bizarre, from practical to practically opaque.

It got me to wondering what sort of trail name I'd choose in the high unlikely (i.e. completely improbable) event that I might consider a thru hike.

You know what? I haven't been able to come up with one. How would I sum up my journey in one or two words?

I'll do more thinking about it, but in the meantime — do you have any idea what your trail name would be?

Limerick & Max

Friday June 22, 2018 — Where does my muse reside?

It depends on what kind of muse you're talking about.

Limmie and Max serve as my inspiration when it's time to think about an afternoon nap. One of these pictures was from when Limerick was a puppy. My daughter took the other one a couple of years later.

Saturday June 23, 2018 —

[**2020 Note:** I'm not including this post, since it lauded a non-profit organization that I found out has been mismanaging their funds for a number of years.]

~ ~ ~

Live in the Moment

Sunday June 24, 2018 — How often have you felt this way?

More Light to Read By

Monday June 25, 2018 — Now that we've passed the summer solstice, the days are getting shorter.

Fortunately, there are still plenty of long daylight hours. I've always thought daylight savings time was one of the stupidest moves imaginable, but for a number of years now I've subscribed to a program offered by my local electric company that allows me to save a substantial amount on each kilowatt I use year-round, as long as I limit my electric consumption during the peak hours from 3pm to 8pm, Monday through Friday from June 1st to September 15th.

So, daylight savings time means that my skylights let in enough light to let me read (and read and read…) the evening hours away.

It's absolutely lovely.

p.s. No, this isn't my skylight – but isn't it stunning?

Credit Tom Balabaud (pexels.com)

Life of a Tree

Tuesday June 26, 2018 — This morning, my neighbor's rooster was crowing into a fine mist, and I could practically feel the trees in the forest behind my house drinking in the moisture.

Clear as Mud

One of my favorite sections in *Lord of the Rings* is the part about the Ents. I've always been partial to trees. Four or five decades ago, I heard someone from The Nature Conservancy being interviewed on WVMT, a Vermont Public Radio station. A woman called in to complain about "all you do-gooders bothering us about politics … Why don't you just go away and let us enjoy our beautiful Green Mountains?"

The man's response was classic. "Those Green Mountains you enjoy looking at every morning are still green due in large part to the work of The Nature Conservancy."

I sat there cheering. There are a few organizations I've supported regularly throughout the years — The Nature Conservancy, Noah's Ark, and the Atlanta Shakespeare Company. I'd say that's a pretty good balance. Oh, and Public Radio as well.

Now, I'm going to go listen to the trees while it's still misty.

Bunny vs. squirrel

Wednesday June 27, 2018 — There was a great American standoff by my front walk yesterday as two wild animals headed for the peanuts at the bottom of one of the bird feeders.

Wish I'd had it on video. As it is, I did get one quick snapshot, but by the time I enlarged it and cropped it so you could see the bunny hiding in the violets and field grass, it was hopelessly grainy. Look carefully and you WILL see the rabbit.

The bunny ducked back into the undergrowth. The squirrel got confused and ran the other direction. The next time I looked, all the peanuts were gone. I guess they both won.

A Special Box

Thursday June 28, 2018 — What else can I say this morning except thank you?

~ ~ ~

Big SUV Saves My Life

Friday June 29, 2018 — Normally I'm not a fan of great big gas-guzzling cars, but I have to admit, the driver of one of them saved my life last Wednesday.

I was returning from having some work done on my little car, and I pulled to a stop in the center lane as the traffic light turned red. An enormous SUV stopped beside me, completely blocking my view of everything to my left.

When the light turned green, I started to ease off the brake, but the big SUV didn't even budge. It sat there, completely unmoving, for two, three, four, seconds. That may not sound like very long, but at a traffic light in the Metro Atlanta area, it can seem like an eternity.

Despite the honking horns from the line of cars behind me, I stayed put. A moment later, a car shot through the intersection from left to right going far faster than the speed limit. If the SUV's driver hadn't sat so absolutely still, I would have been in the middle of the intersection when that third driver ran the red light.

Fran Stewart

Years ago, I was a passenger in a car that turned into the path of an oncoming vehicle. I know what happens when someone plows into my side door at less than 30mph. The red-light-runner on Wednesday was going a LOT faster than that. I woulda been toast.

So, a great big thank you to the driver who must have seen it coming, who sat there completely still. The driver who saved my life.

~ ~ ~

Champ Hikes

Saturday June 30, 2018 — Several people have messaged me asking about how they can find all of my neighbor's videos about his trek up the Appalachian Trail. I'm happy to share it.

Yesterday he posted a short clip of a mama bear with her two cubs outside the Fingerboard shelter.

I went back to the beginning and have been watching two or three of these each day, trying to get caught up to where he is now.

Here's the link to the index of all his videos:

https://www.youtube.com/channel/UCm7sHHPAnmWERwcQXoDSDBA/videos

July 2018

Asparagus Day Again

Sunday July 1, 2018 — When I approach a new scene in WHITE AS ICE, I love the anticipation of not quite knowing the possibilities inherent in writing about that character or that plot point.

Hank Phillippi Ryan, a well-known suspense writer, likes to tell the story of how she and her husband don't celebrate the anniversary of the day they met. They always celebrate the day BEFORE they met, because that's the day of possibilities.

In much the same way, I celebrate Asparagus Day, which is the day before my son's birthday.

I grew up in a vegetable-challenged family, so I was in my late twenties before I ever tasted fresh asparagus. Forty-three years ago, on July 1st my neighbor up the street invited us to dinner to enjoy fresh-picked, lightly sautéed asparagus from her extensive garden.

Ambrosia. I couldn't recall ever having eaten anything quite so delicious.

The next day, I went into labor.

Happy Asparagus Day, Eli.

~ ~ ~

Fuzzy Britches Again

Monday July 2, 2018 — Good morning from Fuzzy Britches.

And from me, too.

I'm looking forward to a day of writing, working on the last-minute tweaks to WHITE AS ICE, the fourth volume of those last four books of mine. Yesterday I realized that there was one nagging question the women in the attic had never found an answer to. That in itself wasn't so much of a problem. After all, when you're rummaging through generations worth of stuff in an attic, there will be a lot of things you won't know the story behind.

The whole idea of this quadrilogy is that as the women find things in the attic, the behind-the-scenes story is unveiled—not to the women in the attic, but to you, the reader.

The entire four-volume story centers around Mary Frances, the woman who was married to the founder of Martinsville. In her diaries, she keeps referring to her "dear daughter-in-law" — but she never mentions that daughter-in-law's name. Never.

Yesterday, I finally found out why not. So I wrote a scene that explains it. Of course, the women in the attic never find that out. But you? You're going to know, as soon as you read *Red as a Rooster, Black as Soot, Pink as a Peony,* and *White as Ice.*

Fran Stewart

August, September, October, and November (or December). I can't wait!

~ ~ ~

Desolation Wilderness

Tuesday Friday July 3, 2018 — Eli and Nima, my son and his love, really do know how to celebrate a birthday. When they go backpacking, they do it the right way—Leave No Trace and love the experience.

Desolation Wilderness is part of the El Dorado National Forest in California, and part of the National Wilderness Preservation System. If you Google *Desolation Wilderness* you'll see some awe-inspiring photos of where they've been for the past few days.

That's what so much of this country used to look like. In the first two books of my WHITE AS ICE quadrilogy, I tell a great deal of the story of how the town of Martinsville was founded in the mid-1700s, including a very long trek through land that had few towns and no cities. I've enjoyed imagining our country the way it must have been.

Of course, people haven't changed in the past 250 years. Manners may be different; dress may be different. Vocabulary has changed; customs have changed. But underneath, there are still the same passions that rule people's actions, the same yearnings that drive people forward, the same fears that may either motivate or paralyze. My books are about people (and murders) that those of us in the 21st century can identify with in the 18th, 19th, and 20th centuries.

What would it be like to go back in time? You can do it in a good book.

Have you ever taken a trip where you haven't seen any power lines?

Have you ever traveled without electronic devices?

Have you ever spent a day without hearing a phone ring?

You can get lost (and find yourself again) in the beauty of nature. Or you can get lost (and find yourself again) in a good book.

~ ~ ~

If You Must Pop Something

Wednesday July 4, 2018 — I'm getting ready to start reading the Declaration of Independence, now that my early morning walk through the neighborhood is complete.

Fuzzy Britches is reminding me that I have to feed her and her sisters first, so maybe the declaration will have to wait just a bit, unless I want Fuzzy tromping across the ersatz parchment and putting nose prints on my magnifying glass.

Yes. Magnifying glass. Time was when I could read the facsimile of the 18th-century writing with no difficulty. Now, though? Even with reading glasses, that print could use some help.

Okay, okay — I hear you. It's my EYES that could use the help.

historical note: Are you aware that our national anthem isn't talking about the American Revolution? It was written in 1814 (during the war of 1812).

So why do we have to have noisy fireworks? The cats and I will be curled up inside tonight. With popcorn.

~ ~ ~

Alan in snow tunnel

Thursday July 5, 2018 — Now that the humidity of July is upon us, I like to look at old photographs like this one of my son in the 1970s.

One winter in Vermont the snow was so deep the pickup-truck-mounted snowplow couldn't handle our driveway. The solution? A bucket-loader that piled the snow into a twelve-foot heap. We couldn't even glimpse our neighbor's house unless we went upstairs.

What to do with such a huge pile? Make a tunnel, of course.

~ ~ ~

Defining You

Friday July 6, 2018 — If you scroll back through my last few posts, you'll see that I got the day of the week completely wrong. [**2020 Note:** I went back and corrected them before *Clear as Mud* went to print.]

How did that happen?

Was I too busy? Well, no. I don't have an excuse, other than I just lost track of what day of the week it was.

I've been writing like crazy but enjoying it thoroughly. I've taken time to talk with friends. Yesterday, when I'd planned to go to the grocery store — and that was about it — I decided at the last moment to take a couple of boxes of books I've culled from my bookcase up to the new and used bookstore in Cumming. I left my house at 9:45. I finally got back into my driveway at 2:53.

Yes, I got a lot accomplished yesterday, what with dropping off the books, stopping at a fabric store I've wanted to investigate, calling a friend and spending an hour or so with her . . . Oh, and sharing a couple of hours—mostly just listening—with another friend whose mother is in the process of dying.

Sometimes, when somebody needs to talk, all the errand-running in the world isn't worth a hill of beans.

I still got a lot done, but it was a very calm day, mainly because I chose to be calm throughout it.

But I never did get to the grocery store.

~ ~ ~

Garden in Scotland

Saturday July 7, 2018 — Years ago I took a trip to Scotland and ended up in an amazing garden (the name of which I can't for the life of me recall. That's what comes of not labeling old photographs.)

When I started writing the Biscuit McKee Mysteries, I wanted Biscuit's front yard to look like what I remembered. That's one of the coolest things about writing. I can create the world I want.

Wish I could do the same with my own front yard . . .

~ ~ ~

Lion sleeps

Sunday July 8, 2018 — If you signed up for my newsletter (on the home page of my website), you will have received a newsletter this morning giving a snippet from RED AS A ROOSTER and a confession on my part.

If you didn't sign up for the newsletter yet, you'll need to wait a bit before the big unveiling.

What does this have to do with a lion?

Uh . . . um . . . er . . . nothing, I guess.

But I really like this lion. And the song reference.

Hope you do, too.

Clear as Mud

~ ~ ~

I Was Duped

Monday July 9, 2018 — I owe you an apology for misinformation. On June 23rd I posted something about the death of Koko, the gorilla who speaks in sign language. [*2020 note: That's the post I deleted for the publication of this book.*] One of the previous caretakers at the Gorilla Foundation replied to that email with a number of links that show how I have been duped for many years now.

You see, although I have for years preached that one should not automatically believe everything one reads on the Internet, I failed in the due diligence I should have used. All that stuff about Koko wanting to have a baby sounds heart wrenching, doesn't it? It turns out, though, that Koko hasn't ovulated in 20 years, but the foundation keeps using a possible baby as a fund-raising gimmick.

And I bought into it. I signed up to donate each month. They debit my account. The money goes from my bank account to theirs. I've emailed them asking to be removed from that process, but have not yet had a confirmation.

Meanwhile, Koko is dead. It turns out she and Ndume, the male silverback at the same facility, were not directly cared for by a veterinarian, but by a homeopathic psychic, who diagnosed them via the telephone and who prescribes supplements that cost one or two thousand dollars each month. I went to the link in this chimp trainer's daughter's blog post and read through the foundation's 2010 tax return to verify that little bit of information. The veterinarian visits (in response to a complaint registered by a previous employee) occur, but do not involve hands-on examinations, but viewings through a fence from 15 feet away. The list goes on and on.

Fran Stewart

Here is a portion of the comment Bill left in my 6/23/18 posting. I've deleted his last name because I don't want to put him at risk for a lawsuit.

Bill: It is so hard to get the truth out. Anything you post on their page that asks a critical question is blocked and previous staff that were paid next to nothing are afraid of being sued if they speak up. There has been talk on several occasions regarding the relocation of Ndume. But then the dust settles and nothing changes. The same story repeating for 40 years. I am working to get the word out over the next couple of weeks while I wait to see if Cincinnati steps up and finally does the right thing. The more people that know the truth the better.

If you lived in a 12' x 20' trailer day in and day out, frequently with no access to fresh air, don't you think you might go a little crazy?

Where do we go from here? I don't know. But I do know now that the life of a magnificent silverback depends on getting him away from the Gorilla Foundation and into a rehabilitative situation.

I truly apologize for anything I've done in the past to promote an organization that is so very deceitful and downright harmful to the animals in their supposed care.

[**Another 2020 note**: Eventually I sent the foundation a registered letter demanding that they remove me from their automatic debiting process, and they did so.]

~ ~ ~

triple daylilies

Tuesday July 10, 2018 — Look what's blooming!

A bunch of years ago, as I was planting some lilies (*Lilium*) in my front yard, and bemoaning the fact that the folks I bought my house from had planted a bunch of daylilies (*Hemerocallis*, a completely different sort of flora), a neighbor of mine stopped by and said they'd just dug up a bunch of lilies — did I want them?

Sure, I said, thinking he meant LILIES - like the ones I was planting.

I forgot that not everybody has the same knowledge of or respect for plant names that I have.

I came home later that day to find a wheelbarrow full of dug-up daylilies waiting for me. He had half the name right, I guess.

Part of me wanted just to throw them out. The other half said, "Oh come on, Frannie. You've got that big open area over there beyond the mailbox."

So I planted them, and they turned out to be these triple-flowered beauties.

Now, ordinarily, I avoid fancy hybrids with such convoluted blossoms, simply because honeybees can't get into them to retrieve the nectar. But I've never seen a honeybee on any regular daylilies either, so what difference would it make that these were too fat for the bees?

Still, I like seeing these particular daylilies. I just wish I'd planted lilies instead.

Or better yet, some cosmos and zinnias and coreopsis for the butterflies and bees.

~ ~ ~

Red's Ready!

Wednesday July 11, 2018 — If you signed up for my newsletter (on the home page of my website (franstewart.com), then you've already read some advance chapters of my next four books (the WHITE AS ICE quadrilogy), and you've already seen the cover, but here's the big unveiling in case you're not yet on my newsletter list.

It's available for pre-order in a lot of the usual places — and as of yesterday, the e-book is available for pre-order as well (everywhere except—according to my e-book publishing program—at the great big A).

Anyway, I just had to share this marvelous cover with you.

If you want to make it to one of my book launches, they're set for 3pm Saturday August 18th at Liberty Books on the square in Lawrenceville, and Sunday the 19th at Another Chapter Bookstore in Cumming GA. I'll be at that one from 1 to 5, with the grand drawing for "Your Name in WIIITE AS ICE" planned for 3pm.

One of my fans is flying in from Indiana to attend the one at Another Chapter Bookstore. [Thank you, Janice!] What fun it will be to meet her in person.

Fran Stewart

What about you? How far do you plan to travel to get a signed copy of RED AS A ROOSTER?

[**2020 Note:** this year I revised and published the updated versions of all my Biscuit McKee Mysteries through My Own Ship Press. Over the years of writing the eleven books in the series, various discrepancies crept in. Uh . . . hmmm . . . okay. I admit it. The discrepancies (like the size of Biscuit's house) happened because the author wasn't paying attention. This is the cover of the new edition. See where it says "revised edition" right under the top line? You might want to look for that note if you buy any of my Biscuit books in the future. To be sure you find the revised editions, head to the book buy links on my website.]

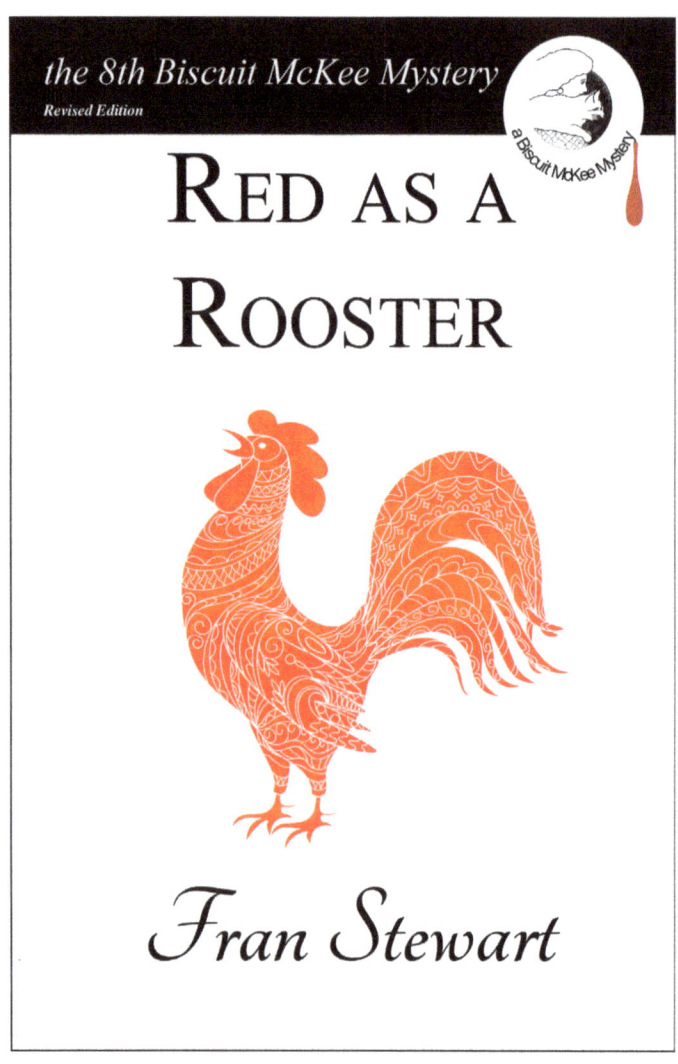

~ ~ ~

Turning People Into Trees

Thursday July 12, 2018 — Turning people into trees. I like that.

At the same time, if a tree has a thick prolific poison ivy vine twining around it, I may appreciate that tree from a distance, but choose not to go near it anymore.

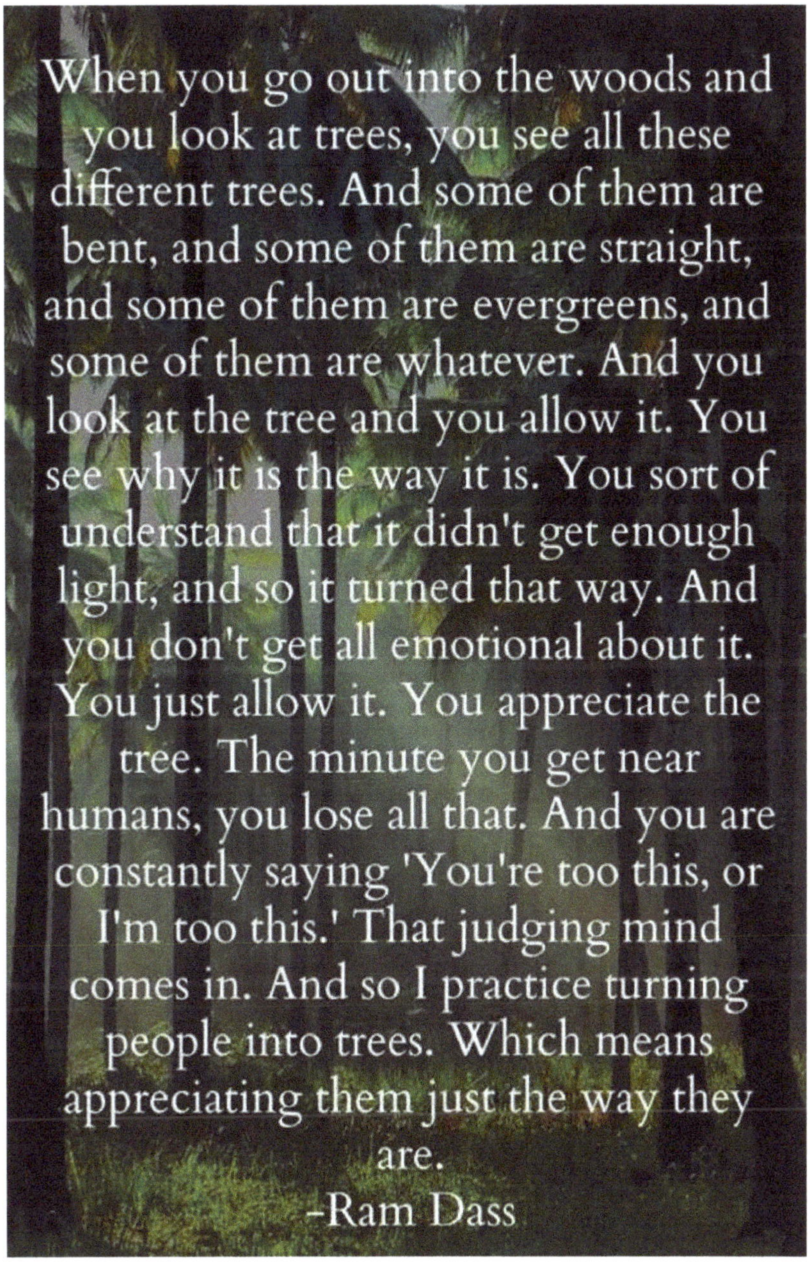

> When you go out into the woods and you look at trees, you see all these different trees. And some of them are bent, and some of them are straight, and some of them are evergreens, and some of them are whatever. And you look at the tree and you allow it. You see why it is the way it is. You sort of understand that it didn't get enough light, and so it turned that way. And you don't get all emotional about it. You just allow it. You appreciate the tree. The minute you get near humans, you lose all that. And you are constantly saying 'You're too this, or I'm too this.' That judging mind comes in. And so I practice turning people into trees. Which means appreciating them just the way they are.
> —Ram Dass

~ ~ ~

Snack Time

Friday July 13, 2018 — Snack time. Golden cherry tomatoes fresh from the bush in the front yard with a couple of green beans from the side yard.

Before breakfast?

Yes.

Then a bit of writing.

Fran Stewart

Before breakfast?

Yes. Have to get those ideas out before they drift away.

Now? Breakfast?

Yes!

~ ~ ~

Oak Leaf Hydrangea detail

Saturday July 14, 2018 — I've been re-reading all my Biscuit McKee books.

What does this have to do with an oak leaf hydrangea flower?

I'm glad you asked, but I need to give you a little background first.

A month or so ago I spoke to a book club at the Auburn GA library, and one of the women asked me a question about Susan. "Susan?" I said. "Who's Susan?" I had completely forgotten about that character, even though I'd woven her as a sub-plot through several of my books.

Clear as Mud

I'd written her, for criminey sakes, and I had no idea who she was.

So I re-read my books and found all sorts of interesting things I'd forgotten over the years.

Now, about this flower. Can you see the sort of pinkish tone off on the left central side of the blossom? That's my finger holding the bloom in place. The petals are so delicate, the color of my finger shows through—but you'll see it only if you pay attention.

I realized that the subplots of my mysteries are like that — it's easy to miss them unless you (or I) look for them.

But if you REALLY want an oak leaf hydrangea sort of book, just wait for RED AS A ROOSTER, where stories from the previous 250 years weave and interweave. It's not a casual read. Or rather, you can read it as casually as you'd like. Take it to the beach and race through it if you want to. Or spend time relishing the little glimpses of fingertips through the petals.

~ ~ ~

Wooly Bear atop the desk

Sunday July 15, 2018 — Good morning.

For the next couple of days, I'll be checking the proof copy of RED AS A ROOSTER. Line by line, word by word.

I hope there aren't any typos, but if there are, I hope I find them. I truly want you to have a perfect copy in August!

Wooly Bear has informed me that she'll help me, once she decides to get down from her perch.

~ ~ ~

Life is about Balance

Monday July 16, 2018 — Balance. Right.

At the moment I'm balancing a couple of kazillion projects. Do you have days like that? Things swim along for a while in a fairly peaceful stream, and then KABOOM – all these things to do — and deadlines for every single one of them.

It'll all work out. It'll all get done. It'll all be okay. And every day is perfect the way it is.

Breathe, Frannie.

~ ~ ~

Expect a Miracle

Tuesday July 17, 2018 — Today I plan to be realistic.

Like this.

What about you?

Beagles and Handwriting

Wednesday July 18, 2018 — I couldn't resist this as a day-starter.

But what I really wanted to mention is that yesterday evening, Sheila Lowe was the guest author for the Virtual Book Club that Donna van Braswell and I host for our Atlanta Chapter of Sisters in Crime.

Sheila joined us from California via televised conference call to talk about her most recent forensic handwriting mystery, *Written Off*. She's an internationally recognized handwriting analyst, so naturally her main character, Claudia Rose, is a professional handwriting analyst and uses her skills to help her solve mysteries. *Written Off* is a beautifully crafted book that I thoroughly enjoyed reading.

While I was at it, preparing for last evening's event, I bought Sheila's *Idiot's Guide to Handwriting Analysis*. At some point, I'm going to send a sample of my writing to Sheila and pay her $200 to analyze it (there are directions on her website SheilaLowe.com). After all, the more we can learn about ourselves, the better, right?

In the meantime, I'm going to have some breakfast and laugh about Lot and the flea.

~ ~ ~

Goat Yoga

Thursday July 19, 2018 — Have you ever tried goat yoga?

I had so much fun researching INDIGO AS AN IRIS because I visited a goat dairy farm. It is absolutely impossible to be around baby goats without laughing.

I've never tried goat yoga, but I can certainly imagine how fun it would be

Do a search and see what you find!

~ ~ ~

What Tea Can Do

Friday July 20, 2018 — Here I sit with my mug of licorice root tea, reveling in the morning. I woke up thinking, "Ah, it's Saturday!" only to find that "Whoops, it's Friday."

Perhaps it's because I stayed up later the usual last night watching a Netflix DVD. Even though I work on my Apple laptop, I keep the old desktop up and running because it has a DVD drive. I'm a bit upset with computer manufacturers nowadays because somebody decided DVDs are a thing of the past.

Confession time. I admit it. Without a TV set (haven't had one for more than 25 years) I missed all the Downton Abbey furor that went on a number of years ago. I honestly could not understand my friends who scheduled their week around whatever time slot that show had. "Can't make dinner — that's Downton Abbey time!"

Now I've spent an inordinate amount of time watching my way through the series. I'm about halfway through Season 4 now. It's a good thing I get these things in the mail (one DVD with 3 or 4 episodes on it). Otherwise I'd be tempted to forget about everything else in the world (even my writing) and vegetate in front of my old iMac.

Fran Stewart

I hope my readers get as involved in the life of the characters in my WHITE AS ICE quadrilogy as I have in the inhabitants of Downton Abbey.

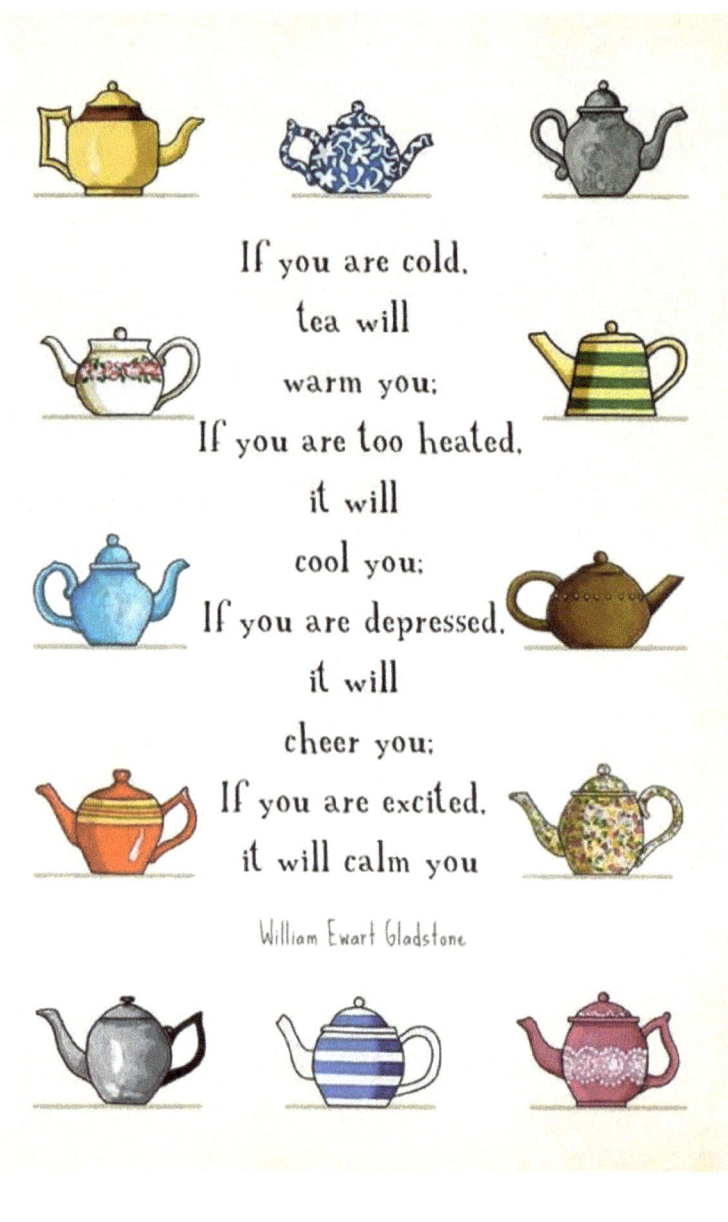

~ ~ ~

Damaging Ignorance

Saturday July 21, 2018 — I just finished reading *Brain Damage* by Frieda McFadden. Sheila Lowe recommended it last week when she spoke to our Sisters in Crime virtual book club. It's one of those thoroughly satisfying mysteries — good characters involved in a well-thought-out situation. I spent most of the book thinking I'd figured it all out, only to be delighted with the twist near the end.

I also learned a fair amount about how damaged brains work (or don't work, as the case may be).

Remember, reading can seriously damage ignorance.

~ ~ ~

Layers of Fur

Sunday July 22, 2018 — Look what happens when you brush a light-colored cat, and then you brush a dark-colored cat, and then the first one comes back for another few swipes of the fine-bristled brush. And so on . . .

Fuzzy Britches and Callie love to alternate their brushing sessions. Do you ever get layered fur like this to put out so the birds can line their nests?

Instead of "very"

Monday July 23, 2018 — Does your inner editor ever cringe when you use the v-word over and over again?

Here's a helpful chart:

WORDS TO USE INSTEAD OF "VERY"

✘ very noisy	✔ deafening
✘ very often	✔ frequently
✘ very old	✔ ancient
✘ very old-fashioned	✔ archaic
✘ very open	✔ transparent
✘ very painful	✔ excruciating
✘ very pale	✔ ashen
✘ very perfect	✔ flawless
✘ very poor	✔ destitute
✘ very powerful	✔ compelling
✘ very pretty	✔ beautiful
✘ very quick	✔ rapid
✘ very quiet	✔ hushed
✘ very rainy	✔ pouring
✘ very rich	✔ wealthy
✘ very sad	✔ sorrowful
✘ very scared	✔ petrified
✘ very scary	✔ chilling
✘ very serious	✔ grave
✘ very sharp	✔ keen
✘ very shiny	✔ gleaming
✘ very short	✔ brief
✘ very shy	✔ timid
✘ very simple	✔ basic

I've found that my writing is better when I use the "Find" facility (or I guess it would be "Search" if you're on a PC) to look up all the times I've written that ubiquitous word. "Very very often" as a matter of fact. Frequently. Continually. Repeatedly. Routinely. Habitually. Oftentimes. Usually. Commonly. Generally.

"Little" is another one of my bugaboos. Tiny, miniature, minuscule, teensy, microscopic, minute, pocket-sized, diminutive.

Or "hurry." Hasten, speed, scramble, sprint, scurry, rush, dash, hightail it.

Heck, I could make my own charts for every one of these.

Math Tricks for Adults

Tuesday July 24, 2018 — What do YOU do when you find yourself wide awake at 3am, with little apparent chance of dropping back to sleep?

This is what I do.

Everyday Math Tricks for Grown-ups by Kjartan Poskitt explains math in a way that not many other books do, building up from how to add and subtract to multiplication and division. Then on to fractions, ratios, roots, and so on.

Now, I've always enjoyed math, so it's not like I'm trying to learn how to add and subtract. I'm reading it mostly for the fun of it. Poskitt peppers the book with little treasures like this:

Pick any three-digit number. The digits should all be different.

Turn it around

Subtract the larger number from the smaller.

The answer will always have 9 in the middle (or it will be 99), and the first digit and last digit will add up to 9.

Example:

724 minus 427 = 297 (9 in the middle and 2 + 7 equals 9)

or

564 minus 465 = 099

Another fun one says that 111,111,111 multiplied by itself equals (*drumroll here*):

12,345,678,987,654,321

If you work that out in longhand, that's the answer you'll get. For some reason, though, there are some calculator apps that replace the last two digits (21) with two zeros (00).

Sometimes you have to trust longhand more than machines…

Fran Stewart

~ ~ ~

Wooly's Scavenger Hunt

Wednesday July 25, 2018 — One of the biggest problems for indoor cats is boredom. That's why I hide Wooly Bear's food.

She has a marvelous cat tree (a well-loved and well-used gift from my friend Linda Bell). It has numerous nooks and crannies, as well as two short ladders which Wooly Bear never uses, preferring to levitate from one perch to the next.

I sprinkle bits of her food on all the various levels, in the nooks, in the tube, behind the scratching posts, and of course, I place a few pieces on that otherwise-unused ladder.

It's fun for me to watch her search.

~ ~ ~

Numeric Angles

Thursday July 26, 2018 — I'm constantly amazed at how fertile the human mind can be.

Who would have thought to work out all these angles, for instance?

Who would have thought to design the first cat tree?

Who first invented any of the musical instruments we use so casually?

I don't know the answer to any of these questions.

Clear as Mud

But as to who first thought of Biscuit McKee, a librarian, and Marmalade, the library cat — I can answer that one. As the series is drawing to a conclusion, I find myself wondering — what's in the works once *White as Ice* is released in December? What will I think of next?

Just like the angles and the cat trees and the instruments, I don't know.

But I'm willing to find out as it unfolds.

And I'll clue you in when I find the answers.

p.s. Did you notice the typo in the zero (and the other one right below it)? Those should be angles, not angels. I imagine there are lots of angels in a zero, simply because there are lots of angels everywhere.

~ ~ ~

Fuzzy's paws in cat tree

Friday July 27, 2018 — Good morning. I'm a little later than usual for today's posting, because I stayed up WAY too late last night finishing *The Memory Keeper's Daughter* by Kim Edwards.

It's one of the suggestions our book club will be voting on next Tuesday, and it's definitely the one I'll be voting for.

As you can see from this photo, Fuzzy Britches wasn't particularly concerned about my late start to the day.

Latin Phrases

Saturday July 28, 2018 — I've decided to put together an ad hoc committee. Its purpose, per se, will be to carpe diem (pro bono, of course). Ergo, the status quo will begin to reflect the vox populi. Mea culpa if the committee ventures into terra incognita. Ergo, the committee et cetera will not be held responsible if such trespass causes them to be held in flagrante delicto. Ipso facto, since I will probably end up in jail (mea culpa, after all), the committee will be disbanded circa 2019 BCE.

Betcha didn't think I could use every single one of these in a paragraph...

Yeah, yeah, I know. Some of these sentences are a bit … uh … forced. But I got in all of those phrases.

Pat myself on the back.

Now go do some serious writing, Frannie.

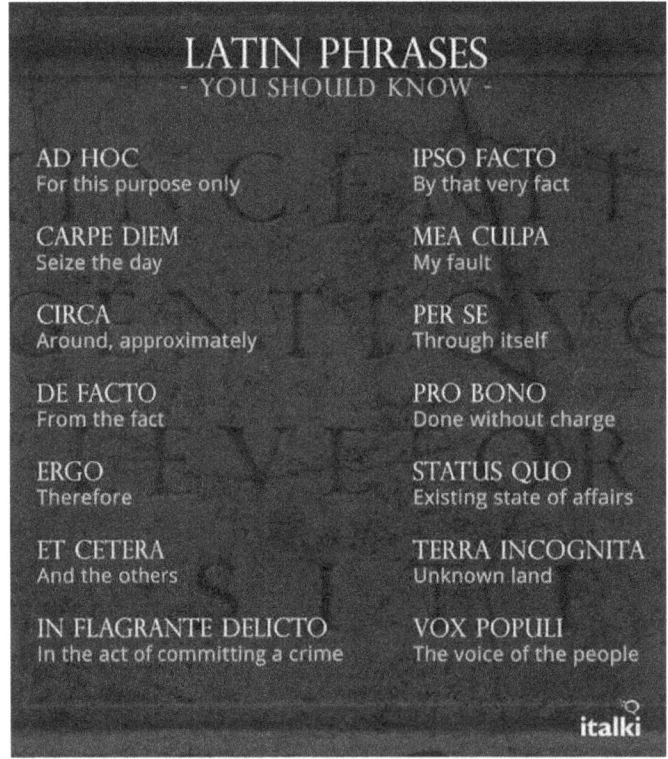

~ ~ ~

Don't Give Up Their Secrets

Sunday July 29, 2018 — I came across this quotation recently and realized how much it applies to my WHITE AS ICE quadrilogy, where the stories and the secrets interweave across numerous generations and thirty decades.

Clear as Mud

The story begins in 1692 when Lucelia Sabriss and her father stumble upon a community in the northern colonies. Three hundred years later in the town of Martinsville GA, the secrets from those early days begin to unfold as more than a dozen women explore the old attic in the house of Biscuit McKee and her husband, Bob Sheffield, where twenty-some-odd people have taken refuge from the ice storm of the century.

Over the span of four books, the secrets are slowly revealed, while the lives of the people who lived in that old house are often masked in mystery.

We're just three weeks from the release of RED AS A ROOSTER, the first of the four books. I'm sorry to say—No, I'm happy to say—RED ends in something of a cliff-hanger, but you'll have to wait only a month for the next book, BLACK AS SOOT (which ends in an even more startling cliff-hanger).

I hope when you read these books, you'll fall in love with the characters and the stories and will tell all your friends about them.

~ ~ ~

Bitter or Better

Monday July 30, 2018 — Yesterday, while I was having brunch at IHOP with a dear friend, two women came in and took the booth right next to ours. An hour or so later, they left, but paused, as women so often do, to say a few pleasant words to us.

Those few words turned into a conversation, and my friend and I came away with a couple of new role models. These women, both in their eighties, were absolute delights, who embodied what today's quote is saying. Bitter — or better. They both chose the latter option—and brightened my day considerably.

Fran Stewart

A good start to the week.

Of course, brunch with my friend was also a good start - so I felt a double winner.

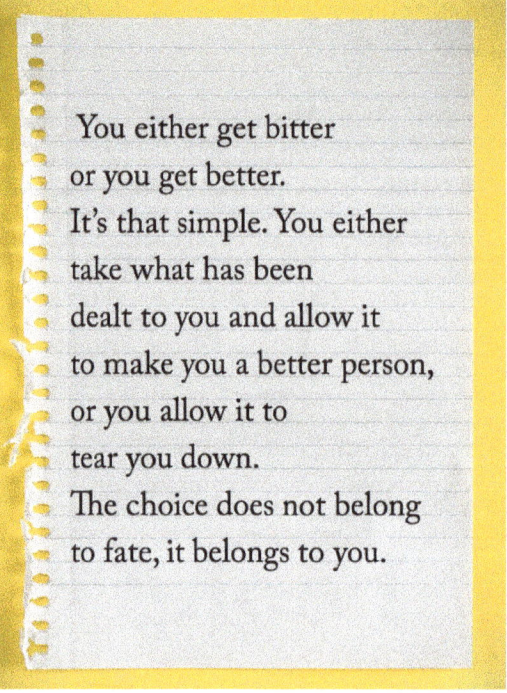

~ ~ ~

Chained Books

Tuesday July 31, 2018 — Have you ever thought about how rich we are, to live in a time where books are so readily accessible? I came across this information about a medieval library where the books were chained.

I hope you find it as interesting as I did.

Now, turn your head and look at the closest book you can spot in your house. Is it within arm's length? Is it on a bookshelf with dozens of other books? Is it in a TBR (to be read) pile? Is it in a stack to be returned to the library?

How very rich you are!

August 2018

Pink Panther

Wednesday August 1, 2018 — As part of my "to-do list," I'll be working most of today on cleaning up any little glitches in PINK AS A PEONY, getting the manuscript ready to send to my publisher. I thought this Pink Panther cartoon was a good place to start.

I hope you enjoy your day. I certainly plan to enjoy mine.

~ ~ ~

Author Reading (7/27/18)

Thursday August 2, 2018 — We're getting closer to the launch dates for RED AS A ROOSTER. My author copies came today, and I can barely contain my excitement.

I can guarantee you that the "Author Reading" on August 18th and 19th will be completely different from this cartoon. You'll get to hear snippets from the various books as well as learn something of how they came about.

And, regardless of which book launch you attend, you'll be able to sign up to have your name used for one of the characters in WHITE AS ICE, the final Biscuit McKee Mystery. Won't that be fun!

You must be present to win.

Fran Stewart

"Don't they usually read out loud?"

~ ~ ~

You Must Be Present to Win

Friday August 3, 2018 — Yesterday's post ended with these classic words:

"You Must Be Present to Win"

You know, that applies to a lot more situations than prize drawings. Everyday life, in fact.

Did you ever drive somewhere and realize at the end of the trip that you couldn't remember making this turn or stopping at that stop sign? Where'd you go? Why weren't you present?

Were you ever in the middle of a conversation and suddenly became aware that your friend's eyes had glazed over? Where did she go? Why wasn't she present? Or maybe you were the one who wasn't paying attention. Where'd you go?

Today, I'm challenging myself to be present every single moment of this day. I want to see every face that approaches me, smell every rich odor that winds past my nose, feel every movement of wind across my face or through my hair, taste the miracle in every morsel that passes my lips.

Would you like to join me in this challenge?

For today, let's be awake.

Let's be alive.

Let's be present.

After all,

You must be present to win

~ ~ ~

Sir Cumference

Saturday August 4, 2018 — Time for a math joke, or rather a math cartoon.

This one got me to thinking about other "Sir's." More about that tomorrow.

~ ~ ~

Photon

Sunday August 5, 2018 — More math related definitions. The cartoon was someone else's creations, but I'm the one who came up with these:

I don't trust what that guy's saying. Who is he, anyway?

    Sir Cumlocution

He sure does take advantage of every possibility, doesn't he?

    Yep. That Sir Cumstance to a tee.

Can I depend on him to be quiet about this?

    Of course you can. He's Sir Cumspect.

Do you think we can get away with this?

    Of course we can, or my name's not Sir Cumvent.

How can we possibly keep these baby goats in the pasture?

Call on Sir Cumscribe.

I love stuff like this. In one of my earlier Biscuit McKee Mysteries, I named one of the characters "Kelvin." Then I had one of the other characters (who obviously didn't like him) describe him as "an absolute zero of a man."

Only the math nerds would get it, but I truly hoped those few laughed uproariously when they read it.

~ ~ ~

squirrel on the skylight

Monday August 6, 2018 — Ever since those big trees were taken down, I haven't seen any squirrels on my roof. Until now. How the heck did this little fella get up there?

I know it seems like a stretch, but wondering how a squirrel could get onto my skylight is a lot like wondering where on earth the characters in my books come from. How on earth did they get into my brain?

There's one character, a little girl, who popped up some time ago when I got to thinking about one of the hatboxes in Biscuit's attic. If you've read this daily journal of mine for any time, you'll know that Biscuit and her friends are exploring Biscuit's 250-year-old attic—and there are LOTS of hatboxes up there.

All of a sudden, Mary Etta Hastings showed up. The name appeared seemingly out of nowhere, the hat appeared as if it had floated deliberately into her life, and then all I had to do was write the story.

This week I'll be sending that particular story to everyone who's signed up for my newsletter (on the home page of my website FranStewart.com).

We're on the final countdown. Just 12 days till the release of RED AS A ROOSTER.

I sure do hope to see you at one of the launch parties.

p.s. And I finally figured out how the squirrels get onto my roof. There's a power wire that goes from the pole to the corner of my house. DUH!!!

~ ~ ~

Thought I Was Cool

Tuesday August 7, 2018 — I tried to think of something to write to go along with this, but I doubt I could top it no matter how long I sit here and ponder.

Buy Cupcakes

Wednesday August 8, 2018 — I agree. You can't buy happiness.

While cupcakes might be a viable alternative, I'd just as soon get a good book.

I just finished reading *The House of Daughters* by Sarah-Kate Lynch, this month's selection for a book club I belong to. It's one of those stories that wrapped me up and transported me to a vineyard in France, taught me a great deal about the making of Champagne—I love a well-researched book!—and gave me a cast of characters who were thoroughly memorable.

What books bring you happiness? (Or, as an alternative, what kind of cupcake?)

Gregorian Chants

Thursday August 9, 2018 — If you'd like to learn more about Gregorian chants, read *The Beautiful Mystery* by Louise Penny, one of my all-time favorite authors.

It will help you understand the characters if you read the other books in her Inspector Gamache series first — begin with *Still Life*.

I always wanted to be a Gregorian Monk

but I never got the chants

~ ~ ~

Breathe

Friday August 10, 2018 — Breathe. Right. My chiropractor today told me that I'm not to sit for more than 45 minutes at a stretch without getting up and moving around. No long car drives. Absolutely no plane trips. For the rest of 2018.

So I had to cancel my planned visit in October to Florida to see my friend Linda Bell.

<<<Sigh>>>

Still, as I sit here icing my back 20 minutes out of every hour, I can be grateful that I still can breathe. After two adjustments in three days, it doesn't hurt to inhale anymore. That's progress.

Stop Being Afraid

Saturday August 11, 2018 — After all my complaining in yesterday's post, it's time to give myself a little pep talk. There truly is a great deal of good going right in my life.

1. Yesterday I had great fun sending out another newsletter with the story of "Mary Etta's Hat" that Biscuit and her friends found in the attic.

2. Heard again from my granddaughter who's settling in at college for her freshman year.

3. Had a text conversation with my daughter. She and I will be getting together for lunch next Friday.

4. Furthering the final plans for the two book launch parties coming up next Saturday and Sunday. There will be a special give-away at both bookstores.

5. Remembered to ice my back 20 minutes out of each hour—and it felt better.

6. Was exceedingly grateful that my sewing machine is on a waist-height table so I could stand up as I worked.

And so on from #7 to the mid-twenties . . .

Gosh! Life is good.

~ ~ ~

Bread and Water (8/11/18)

Sunday August 12, 2018 — Turning bread and water into toast and tea sounds like an exceptionally good idea for today.

Won't you join me?

~ ~ ~

Greek Olives

Monday August 13, 2018 — Last month my daughter took my granddaughter to Greece and Crete for one of those "trip of a lifetime" events. I enjoyed the trip vicariously as Veronica posted dozens of photos on her FB page. When they came back, they brought me a package of olives and a jar of honey.

Oh! Such deliciousness! The honey is—I must admit—even better than what came from the hives I used to have on my back deck. And the olives? Each one is tiny; most are about the size of my pinkie fingernail (for comparison, that's the end of my thumb in this photo). There's a pit inside each one, too, so the edible amount is minuscule. I've been eating four or five for dessert each evening.

Fran Stewart

Olives for dessert?

Yep. Thoroughly enjoying each one of them.

~ ~ ~

A Selfie Each Day

Tuesday August 14, 2018 — Last weekend I went to a funeral service for the mother of a friend of mine. I never had a chance to know Liz, but she was one of those vibrant women who loved life and who never let anything slow her down.

There were dozens and dozens of photos of her, in an album, on a power point slide show, framed, everywhere. Her relatives sighed when one picture came up, laughed at another, exclaimed over this one, wondered about that one.

Nothing was labeled, though. No indication of who the people were, when the picture was taken, where it was taken.

A surprising number of those more recent photos were selfies.

When I came home, I looked through a few of my albums and, of course, the Photo app on my laptop.

First of all, there are very few pictures of me. Most are of my family, my cats, my yard. Few of them are labeled. And precious few selfies. If my daughter doesn't take pictures of me, then why don't I do it myself?

So, I decided to:

take a selfie every day

label everything in the various albums, and

put names with the pictures on my laptop.

Looks like I have a lot of work ahead of me.

I did find one photo to share with you - taken at the Pen Women Nature Garden at Stone Mountain in April of 2017. I love laughing pictures, even if I can't recall just what I was chuckling about at the time.

And here's another one I took in front of a favorite framed print.

~ ~ ~

Selfie with quilt

Wednesday August 15, 2018 — I promise I won't bombard you with my once-a-day selfies, but I thought I'd share just this one for now.

The quilt hanging in the background was created by my sister, Diana Alishouse, and you can read about it in her book *Depression Visible: The Ragged Edge*. Or look at it on her website depressionvisible.com. I wish the lighting in this selfie did justice to the vibrant colors.

Fran Stewart

Meanwhile, I'm counting down to the book launch parties this Saturday and Sunday . . .

~ ~ ~

autumn clematis

Thursday August 16, 2018 — When all those trees had to be taken out of my yard two years ago, the heavy machinery not only ran over my Sweet Autumn Clematis, it compacted the soil, destroyed the whole area, and left me afraid that I'd never see another flowering vine.

Last year a couple of little shoots sprang up amid all the blackberry canes (I don't think anything kills those guys) and some vinca (equally un-killable).

This year? That entire quadrant of the yard is awash with the most delicious scent coming from billows of white blossoms. The vines are entwined all the way up the Washington Hawthorn and the Gingko Biloba tree. It looks like a jungle, and that's just fine with me.

Thank goodness there's no HOA here, or I'd be in deep doo-doo!

~ ~ ~

Rainbow selfie

Friday August 17, 2018 — Tomorrow's the big day, and so's Sunday, with the release of RED AS A ROOSTER and the two launch events. I think this selfie I took is prophetic, all these colors raining down over me.

How did it happen? I have no idea. Some quirk of the morning sun coming in through my skylight, the camera angle — or maybe it was fairies or angels or leprechauns. Who knows? All the colors of my Biscuit McKee Mysteries are in there. All my hopes for these final four volumes. All the joy I feel every day. All the love I'm surrounded by. All the gratitude that pours from my heart.

Selfie on Loveseat

Saturday August 18, 2018 — Today's the day RED AS A ROOSTER is released.

I feel like I've put not just my whole heart, but my whole reputation as a writer into these last four books. I know I keep saying they're the best I've ever written, but the anticipation of waiting to hear from the important folks—my readers—kept me up most of the night (which is why I'm a bit late with my post this morning).

I know it'll be a few days before the comments begin to roll in via email and messenger and text, but I'm practically bouncing off the walls.

[**2020 note:** The embarrassing thing about calling these books the best I've ever written is that when I re-read them two years later, I found all sorts of errors. Doggone it. But that's why they were re-published in revised editions.]

~ ~ ~

6 Out of 7 Dwarves

Sunday August 19, 2018 — Are you Happy today? I sure am. Yesterday's book launch event at Liberty Books in Lawrenceville went so well, and I'm looking forward to the one this afternoon at Another Chapter Bookstore in Cumming.

Clear as Mud

The winner of "Your Name as a Character in White as Ice" turned out to be a five-year-old girl who came with her grandmother. She's going to end up being a merry old lady who makes the best Apple Pan Dowdy in the town. Twenty or thirty years from now, I hope she'll appreciate it!

There'll be another drawing this afternoon. Who knows? You might win if you show up and put your name in the jar.

~ ~ ~

Teapot bird feeder

Monday August 20, 2018 — What a great weekend. Between the two book launch events, I now have the names of FIVE characters to be used in WHITE AS ICE. Here are the winners of the various drawings in the order in which they were drawn:

Liberty Books:

Hannah Heath (whose name was entered by her grandmother)

Veronica Lowe (whose name was drawn by Hannah!)

Another Chapter Bookstore:

Janice Adams Beene (for having traveled the farthest—from Indiana)

Peggy Dixon, and

Mozelle Funderburk

Fran Stewart

Thanks to everyone who showed up! Thanks to both bookstores for having me there, and extra thanks to everyone who bought a book (or two or three or four!)

Let's all have a cup of tea to celebrate, shall we? And I know the birds will join us as they feast from the teapot bird feeder in this photo taken from the Antiques and Teacups FB page.

~ ~ ~

Janice Adams Beene

Tuesday August 21, 2018 — If you really love the work of a particular author, how far would you travel to hear her speak? How many pounds of her books would you lug along in your carryon bag so she could sign them all?

Here's the woman who won the "traveled the farthest for the book launch" prize. Janice Adams Beene flew here from Indiana for the event at Another Chapter Bookstore. Don't you love the slogan on her shirt? "When in doubt, Bloom."

I say amen to that.

Janice is now a character in WHITE AS ICE, and she promised to come back for that book launch three months from now.

~ ~ ~

Adventure or Tea?

Wednesday August 22, 2018 — I'm opting for tea this morning. Had enough delightful adventures this past week.

I'm going to be adventuring vicariously for a while: 1) through my reading, 2) through looking back at the photos my daughter and granddaughter sent from their trip to Greece and Crete, and 3) through the pictures my son plans to post of his trip through northern California, Oregon, and Washington.

He has a van he's outfitted as a home away from home.

He has a job that allows him to work from home (no matter where that is). All he needs is his laptop, various other bits of technology, and a WiFi connection. Hence, the traveling.

Talk about building a life the way you want it to be…

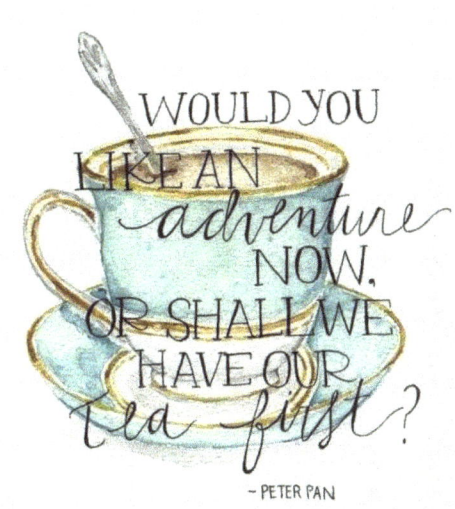

Fran Stewart

~ ~ ~

Dream or Plan

Thursday August 23, 2018 — What'll it be today for you? A dream or a plan?

Wishful thinking or walking meditation?

Sit back and wait or take a few steps?

Those of you who know me, know I've been dealing with a wrenched back for some time now. This morning I decided to forget the dreaming, wishing, sitting back. I went for the planning, meditating while walking, and taking those first steps.

It's still blessedly cool outside from a lovely night of open windows and gentle flow-through-the-house breezes, so I took a walk up the cul-de-sac, around another one, and back. It may not sound like a lot, but considering that last week I could barely get down my front stairs, this felt like a huge accomplishment.

A couple of crows kept me company, following along from phone line to phone line. Now they're scarfing peanuts off the driveway. Yes! I was able to fill the feeders before I went walking.

How much better I feel!

~~~

Halo Selfie

Friday August 24, 2018 — Have you taken a halo selfie lately? Just get the sun behind you. Try it. It's lots of fun.

~~~

When in doubt, drink tea

Saturday August 25, 2018 — Not sure what to do today?

I just brewed myself a pot of licorice root tea. Love that stuff.

Fran Stewart

~ ~ ~

Ancient Grammar Police

Monday August 27, 2018 — Did you ever wonder if there's any sense to the rules about when to use "lay" and when to use "lie"?

You're not alone. About half the books I've read recently have a character proclaiming a need to "lay down and rest."

Grrrrr! It's supposed to be "lie down and rest." You can lie down, or you can lay something down. Think about the old nursery rhyme "Now I lay me down to sleep…" That's correct, simply because of the word "me" in there. The "me" is the something I'm laying down, the same way I might lay down a book when I'm through with reading it, or lay down a child who's fallen asleep in my arms.

On the other hand:

>   Now I lie down to sleep, or

>   I lie here with a book lying next to me, or

>   My child lies sleeping

Does it matter?

I think it does.

~ ~ ~

Things Money Can't Buy

Tuesday August 28, 2018 — Tune back in tomorrow, when I'll mention something else money can't buy.

~ ~ ~

Biscuit on My Shoulder

Wednesday August 29, 2018 — Yesterday I said I'd talk about something else money can't buy. That would be memories. In September and October, I'll be teaching memoirs classes (as in how to write yours) at three different area libraries (Auburn, Peachtree Corners/Gwinnett, and Collins Hill/Gwinnett). If you're in this area and want to know more, send me a FB message.

But, back to the memories. In 2002, a friend of mine snapped this picture when Biscuit and I went for a walk. That is to say, I walked, she perched on my shoulder. She was the cat-family matriarch, the only cat I've ever had who knew the names of all the other cats in the household. If I called Harley, for instance, Biscuit would turn her head to look at the big black cat who purred like a motorcycle. If I mentioned Chaucer's name, she'd level a stare at the champagne-colored one. "Agatha," I'd say, "where are you?" and my amazing orange and white tabby would lead me into another room where Agatha sat on the windowsill.

Those kinds of memories are priceless. Have I written about these particular ones in my own memoirs? No.

Fran Stewart

Maybe I should just copy and paste all these FB posts. They certainly qualify as memoirs…

[**2020 Note:** And that is precisely why I'm putting all these into book format—so my grandchildren will have easy access to them. And so will *you*.]

~ ~ ~

What's a Steve?

Thursday August 30, 2018 — Loved this - and thought you might too.

Wonder how soon it will be explained… Meanwhile, it's magnificent.

If you want to see the original CBC news story, search for "steve-northern-lights-not-aurora"

Why's it called a Steve? It stands for **S**trong **T**hermal **E**mission **V**elocity **E**nhancement.

Yeah, I figure we all need to know that.

~ ~ ~

Cat Loaf

Friday August 31, 2018 — There's nothing like fresh bread right out of the oven. I used to bake bread every week. There was an extraordinary little restaurant in Middlebury, Vermont, called the Bakery Lane Soup Bowl that served soups, breads, salads, and quiches. And cookies.

In 1976 I bought a copy of their "Bakery Lane Soup Bowl Cookbook" and began making a different bread each week. Sometimes I baked two batches in a week, enough to feast on and to gift some loaves. My all-time favorite was "Beverly's Dill Bread," bursting with the flavor of dill seed and green onion. There was some cottage cheese in there as well. Yum.

It's been years since I baked even a single loaf, but the memories linger.

Come to think of it, the recipe for "Virginia's Broccoli Soup" has been getting a little lonely. I haven't splattered it in quite a while. Maybe that and some dill bread … hmm. As soon as the weather cools off a bit.

September 2018

OK to do nothing

Saturday September 1, 2018 — I had one of these do-nothing days yesterday. At least, I thought I had until I began writing in my journal last night.

Not only had I accomplished all the usual daily chores (such as playing a rousing game of "chase the mouse" with Wooly Bear), I'd also proofed a book galley, began reading an ARC (Advanced Reader Copy) for a soon-to-be-published beginning author, completed reading this month's book club discussion book (*The Irresistible Blueberry Bakeshop & Cafe* by Mary Simses, which I thoroughly enjoyed), took a walk, ran a load of laundry, concocted another one of my crockpot throw-together stews—it turned out quite well, by the way—made up several necessary lists, made sure my September calendar was up to date, and wrote a letter. Yes, a real letter. The kind that has to be mailed with a stamp.

Did I write about all these doings in my journal? Well, no. But I thought through them before deciding what to write.

I guess my do-nothing day will have to wait until the next time I go to Sapelo Island.

How about you? Do you have days like this when you "do nothing" ? ? ?

~ ~ ~

It was Tense

Sunday September 2, 2018 — Yesterday I spent a large chunk of the day reading through an ARC (advanced reader copy) of a debut novel by someone whose editor contacted me to request an endorsement. As always, I told her I'd be happy to read it, but would endorse it only if I truly enjoyed the book — which meant it had to be well written, with characters I cared about and a plot that intrigued me.

The good news? The book was marvelous, and I had no problem writing a glowing endorsement of it. The bad news? It won't be published until next April. When we get closer, I'll tell you more about it.

Meanwhile, I thought you might be up for a little pun.

~ ~ ~

Callie's Newest Toy

Monday September 3, 2018 — The best part of ordering my author copies of my books is that they come packed with lots and lots of long trails of paper. They eventually end up in the recycling bin, but usually have a few detours on the way.

Such as their very important usage as cat toys and cat nesting crumples. As you can see, Callie is completely at ease here.

Tomorrow, I'll show you another use of this paper, if I can manage to get a picture of it…

~ ~ ~

Dancing Grannie Poster

Tuesday September 4, 2018 — Here's another good use for long wrinkly pieces of packing paper. Head out to the driveway on a sunny June day with your two grandchildren and a whole box of markers, stretch the paper out, then trace each other. Cut out the figures, color them, decorate them (jewelry, blouse edging, polka dots, and hair squiggles), and either take them home from Grannie's house to show mom and dad — or (as I did seven years ago) put your own portrait up on the back of a door where you can laugh with it every evening as you write in your journal.

One more thing—be sure to date it.

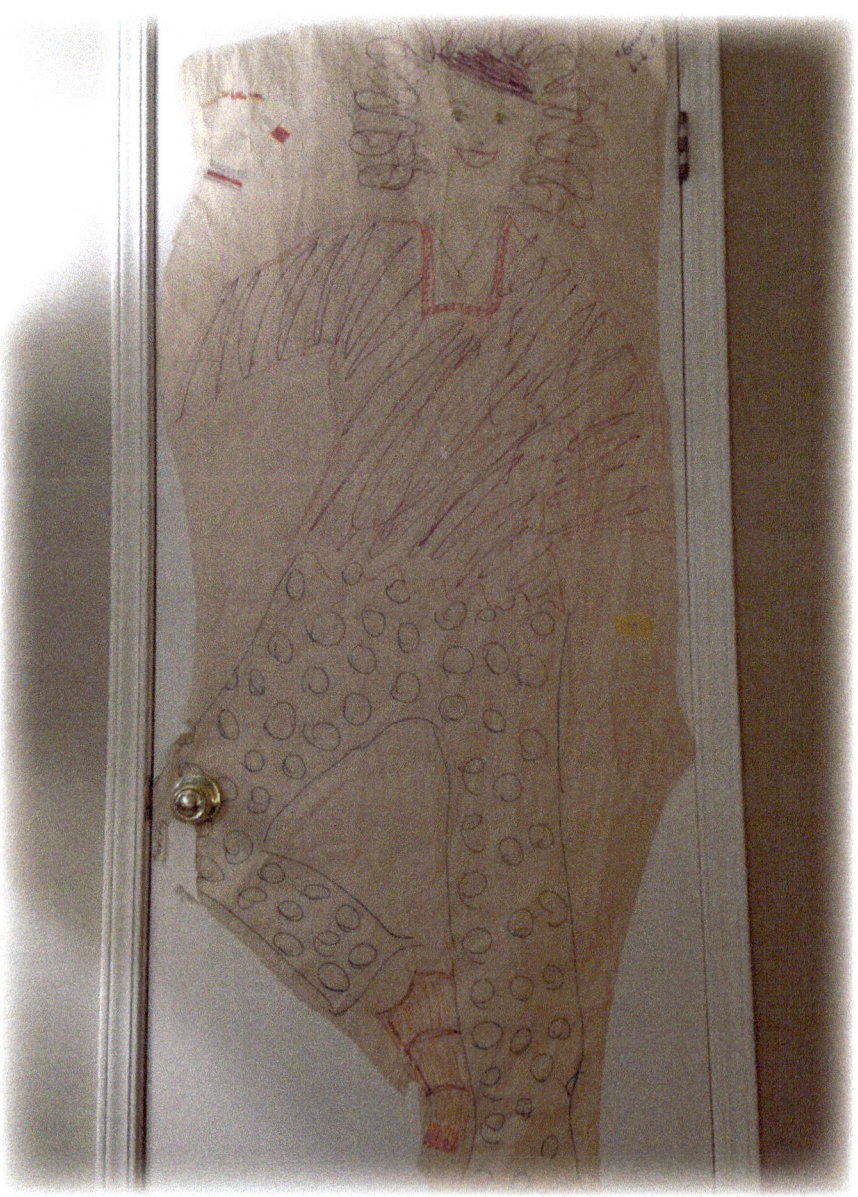

~ ~ ~

Silly Selfie

Wednesday September 5, 2018 — Good morning! It's silly selfie time.

~ ~ ~

Handmade

Thursday September 6, 2018 — While rummaging through a box of odds and ends a while ago, I came across a manila folder that contained four sheets of bright purple (yes—purple) hand-made paper and a couple of marbled envelopes. This photo doesn't do them justice.

Holding that folder in my hands brought back a ton of memories of the summer my children and I made the paper, beginning with collecting onion skins and ending with placing leaves and flower petals into the mixture. The leaves and pine needles looked quite festive when they were still green. I can't recall what caused all those tiny blue dots. Somehow or other, I think there were fresh-picked blueberries in the process.

Fran Stewart

I do (sort of) remember marbling the envelopes (another project that we took on the following summer). It involved a lot of water, a great deal of ink and various other substances, and lots of laughter.

We used the paper and those envelopes for years, sending letters to the grandparents and to friends.

I wonder if my kids even remember …

~ ~ ~

So Much Time on Somebody's Hands

Friday September 7, 2018 — Do you like to put lists together?

So do I.

But this list took a lot longer, I'm sure, than most of the ones I dash off.

Still, it's a lot of fun.

I'm still trying to work out three of these. How many can you identify?

Can you name the famous book?

1. The Geezer And The Caribbean
2. An Elm Develops From A Sapling Where The Dodgers Once Played
3. Brilliant Red Communication No One Writes Anymore
4. While I Was In The Bed Croaking
5. The Muscadines Belonging To Anger
6. Armed Conflict And The Kind of Train Cat Stevens Used To Ride
7. Out Of Here In The Current Of Air
8. The Purple Rain Singer Associated With the Rising & Falling Of The Ocean
9. Tremendous Anticipations
10. What Comes Before A Fall & Preconceived Judgement Towards A Group
11. Mitt-Wearing Home Plate Squatter Enclosed By Reuben Sandwich Bread
12. Murder A Derisive, Taunting, Feather-Covered Creature
13. An Au Revoir For Everything Inside The Shirt Sleeves
14. Y2K Minus Number Of Candles On Molly Ringwald's Cake
15. Felonies And Misdemeanors Coupled With Spankings
16. That Audio And That Rage
17. Toward What Person Or Persons A Recess-is-Over Sound Is Directed
18. One Who Domineers Over Things Stuck To The Swatter
19. Scoliosis Sufferer At The Fighting Irish School
20. Courageous Globe With The Tag Still On It
21. Pirate Loot / Counter In The Center Of A Kitchen
22. Story Of A Duo Of Municipalities
23. About Little White Rodents And Grown Boys
24. Ruby-Colored Nametag Indicating Bravery
25. The Star In Our Solar System Comes Up, Too

Copyright © 2016 by Laurie Parker   www.laurieparkerwriter.com

2020 Note: I finally figured them all out!

~ ~ ~

Maze Quilt

Saturday September 8, 2018 — There are mazes, and there are labyrinths, and then there are enclosed creations like this quilt that a friend of mine found somewhere on the Internet. While it's gorgeous and technically amazing, the pattern would drive me crazy after a short while.

Why? I'm glad you asked.

You see, a maze may be frustrating, but eventually one should be able to find a way out of it. A labyrinth is a meditative path—no frustration involved whatsoever. But the walls on this quilt? Good grief! There's no way out of the five foundation squares at all, short of climbing those walls.

The other thing is that nothing's growing in there. I'd want a few green vines and a tree or two, wouldn't you?

Still, it IS a beautiful quilt, and I acknowledge the work that went into designing and creating it.

But—would you want it in your bedroom?

~ ~ ~

Think Bigger

Sunday September 9, 2018 — I am moving SO far beyond my comfort zone, and I'm glad you're coming along with me on the ride. These final four Biscuit McKee books are quite a departure from what I've written before. It's not scary exactly, but it sure is a growing place!

Have you read RED AS A ROOSTER yet? If so, you'll know it ends on something of a cliffhanger. What's going to happen next? Less than a week to find out, because BLACK AS SOOT's release date is this coming Saturday!

~ ~ ~

Call Up the Author

Monday September 10, 2018 — I've always felt this way. That's why when I own a book that I enjoy, I tend to make marginal notes of the questions I'd love to ask the author. Who knows? Maybe someday I'll meet Louise Penny …

"What really knocks me out is a book that, when you're all done reading it, you wish the author that wrote it was a terrific friend of yours and you could call him up on the phone whenever you felt like it. That doesn't happen much, though."

~ J.D. Salinger, The Catcher in the Rye

The good thing is that nowadays you can message an author through their FB page. And most of us are more than happy to answer. I made a new friend that way when someone in Indiana contacted me.

How many times have you contacted an author whose work you love?

Did it ever occur to you that authors frequently hear from people who complain about their books, but so often never hear from people who enjoy them, who've learned from them, who like to re-read the stories, who'd love to discuss them.

[**2020 Note**: Just a couple of weeks ago I had someone ask me if we could do a Zoom conversation about *Orange as Marmalade*, which she had just read for the first time. She had a whole lot of GREAT questions about it, about the motivations of the characters, about the nuances of the plot. She'd even seen some underlying themes I hadn't been aware of myself.]

~ ~ ~

One Day at a Time

Tuesday September 11, 2018 — Do you ever end up with a to-do list that looks a bit overwhelming?

That's what this week started out like for me. Each individual task to be accomplished isn't that difficult - but the sheer volume of tasks looms like an ocean liner heading toward a sailboat.

Luckily, I glanced to my left when I walked past the magnet on my fridge this morning.

Okay. Now I remember how to do it.

Moose in Alaska

Wednesday September 12, 2018 — Years ago, when my son was studying at the University of Alaska in Anchorage, he took a photo of a moose on the snowy lawn of one of the buildings. The quote etched into the wall of the building says:

Two things fill me with awe: the starry heavens above and the moral law within. Immanuel Kant

Of course, in the photo it looks like "the starry heavens above and the moose below."

Think about it. What fills you with awe?

Different Lessons

Thursday September 13, 2018 — The memoirs classes I'm teaching this month and next call to mind the past, present, and—yes—even the future. Our memories, those stories we want to remember or that we want to pass on to our children or grandchildren, can't help but call up thoughts of "what will I do if and when I'm up against a similar circumstance?"

Of course, we'll probably make different choices if that happens.

Fortunately, if we've made peace with our past, we won't be given those same lessons a second time.

We'll be given different lessons.

Oh dear! What do I do now?

Take a breath, that's what.

~ ~ ~

Back yard trees

Friday September 14, 2018 — As you can see from this photo of part of my backyard, which I've shown you before in these posts, the tiny creek isn't usually visible unless you're standing right next to it because of all the lush ferns. I'm remembering back to the last time (when was it?—seven years ago?) when the leading edge of a hurricane came through the Atlanta area and this placid meandering creek became a raging torrent well more than 30 feet wide. It swept away the chair where I used to sit and write, along with the 14-foot long plank that kept me from sinking into the always-damp fern-filled swale.

In its wake, there were sandbars amongst what was left of the ferns. Yes! Sand piled 6 to 8 inches deep.

Of course, everything recovered. I'm waiting to see what will happen with Hurricane Florence on her way.

Also, the book launch event for BLACK AS SOOT is tomorrow at Liberty Books in Lawrenceville at 3 pm — weather won't be a problem and the movie folks are finished shooting their monster film in the middle of town, so traffic will be back to normal. Sunday from 1 to 5 I'll be at another launch. Rain is predicted, but with Florence moving so slowly, there shouldn't be any disruption. I hope you'll join me if you can.

But then will come Monday and Tuesday . . . and I'm wondering what my creek will look like by this time next week.

I'll let you know. In the meantime, stay safe.

It's Here!

Saturday September 15, 2018 — Today's the big day! BLACK AS SOOT's release day!

Yesterday I was talking with my daughter, who is a voracious reader, and she gave me the highest compliment imaginable. It's hard for me to express how delighted I was to hear how much she loved RED AS A ROOSTER, and is looking forward to getting her hands on BLACK AS SOOT today.

Whether you read it as an e-book or a print copy, please, please know that word of mouth helps authors keep food on their table. Please, please tell your friends, your family, your colleagues, even your casual acquaintances. And please, tell them to start with RED AS A ROOSTER. Otherwise they won't know what's going on up in that attic.

I've talked about a number of fine writers in these daily posts of mine—people whose books I can thoroughly recommend. I'd like to think I've introduced you to a few of your new favorite authors. I'd like to be your best friend's new favorite author.

Pretty please?

~ ~ ~

An Echo

Monday September 17, 2018 — This picture has nothing to do with what I'm going to write about this morning, but I like it—and I completely agree with the sentiment—so I thought I'd share it.

The launches for BLACK AS SOOT this weekend went well, and I was gratified at how many people said they'd just finished reading RED AS A ROOSTER and couldn't wait to start BLACK so they'd know what happened.

"Just wait," I told them. "The cliff-hanger at the end of BLACK is a doozy."

I still remember the old Mission Impossible (the original hour-long weekly TV show) that ended once on a real cliff-hanger, showing feet and legs creeping down a hallway. We knew who the legs were attached to, and we knew the weapon he held, and we knew he was approaching a room where one of the good guys was trapped . . . but then the screen dissolved to a message that said, "To be continued." AARGH!!!!! We had to wait a whole week to find out what happened.

As I recall, the next show was something of an anticlimax, but—oh—the anticipation during that week of waiting was delightful.

What about you? Do you have some favorite cliffhangers?

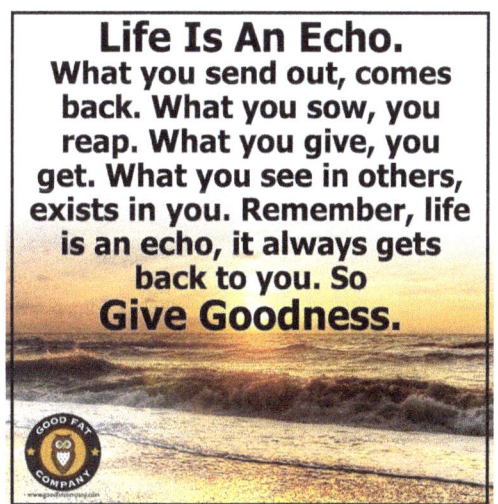

~ ~ ~

Inside the Box

Tuesday September 18, 2018 — There are so many times when "inside the box" doesn't work. Ditto with "outside the box."

Today, maybe I truly don't know where the box is. That's sort of the way I'm feeling, what with the end of the Biscuit McKee series looming.

This coming Saturday, I'll be at the Brenau Literary Festival, but I won't even be talking about my books. Instead, I'll be introducing people to memoir writing – sort of a highly condensed 45-minute version of the classes I teach at various libraries.

I really do need to develop an online version of these classes, since I've had so many requests for memoirs webinars. Trouble is — I'm not sure where that box is!

[**2020 Note**: Those online memoirs classes are now a reality—thanks in large part to the COVID-19 pandemic that forced my hand and made me learn how to use Zoom. If you're interested, head for my website franstewart.com to see what classes are available.]

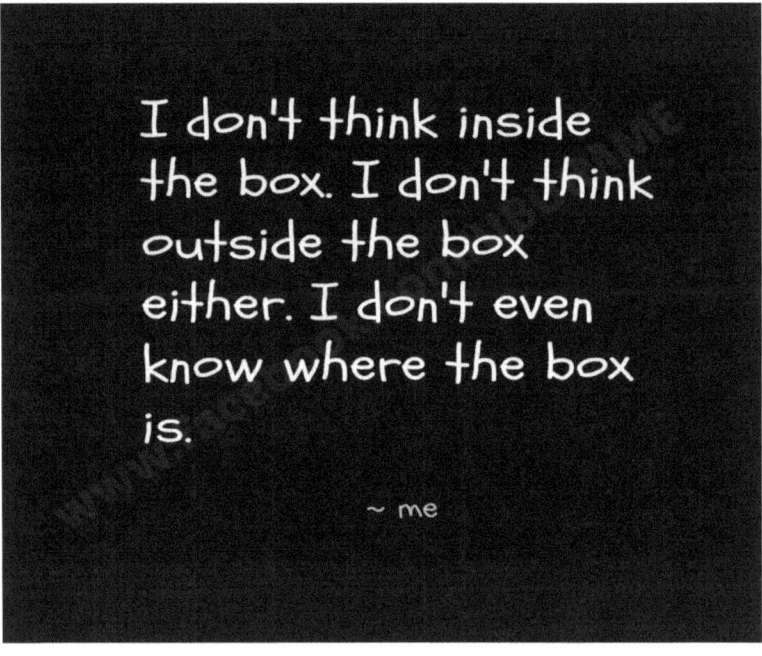

~ ~ ~

26 Cats

Wednesday September 19, 2018 — I need some advice. Last evening, I hosted a virtual book club on FreeConferenceCall dot com. There were so many problems with the connections and the audio, it was hard for the attendees to hear Sherry Harris, our wonderful guest, whose Sarah Winston Garage Sale Mysteries are lots of fun (especially if you need tips on how to run a garage sale!).

Have you had any experience with other video conferencing outfits? I'm looking into offering my memoirs classes online, but I don't want to start them until I have a really good video conference platform with which to work.

What does this have to do with the 26 cats? Nothing. Absolutely nothing. Just thought I'd share a laugh before I asked for help.

Clear as Mud

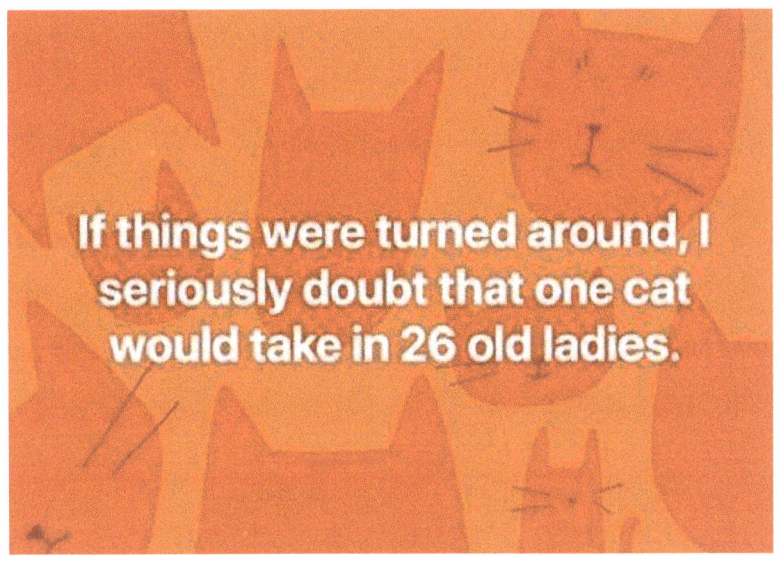

~ ~ ~

Try to Identify

Thursday September 20, 2018 — It doesn't matter how full, how involved, how frantic my day becomes, I can always find the time to take three deep breaths. In those few moments, I can reach the calm sure center of the storm.

Try it yourself. Three slow breaths.

Almost like magic.

Wooly Bear Again

Friday September 21, 2018 — Talking about taking three deep breaths (as we were discussing yesterday), another regular moment of peace in my life is when I brush my teeth. I've learned to leave just a dribble of water running for a very short time, while Wooly Bear laps at it with great gusto.

Then she runs out and dives into the pile of paper wrapping material I leave out for her.

Yes, you're right. She has me very well trained.

Bumblebee on Goldenrod

Saturday September 22, 2018 — I love bumblebees. As I'm sure you've heard or read over the years, engineers have proven that bumblebees should not be able to fly because their bodies are too heavy for their wings to support. Of course, nobody ever told the bumblebees that, so they just keep flying.

They love the goldenrod in my yard. I'm happy to supply the bees the food they need for the winter.

For years I told myself I couldn't possibly write the mysteries I always wanted to write. But then one day I ended up trying to recover from surgery and began writing, and look what's come about? I could fly!

What have you been telling yourself you couldn't possibly do?

Why not try listening to the bumblebees instead?

~ ~ ~

I Forgive Myself

Monday September 24, 2018 — Yesterday I spent time with a friend who has been holding a grudge for the past thirty years or so.

It's a very heavy weight to carry.

It reminded me of the weight of resentment I used to tote around, first against another person and then, once I'd cleared that away, against myself.

In these last four Biscuit McKee mysteries, Biscuit the librarian comes up against a load of resentment she's been hanging onto. Eighty-something-year-old Sadie Masters finally calls her on it, when she mentions—rather pointedly—that "holding a grudge is like taking poison and expecting the other person to die."

Biscuit remembers then about a technique for releasing such garbage. She lights a candle, imagines all the resentment balling up inside her lungs, and then blows it all out toward the candle flame. As the wisp of smoke curls upward, all that yucky energy dissipates.

It works. And it doesn't matter whether you're releasing anger toward someone else or toward yourself.

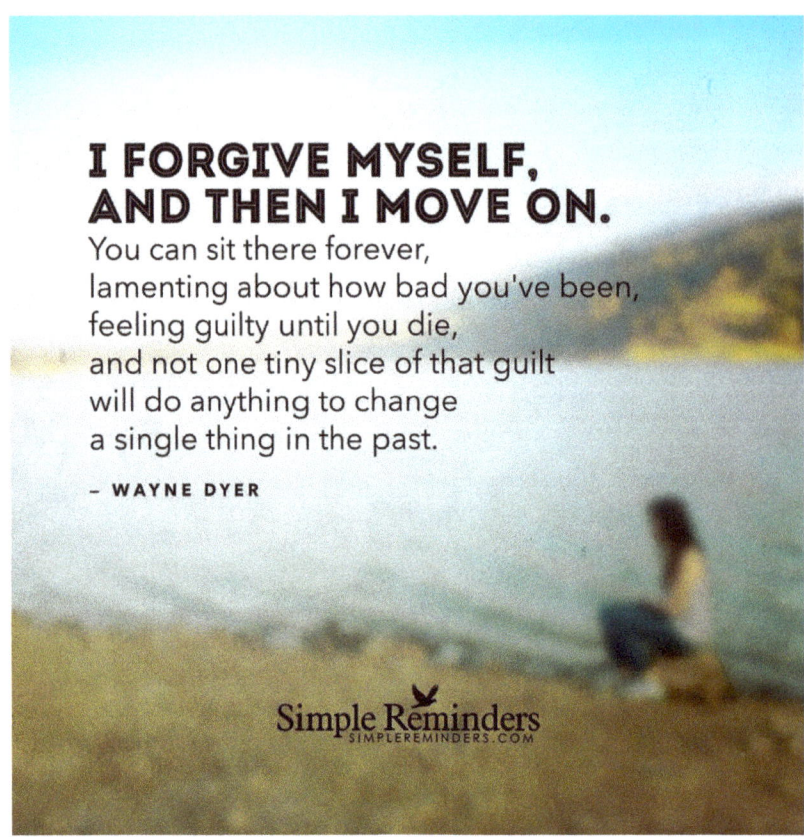

~ ~ ~

Fire Ladder

Tuesday September 25, 2018 — In one of the memoirs classes I've taught, we talked a lot about reaching new heights. There are a lot of ways of doing such a thing.

When my sister was eight years old or so, she had a chance (at an Armed Forces Day celebration) to climb a ladder on a fire truck. Those were the days before OSHA rules and liability regulations. I was so in awe of her as I watched her scale the ladder hundreds—maybe thousands!—of feet into the air. I thought she was the bravest person I had ever known.

I was also envious as heck, but I suppose even back then, somebody drew the line at letting a five-year-old head up a ladder.

Two years ago, when she came here for a visit, I mentioned that magnificent ladder-climb, and found out that she'd felt completely terrified, both on the way up and on the way down. I also realized how my viewpoint had seen a sturdy pathway almost to the stars, while her view had been of a wiggly thirty-foot wooden ladder that was sure to be her doom.

What a difference in perspective. When you write your memoirs — you are going to do that, aren't you? — be sure you take into account how two differing viewpoints can entirely change a picture.

Clear as Mud

~ ~ ~

10 Things to Say

Wednesday September 26, 2018 — The next time somebody tries to tell you to buck up, try sending this list to that person.

Sadness happens.

In one of the memoir classes I'm teaching, several of the women told us at the first class that they were trying to figure out how to deal with—and write about—the death of someone dear to them.

Grief happens.

Sometimes, if you're on this side of that divide, simply listening to your friend's story is enough, rather than trying to "fix" your friend so that *you* won't feel uncomfortable.

Fran Stewart

Death happens.

If you're on that side of the divide, having lost someone and had your world turn upside down, writing about it can be therapeutic.

I'm not a grief counselor, but it makes sense to me that "It doesn't feel fair" is a kinder thing to say than "You'll get over it."

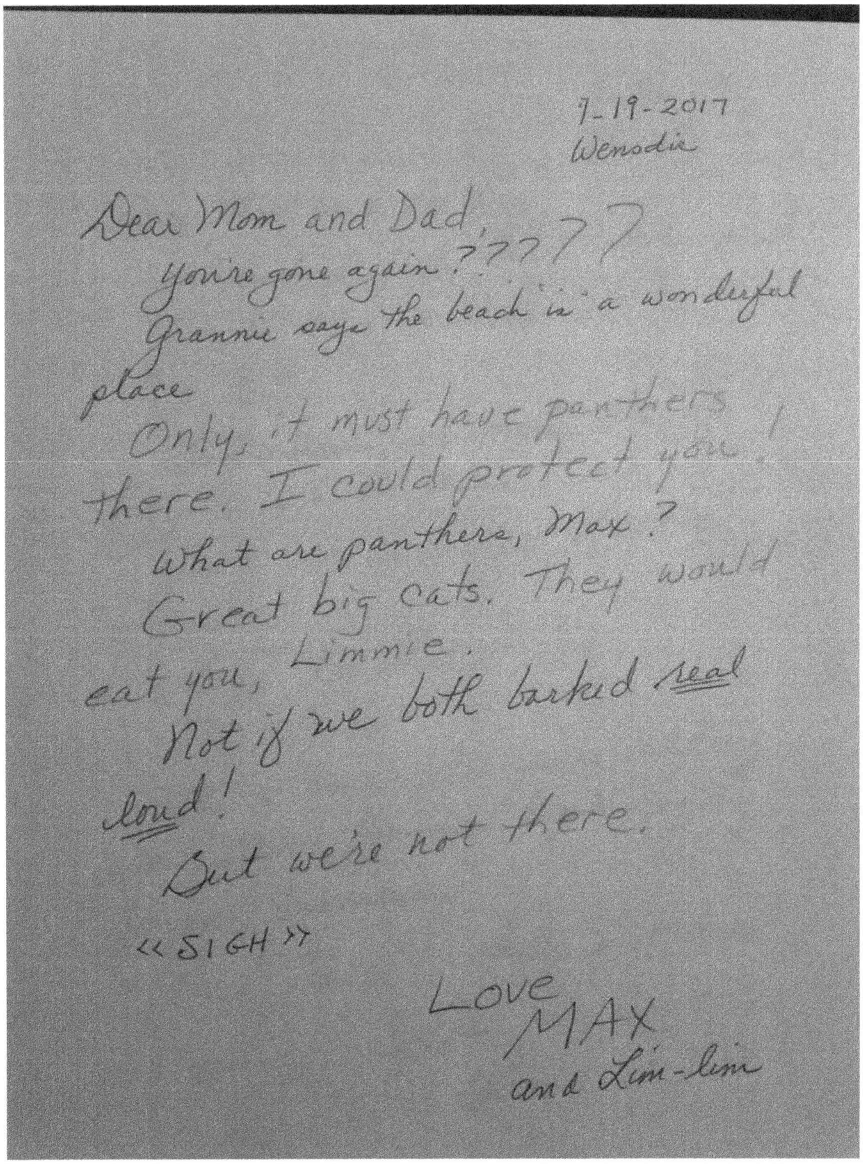

~~~

Dog Diaries

Thursday September 27, 2018 — Last year, my daughter and her husband went hiking at Panther Creek. I got the name wrong when I told my grand-dogs (Max and Limerick) they were at Panther Beach, so their letters to Mom and Dad were somewhat skewed.

This whole correspondence is a perfect example of how misunderstanding one word (or two words) can throw off one's perception of what's going on.

> 7-19-2017
> Wensdia
>
> Dear Mom and Dad,
> You're gone again??????
> Grannie says the beach is a wonderful place.
> Only, it must have panthers there. I could protect you!
> What are panthers, Max?
> Great big cats. They would eat you, Limmie.
> Not if we both barked <u>real</u> <u>loud</u>!
> But we're not there.
> « SIGH »
>
> Love,
> MAX
> and Lim-lim

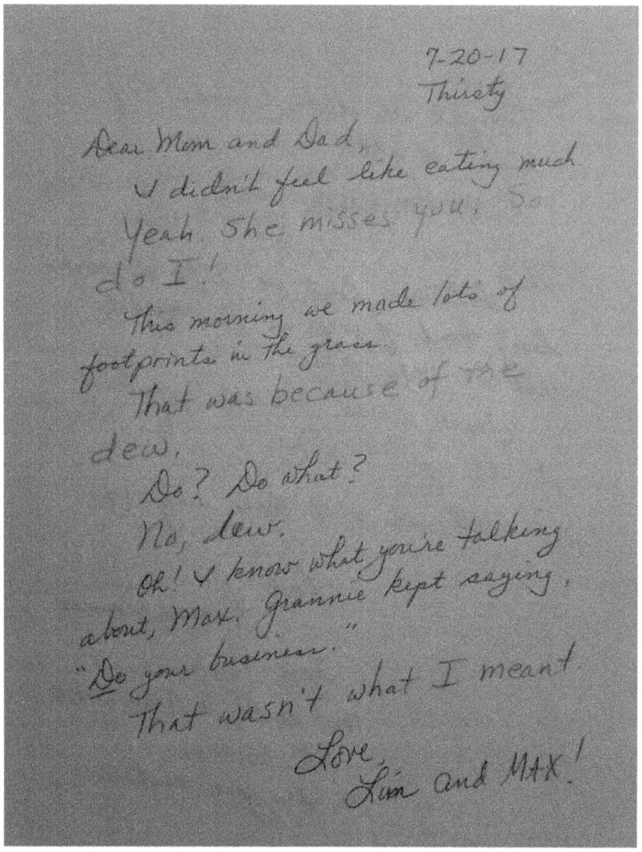

Fran Stewart

7-20-17
Thirsty

Dear Mom and Dad,
　　I didn't feel like eating much.
　　Yeah. She misses you. So do I!
　　This morning we made lots of footprints in the grass.
　　That was because of the dew.
　　Do? Do what?
　　No, dew.
　　Oh! I know what you're talking about, Max. Grannie kept saying, "_Do_ your business."
　　That wasn't what I meant.
　　　　　　Love,
　　　　　　Lim and MAX!

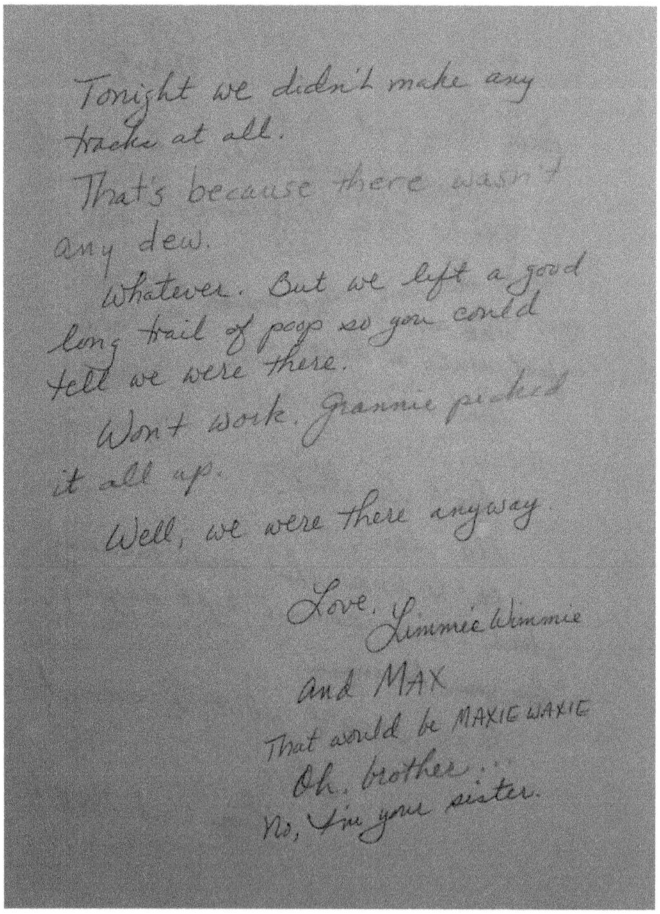

　　Tonight we didn't make any tracks at all.
　　That's because there wasn't any dew.
　　Whatever. But we left a good long trail of poop so you could tell we were there.
　　Won't work. Grannie picked it all up.
　　Well, we were there anyway.
　　　　　　Love,
　　　　　　Limmie Wimmie
　　　　　　and MAX
　　That would be MAXIE WAXIE
　　Oh, brother.
　　No, I'm your sister.

Clear as Mud

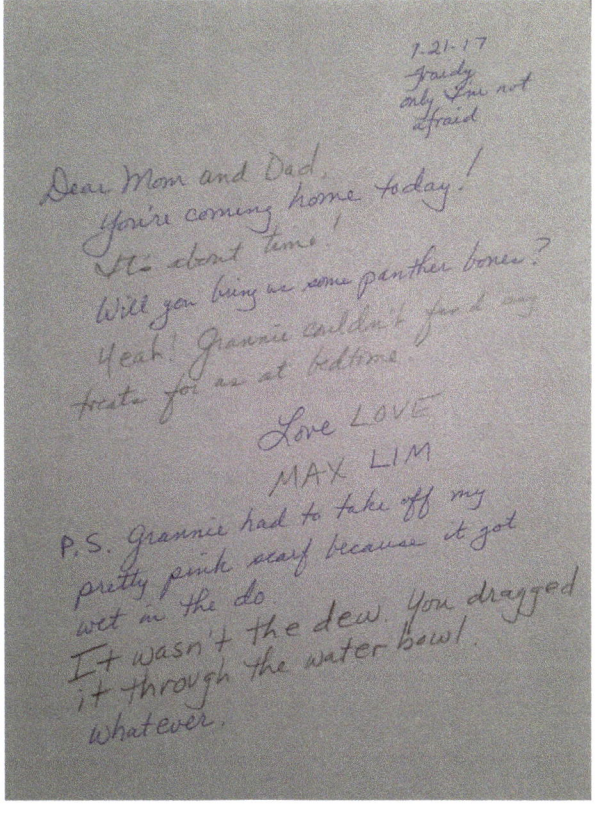

~ ~ ~

Goodbye to Summer

Friday September 28, 2018 — I guess it's time to say goodbye to summer. I barely got used to February, and now it's almost the end of September. Where on earth did 2018 speed to so fast?

When I was younger—MUCH younger—the years seemed interminably long.

Now? Psssst! Just like that, they're gone. Thank goodness for photos. Thank goodness for memories.

Pizza with Veronica

Saturday September 29, 2018 — Yesterday I had lunch with my daughter at Alino's Pizzeria in Buford GA. Real pizza. This is the Bianca Pizza, made with four cheeses, plus fresh basil, and fresh garlic. The simplicity of it was refreshing.

It reminded me of a well-written story – just enough detail, not too much. And the re-reading (like eating the leftovers) is thoroughly satisfying.

October 2018

Bumblebee on Goldenrod

Monday October 1, 2018 — The bumblebees are getting prepared for winter. I love this time of year when the goldenrod is so abundant. The bumblebees were positively swarming all over this patch near my mailbox. Somehow or other, I managed to find the one place where only one bumbler was visible.

I know I used this same photo just a couple of weeks ago, but isn't it magnificent and well worth looking at again?

Clear as Mud

~ ~ ~

Won't Solve Your Problems

Tuesday October 2, 2018 — I hereby confess: I've been a lazy bum for a number of days. Well, weeks.

The amount of paper piled on my writing surface(s), the volume of cat hair entwined in the carpet, the bag of canned goods still not put away from the last trip to the grocery store. Maybe I should decorate the canvas bag so it looks more festive.\

Fran Stewart

~ ~ ~

Eagle Rock Studios

Wednesday October 3, 2018 — The Gwinnett Citizen Fire Academy Alumni Association took a tour of Eagle Rock Studios yesterday evening. Not only did some friends give me a ride in their new Tesla - and let me sit in the front seat so I could ooh and aah over all the electric car miracles, I also got to ooh and aah over the sets at Eagle Rock as we were given a tour of about half of the 470,000 square feet of studio space.

We walked through the sets of Ozark and Greenleaf, which aren't shooting now, so everything was draped in plastic. I don't have a TV set. Haven't had one for 26 years or so, so I had no idea what these two shows are about, but the sets were gorgeous. Of course, on the outside of each individual set room is nothing but bare wood and lots of space for cables and cameras. The magic of theater.

We weren't allowed to take any photos inside the building, so I don't have anything to show you.

And then, a ride home in the Tesla!

Sheer comfort.

~ ~ ~

I Believe Her

Thursday October 4, 2018 — I believe Dr. Ford.

Just thought I'd let you know.

~ ~ ~

It Helps

Friday October 5, 2018 — No matter what's going on in our human world, the bees just keep going about their business, gathering nectar and pollen, getting ready for winter. I plan to spend some time today standing out in my yard just watching them and breathing.

It helps when the craziness around us seems overwhelming.

Tomorrow I'll show you the evidence of some other critters who've been quietly attending to their business.

~ ~ ~

Used Chrysalises on My Front Porch

Saturday October 6, 2018 — How many times a day do you look up? I'm not talking about looking at the sky. I know we all do a lot of that.

I'm talking about the corner of the porch overhang.

Look what I found several days ago. I have no idea how long these empty chrysalises have been hanging there, no idea how long it's been since the butterflies emerged and flew away.

Next year, I'm going to look up more often. Maybe I'll see a caterpillar building its chrysalis around itself.

By the way, I'll be at the Decatur Library today taking part in an all-day event (8:30 to 4:30) about the Psychology of Writing. The panel I'm on will be discussing "Writers' Minds and Killer Characters."

Fran Stewart

~ ~ ~

The purpose of life

Monday October 8, 2018 — Exactly one year ago I posted the first of these daily author Facebook posts. At first it was every single day, but you may have noticed that lately I've been posting only six days a week, leaving Sundays alone.

This quote from Kevyn Aucoin struck a chord with me, since I'm in the process of switching from a life of writing mysteries to another one, as yet rather undefined. By the way, I did a search for Kevyn Aucoin and was fascinated by the story of his life. Thank you, Wikipedia!

I recently finished reading *Man's Search for Meaning* by Viktor Frankl, a psychotherapist who survived years in various concentration camps and came out of that experience with an in-depth understanding of what helped him to survive when so many others succumbed.

According to Frankl, the deciding factor was the belief that there is a purpose to one's life. People who feel they have no purpose ultimately begin to question whether there is any reason for them to live. I do wonder if that's why so many people retire and then croak. A belief that one's work (i.e. one's paying job) is the only reason for existence plunges one into a vacuum when that work no longer exists.

Believe me — although I have thoroughly enjoyed writing mysteries, and although I know that my writing has brought me a good deal of joy and a great sense of accomplishment—mystery-writing has never been the driving purpose of my life.

Perhaps that's one reason why I chose early on to deal with specific social issues in my mysteries, such as bipolar disorder, suicide prevention, the long-term effects of childhood abuse, and so on. By educating at the same time I entertained my readers, I found a higher purpose than merely the fun of crafting a story.

Keep checking in each day, Monday through Saturday. You and I together may just discover where our on-going purpose lies.

~ ~ ~

National Book Month

Tuesday October 9, 2018 — Do you ever wonder who decides what month is dedicated to what organization, concept, product?

I sure do.

But this month it doesn't really matter who decided, National Book Month is a concept I can readily endorse.

I simply can't imagine a life without books.

~ ~ ~

Six Examples

Wednesday October 10, 2018 — I've been looking through old photo albums. Just the change in the length of my hair over the years — long to short to medium to short and back, eventually to long again — show a journey in and of itself, not even to mention to change in silhouette. Here are forty-plus years of my life encapsulated in six photos. Sometimes it's hard for me to believe I'm still the same person. Of course, in many ways, I'm not the same. For one thing, I like who I am better now than I did back then, and it has nothing whatsoever to do with what I look like.

I'd encourage you to look back through your photo albums and think about the length, breadth, and depth of your path through life. In the memoirs classes I teach, we talk a lot about the differing perspectives as we reach new stages. The changes are there. The photos merely reflect them.

Fran Stewart

~ ~ ~

Step over ants

Thursday October 11, 2018 — Rescue worms and caterpillars and spiders? Absolutely! Step over ants? Well, yes. I do step over ants when I'm outside, but recently a veritable army of teeny-weeny ants has invaded my house. They seem to congregate in three different areas, and then they trail around looking for odd bits of detritus, I guess, such as bits of cat food Callie and Fuzzy Britches have scattered.

They found a butterscotch candy, still wrapped in its bright yellow cellophane, that I had somehow missed removing from a canvas grocery bag. For that treat, they came in under a floorboard near the bay window, trekked all the way across the dining room and kitchen, and then three-fourths of the way across the living room, to where the bag sat by the door where it awaited my transferring it back into the car.

Such dedication!

I've asked the cats repeatedly please to eat the ants, but they simply won't — not until I've squashed the little guys and left them, like an offering, in a tiny pile. Then Callie finds them most tasty.

What I can't figure out is why the critters have to be dead before she'll eat them. It's still the same protein, isn't it?

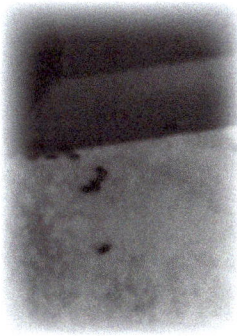

All Booked

Friday October 12, 2018 — I'm late this morning getting around to posting. Usually I sleep well, but I had a hard time staying asleep last night because I kept thinking about what was going on in a book I'm reading. I finally turned on the light around 2:30 and read until I was so tired I started dropping the book …

That reminds me of something my friend Kathy Pate told me yesterday. She hadn't gotten much sleep the night before because she was reading BLACK AS SOOT and couldn't put it down.

Do you have any idea how much authors love hearing those words? It's not that we want to deprive you of sleep. But by golly when you tell us our story involved you so much that reading became more important than sleeping—well, hearing that is an incredible gift.

I need to contact Louise Penny and tell her how much she is responsible for my droopy eyelids this morning.

Which books do you lose sleep over?

~ ~ ~

Before You Speak

Saturday October 13, 2018 — Can you imagine how much more peaceful our world would be if everybody paid attention to passing these three gates before they spoke? Those same three gates could apply to our actions as well—is this action based on truth / is it necessary / is it kind…

I'm going to pay particular attention to my words and actions today and through the upcoming week. Will you do the same?

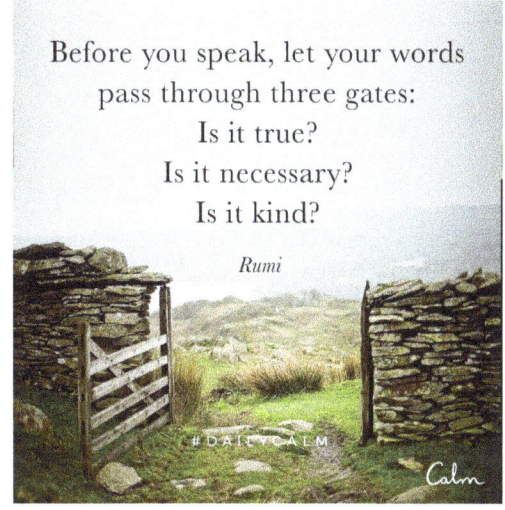

~ ~ ~

Bunny in the Yard

Monday October 15, 2018 — If there's one bunny in the yard, how many more will there be eventually?

I've seen only one - or at least, I've seen only one at a time.

And I haven't found any big holes in the yard.

Does that mean this bunny has its den in a neighbor's yard and comes over here only to visit and to nibble on the clover? Maybe the den is on the hill behind my house where it slopes down to the creek?

Hmmm. I don't have any answers to that.

~ ~ ~

Changed my Thinking

Tuesday October 16, 2018 — One of the women taking my memoirs class told us that she'd had a serious eye infection and was only now beginning to be able to drive again. Her driving was, of necessity, slower than what it had been, simply because focusing her right eye took longer — and hurt more — than it used to.

She'd been startled on numerous occasions at the impatience and inconsideration of other drivers.

She changed her thinking, and it changed her whole outlook.

"How often before this," she asked, "have I been exasperated by drivers going slower than me? What if they had an eye infection, or an injured arm, or a stiff leg that made driving difficult?"

The next time I'm tempted to feel irritated at someone else, I hope I can change my thinking the same way she did.

~ ~ ~

12 Symptoms

Wednesday October 17, 2018 — I love number 6 on this list.

Which is your favorite?

12 Symptoms of Spiritual Awakening

1. An increased tendency to let things happen rather than make them happen.
2. Frequent attacks of smiling.
3. Feelings of being connected with others and nature.
4. Frequent overwhelming episodes of appreciation.
5. A tendency to think and act spontaneously rather than from fears based on past experience.
6. An unmistakable ability to enjoy each moment.
7. A loss of ability to worry.
8. A loss of interest in conflict.
9. A loss of interest in interpreting the actions of others.
10. A loss of interest in judging others.
11. A loss of interest in judging self.
12. Gaining the ability to love without expecting anything.

http://recoverytradepublications.com/blog.html?entry=12-symptoms-of-a-spiritual

~ ~ ~

When You Feel Down

Thursday October 18, 2018 — Yesterday I had the great fun of attending an 80th birthday luncheon for Barbara Hall, a woman I met almost 20 years ago, who is one of the best role models imaginable.

She is interested in everything, interesting in so many ways. She's been a realtor for more than thirty years and still works actively, not only selling houses, but mentoring younger women.

Does she have aches and pains periodically? Probably so, although I've never heard her issue a word of complaint. She lives up to this dictum about going out and being a blessing.

At the restaurant, yesterday, I sat across the table from a woman who has experienced what it is to live with several people who deal with depression. Naturally, I told her about *DEPRESSION VISIBLE: THE RAGGED EDGE*, by my sister Diana Alishouse.

I felt like I was a blessing to that woman, since I was able to give her practical information about where/how she could get information to help her with her life situation. Isn't it funny how the people you need to meet show up right on time?

Thank you, Barbara, for having a birthday and for inviting me to participate.

First Nine Books

Friday October 19, 2018 — The wonderful folks at Liberty Books in Lawrenceville took this photo of the first nine Biscuit McKee Mysteries. They're lined up on the sidewalk beside the store. Great photo, isn't it?

I've had a couple of people ask why I list all the toll-free numbers and websites where my readers can get more information about the social issues I deal with in the first seven mysteries, but I'm not listing them in these last four books.

Good question.

This final quadrilogy is wrapping up all the questions, all the mysteries, all the loose ends from the previous books. If you need to find a resource list for depression, suicide prevention, the long-term effects of abuse, or you just want to find out more about green funerals, then look at the end of INDIGO, VIOLET, or GRAY.

Enjoy your reading. I hope it will be one of my books, but whichever authors you choose, I hope you'll buy from an independent bookstore.

In the meantime, drop by Liberty Books tomorrow (Saturday) at 3pm or Another Chapter Bookstore in

Cumming on Sunday (the 21st) from 2 to 4pm and take a look at PINK AS A PEONY. I'd love to autograph a copy for you!

~ ~ ~

Don't Complicate Life

Saturday October 20, 2018 — An acquaintance of mine said at the end of an email that she would love to "catch up" with me, so I emailed her right back giving her the days and times over the coming week when I'd be available for a phone call.

No reply.

Not that day, not the following day. Zip. Nada. Nothing.

Why? Does "I'd love to catch up with you" not mean now what it used to mean?

I'm not complaining. I'm just asking.

Fran Stewart

Don't complicate life

Missing somebody?	CALL
Wanna meet up?	INVITE
Wanna be understood?	EXPLAIN
Have questions?	ASK
Don't like something?	SAY IT
Like something?	STATE IT
Want something?	ASK FOR IT
Love someone?	TELL THEM

Keep your life SIMPLE.

~ ~ ~

Hill Areas

Monday October 22, 2018 — Erica, my niece, periodically drives past the Indian Hills Community Center in the Colorado mountains. She sent me this photo of their most recent sign. It sort of reminds me of the scene in BLACK AS SOOT when everyone sitting around the dinner table at Biscuit and Bob's house begin discussing their favorite signs on the signboard at the Old Church in Martinsville, and Henry, the pastor, explains how or why he preached about what he preached about that particular Sunday.

The one that said "EVERYBODY WHO BELIEVES IN TELEKINESIS RAISE MY HAND" elicited a sermon about Doubting Thomas. Then Pat spoke up. Here's what followed:

"Maggie had a favorite," Pat told us. "It was MY SUPPORT GROUP FOR PROCRASTINATORS HASN'T MET YET, but she never did tell us what you preached about that week."

Henry shrugged. "About the only thing I could come up with was the parable of the loaves and fishes."

"What on earth," Ida asked, "does that have to do with procrastinating?"

"An awful lot of people must have forgotten to bring food with them to the Sermon on the Mount." Henry made a wry face. "Neglecting to plan ahead is sort of like procrastinating. I thought it was appropriate. Kind of."

Amazing what you can work into a murder mystery, isn't it?

~ ~ ~

My Closet Has Eyes

Tuesday October 23, 2018 — If you've ever been owned by a cat, you'll know how very good they are at hiding. Wooly Bear is particularly good at it, since she's pure black. I spend a great deal of time looking for her while she looks down at me from the top of a six-foot bookcase or from a basket or from under a pile of afghans.

Her latest perch is on the shelf in my closet where I keep my old comfy sweatpants — comfy for me and now, apparently, comfy for her. This is where I finally found her a few days ago. Imagine how startled I was when I tried to pull a pair of pants off the shelf. They were stuck somehow, and I bent to see what the problem was. I hadn't turned on the light in there — I knew exactly what I wanted and where it was, so why waste electricity?

My closet shelf had sprouted eyes!

Over the years I've had numerous cats crawl into unexpected places. Now that my Biscuit McKee Mysteries are completed—except for the release of the final one, WHITE AS ICE, in just a month—I wish I'd written a "where's Marmalade?" scene into at least one of them.

Fran Stewart

~ ~ ~

Minimalism

Wednesday October 24, 2018 — A dear friend of mine suggested very strongly that I buy some lottery tickets, now that the prize is up over a billion dollars.

I'm not a lottery-ticket kind of person. But just for the fun of it, I bought two tickets for a grand total of $4. When I mentioned that to my son during a phone call, he asked what I was going to do with all that money once I won it.

Good question.

You know me and spreadsheets — at least you do if you've been reading these daily blogposts for any length of time.

So, I put together a spreadsheet for how to invest/spend/distribute the money. I felt so darn philanthropic. I took off a healthy percentage for taxes, then divided it into columns showing who gets what (each column a percentage of the net so the computer would do the figuring for me). Let's see, twelve million to the Atlanta Shakespeare Tavern (2 percent), another twelve million to the Nature Conservancy. Hefty amounts to the Red Cross and the Owens Foundation, Planned Parenthood and Heifer International. Eight million here, six million there, four million somewhere else.

Did you know that 0.07 percent of 1.6 billion dollars is still a hefty $424,130.56? Quite a nice gift for the person in Column U. A Tesla — I definitely want a Tesla— will take 0.00610661019 percent of the haul. The person in Column AT will receive $60,590.08. That's 0.01 percent.

Even after all that investing/giving/spending, I'll still have more than $477 million dollars left over. Hmmm. Scholarships. Women's shelters. My alma mater. More decisions to be made before I claim that prize.

Don't worry—I set aside a certain percentage so I won't ever be a financial burden on my children. Of course, I've already taken that into account, even with my budget the way it is without the billion dollars.

Your Own Voice

Thursday October 25, 2018 — I like this thought.

I spent way too many years ignoring that still small voice within me. Thinking back, I realize how much pain I could have avoided if I'd paid attention. On the other hand, I wouldn't be who I am today without all those choices I made, even though in hindsight I know they were truly dumb decisions.

It's taken me a lot of years, but I'm on pretty good terms now with that inner voice of mine.

It took one step at a time to get to this point.

How about you?

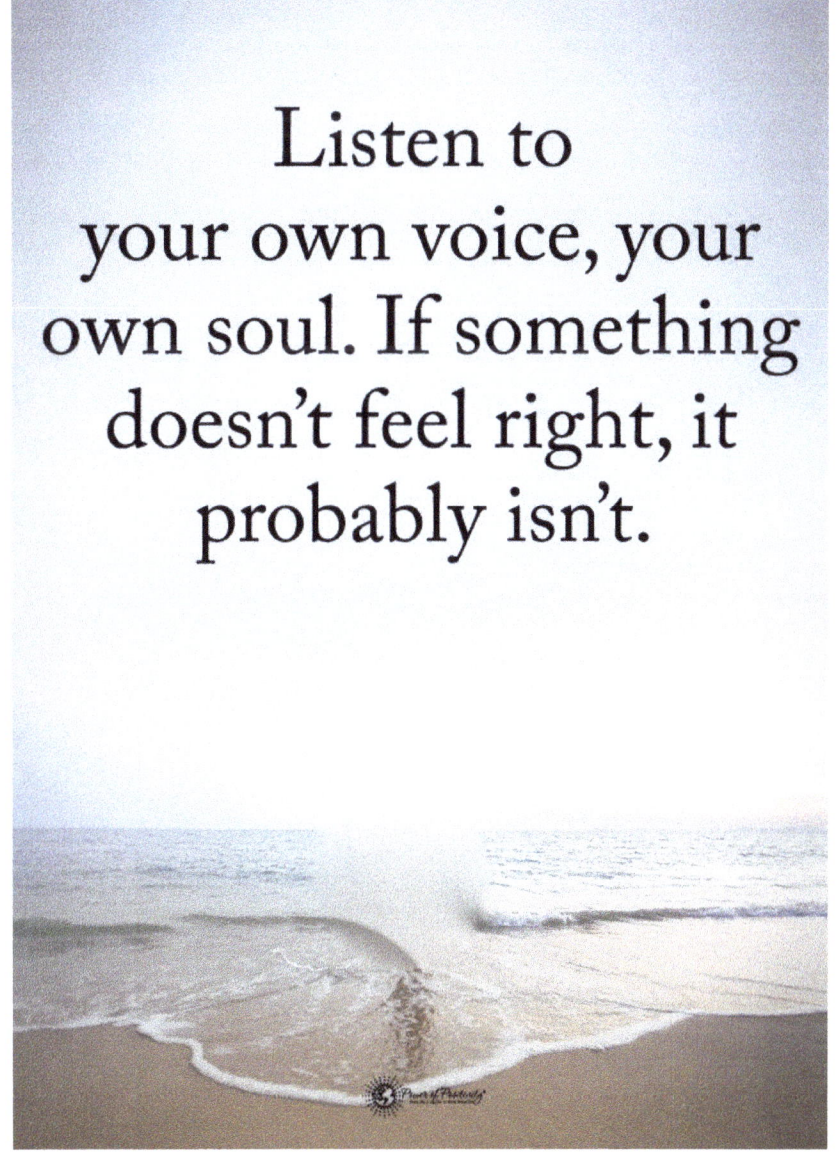

Tall Tales

Friday October 26, 2018 — Tomorrow, I'll be appearing at Tall Tale Books in Toco Hills with three other Sisters in Crime to tell Macabre Mysteries. I'll be reading from RED AS A ROOSTER - and maybe telling a tale about ghost stories from my childhood.

If you're anywhere in the Atlanta area, drop on by from noon to two tomorrow. Grab some goodies—including some great books, of course—and listen to Macabre Tales!

Candy Corn Cob

Saturday October 27, 2018 — I'm definitely going to have to try this - this afternoon, after I get back from the Tall Tales Book Store "Macabre Tales" event. Be sure you drop by LaVista Road from noon to 2pm to hear ghoulish tales. There'll be a scavenger hunt, too.

Then stop by my house to see my corn cobs – if I haven't already eaten them …

~ ~ ~

Autumn Scene by Veronica

Monday October 29, 2018 — Do you ever feel like you could simply walk into a painting and live there?

My daughter painted this Autumn Scene just because she loves this time of year.

I'm in utter awe of her.

Authors You Should Know

Tuesday October 30, 2018 — Put this coming Friday on your event calendar! Doug Dahlgren hosts a monthly event at the Georgia Center for the book (located in the Decatur Public Library) where he interviews a panel of four select authors. It's always the first Friday of the month at 7:15 pm. Doors open at 6:45.

I attend these as often as I can, and they're always informative and great fun. This Friday (November 2nd) I'll be one of the four featured authors, along with Lori Duff, Bobby Nash, and Haywood Smith.

If you're anywhere in the Atlanta area, drop on by. I'd love to see you.

p.s. Doug also hosts a weekly internet radio show every Friday morning at 11 Eastern time. He's a darn good interviewer.

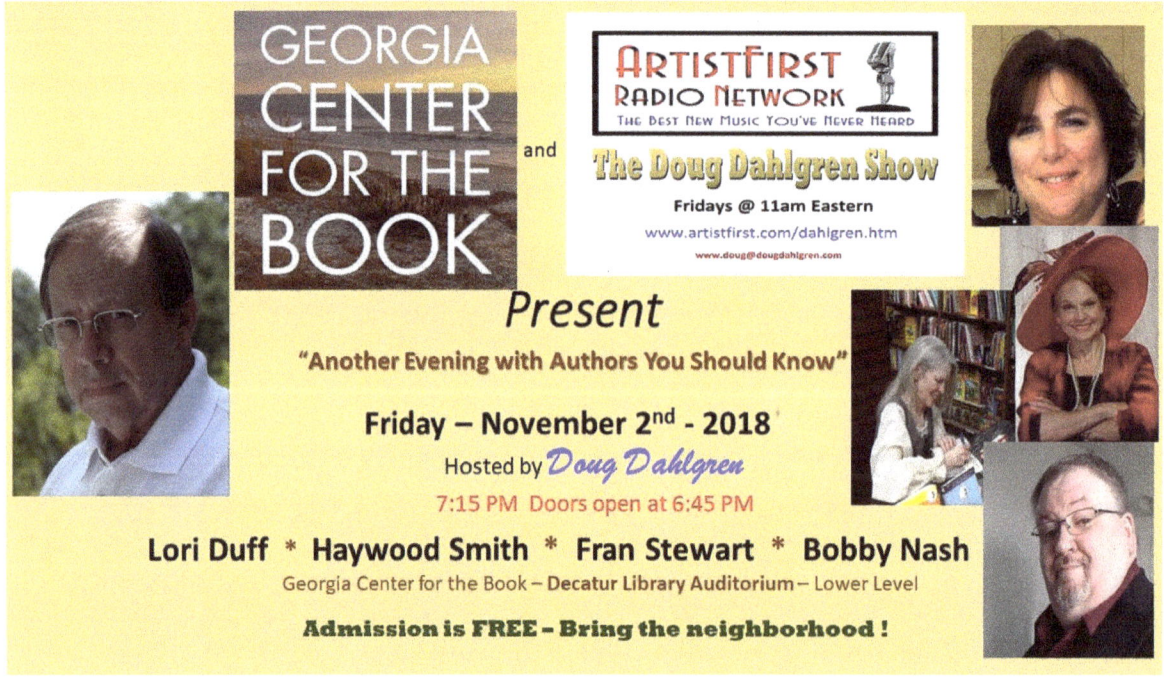

~ ~ ~

Crazy Pumpkin & Sweater Pumpkin

Wednesday October 31, 2018 — Happy Halloween from Larry (the creation of Veronica, my daughter), and from the brown pumpkin I made for my granddaughter from an old sweater.

November 2018

Skeletons

Thursday November 1, 2018 — We're (almost) all alike once we croak. Here's one of the leftovers from my Halloween this year.

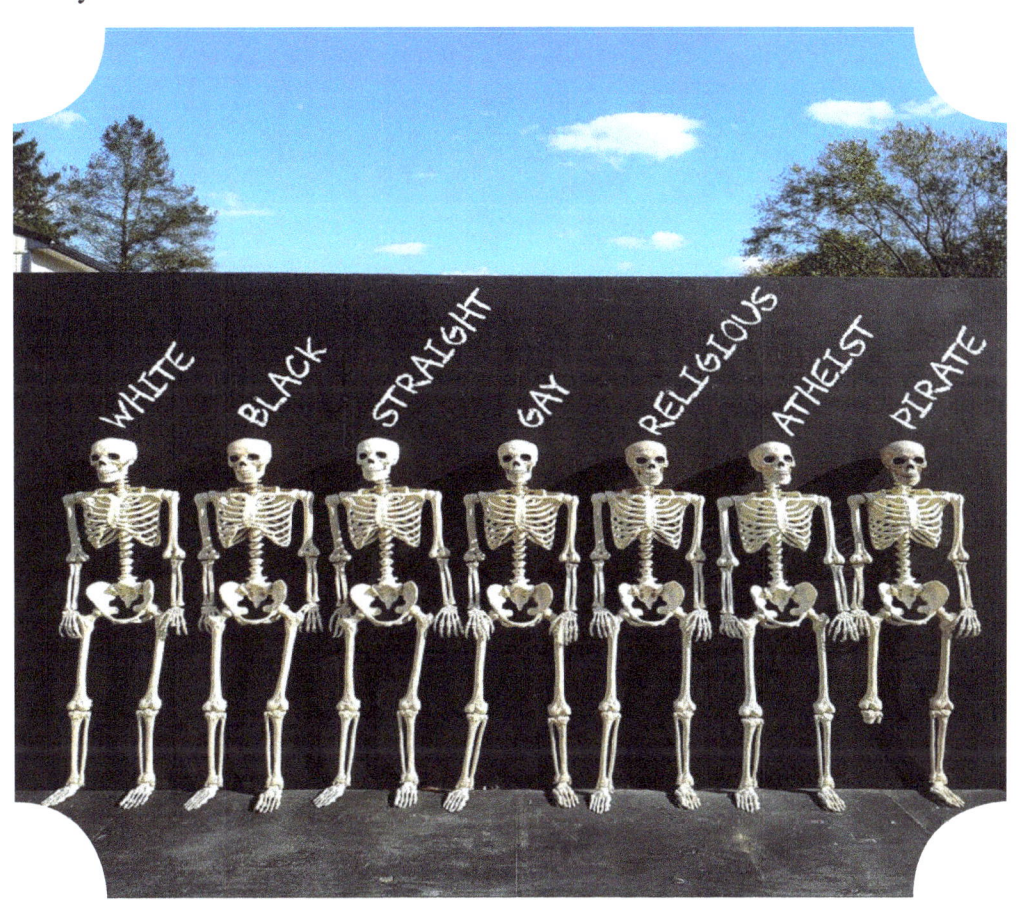

Let the Dead Things Go

Friday November 2, 2018 — What lovely advice from this time of year. Now, if you live north of Georgia, you already got this message a month or two ago. I remember those 26 years I lived in Vermont, when tourists always seemed surprised that they'd traveled to do some "leaf-peeping" in October to find that most of the leaves were on the ground — not quite the visual image they'd been hoping for.

My Faith is Not Your Faith

Saturday November 3, 2018 — There's nothing like a good discussion in which opposing viewpoints are put forth reasonably and logically and without rancor.

Last night at the Georgia Center for the Book in the Decatur Library, our host Doug Dahlgren asked the four panelists about the pervasive appearance of profanity throughout our culture — movies, TV, music, and print. I'll try to sum it up briefly:

Bobby Nash asserted that a lot of words that used to be considered profane have lost their shock value simply because they are used so often people have become used to them. He also said that oftentimes publishers require him to use a certain number of those words because the reading public has come to expect it.

Lori Duff compared the use of profanity to the percussion section of an orchestra. Some words are a simple brush across the rim of a snare drum, used as a gentle backdrop, while other words seem like a bass drum attacking the senses.

Haywood Smith said she had only 16 swear words in one of her books, but they were all there for a reason.

I said that I choose not to speak with profanity, and I choose not to write with profanity, in the same way that I refuse to dumb down my vocabulary to the lowest common denominator.

We all agreed that the use of profanity is frequently a lazy author's approach to writing.

It is, after all, much easier to sprinkle the F-bomb around like too much pepper in a stew rather than searching for the precise herbs to flavor the entree.

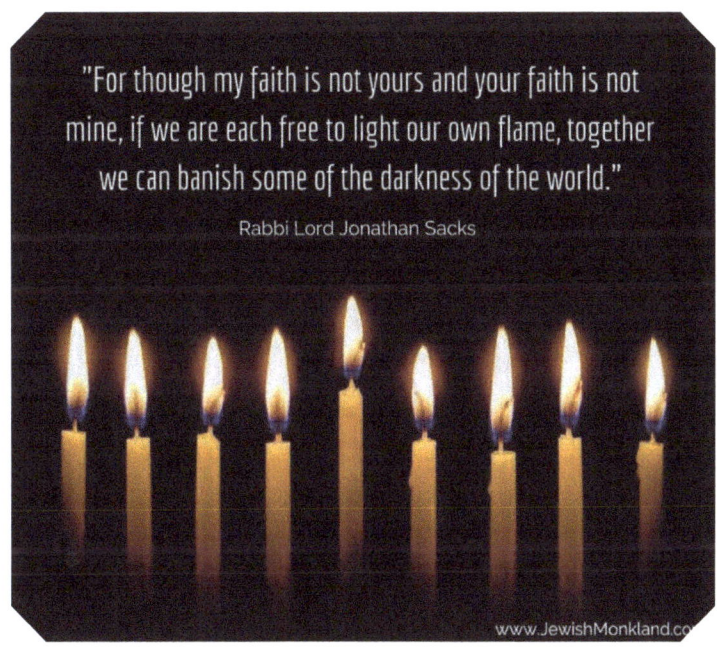

~ ~ ~

Fire in the medieval manuscripts

Sunday November 4, 2018 — When I was researching my 14th-century Scottish ghost for my ScotShop mysteries, I found a fascinating website, originating in the UK, called Medieval Manuscripts, and subscribed to their blog.

A few days ago, they talked about calendars — illustrated calendars — and included these two images from two different calendars, created at different times and in different places. Each one is a November calendar page. In both of them there are five figures gathered around a fire. The three men on the right (as you can see and as is mentioned in the post) are warming themselves, while the two on the left are working. A blacksmith has his tongs in the fire, while the other guy is toting a bundle of wood.

Now notice the fellow in the center. Not only is he bare-legged and bare-footed (brrr!), but what clothing he has on looks totally inadequate.

Both illustrations have:

Fran Stewart

- a stack of wood over on the left
- almost identical hand positions for each of the five people
- (even their feet are pointed the same way)
- the same sort of drapes to their clothing

Sure looks like plagiarism to me. There are a few differences such as hair color and how far apart the feet are spread, but doesn't it look like the artist in the second drawing copied the first one?

And why the bare-legged guy?

Have to admit - I love a good mystery.

~ ~ ~

Balance

Monday November 5, 2018 — Balance comes in many forms. There's a community theater in my area that used to present a very satisfying yearly Christmas program. Even though I don't celebrate Christmas, I attended each year because I enjoyed the mix of happy songs with thoughtful songs, the blend of snappy repartee with calm reflections.

Something changed, though, as the shows became goofier, sillier, more frenetic. There was hardly a calm moment in the entire production. I put up with it for two years, gave away my ticket for the next two years — and received reports that those shows had been just as frenzied as the previous ones.

Finally, I canceled my season ticket because the musicals they put on during the year featured volume more than plot. The plays they presented were increasingly thoughtless "comedies" — I use the term loosely — so peppered with F-bombs that I found myself cringing repeatedly.

Whatever happened to balance in the entertainment industry?

How can there be re-takes on reality shows? What's "real" about something that has to be re-staged multiple times to get the best camera angle or the best *spontaneous reaction*? Where is the adventure when people "forge" their way into the wilderness while someone's walking ahead of them down an obviously pre-cleared path wielding a camera (and probably having to walk backwards to do it, which is why the path had to be pre-cleared).

I know our lives are increasingly fast paced. I would suggest that such a tempo leaves precious little time for thought. Let's get some balance back in our lives by setting aside time each day simply to breathe for a few moments.

It's a start.

~ ~ ~

Vote

Tuesday November 6, 2018 — I was the second person in line at the polls this morning when I got there at a little past 6am.

The first 15 of us in the line had the pleasure of standing underneath the overhang while everyone after us had to get drenched.

Getting up extra early was a small price to pay for a chance to read my book where it was dry.

~ ~ ~

The Better Side

Wednesday November 7, 2018 — I don't care who you voted for yesterday.

I care whether you act with integrity, whether I can rely on your word, whether you withhold judgement until you know the truth, whether you do what you say you will do, whether you choose the better side of life.

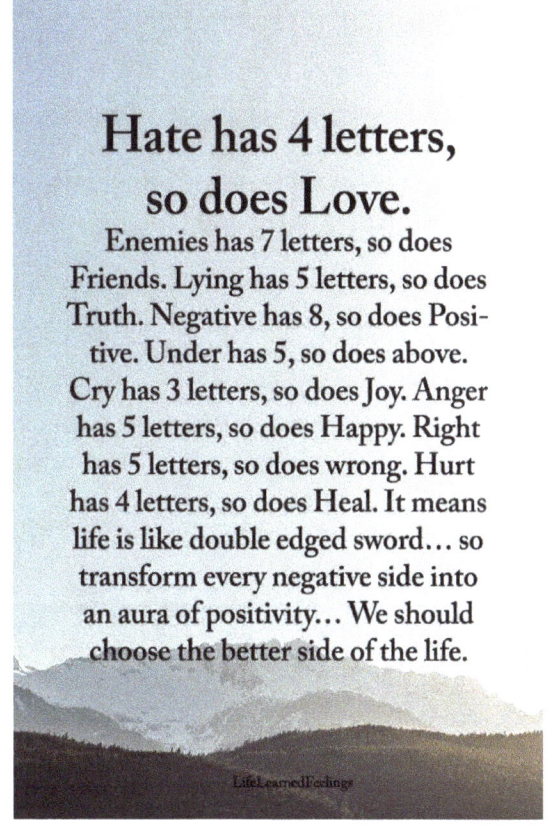

~ ~ ~

Gratitude

Thursday November 8, 2018 — I'm doing a daily gratitude challenge with a friend of mine, listing three things for which we're grateful. It's funny how when I concentrate on what's right with my life, it's harder to see what I may in the past have perceived as what's wrong.

Gratitude every day.

Give it a try!

Fran Stewart

~ ~ ~

Clean-out Time

Friday November 9, 2018 — Clean-out time! I went through a major clearing out two years ago in connection with a remodeling job, and guess what? Now it's time to do it again.

Part of the problem is sheer laziness on my part. One end of my living room reminds me of Biscuit McKee's attic in my mystery series, except that the stuff in her attic is a great deal older (and a heck of a lot more interesting!) than my things. It's so much easier to just add it to the pile.

That old saw about having a place for everything and everything in its place doesn't apply in this house of mine that has limited closet space. Of course, I should pay attention to this quote I pulled from my niece's FB page. Time to start recycling, giving away, re-purposing!

> If you're not using the stuff in your home, **get rid of it.** You're not going to start using it more by shoving it in a closet somewhere.

Wooly Bear

Saturday November 10, 2018 — What does Wooly Bear and her two bright eyes have to do with the value of counting? Well, nothing. I just like this photo of her and wanted to share it with you.

But here's what I really want to show you today:

- 24 words   Pythagoras' Theorem
- 66 words   Lord's Prayer
- 67 words   Archimedes' Principle
- 179 words   Ten Commandments
- 286 words   Gettysburg Address
- 1,300 words   US Declaration of Independence
- 7,818 words   US Constitution with all 27 Amendments
- 26,911 words   EU Regulations on the sale of cabbages

On Monday, I'll share with you a little snippet from one of my books about how many pages there are in the income tax forms.

In the meantime, have a great weekend.

Fran Stewart

~ ~ ~

Income Tax

Monday November 12, 2018 — As you may know, my WHITE AS ICE quadrilogy of books has Biscuit in the attic with a bunch of her friends during the ice storm of the century. For each item they find, the story merges into the time that item was placed in the attic — and tells us why.

In 1913, Young Gideon, the town vet, and his wife Amelia are discussing one of the new Lincoln pennies their son has shown them. The penny was first released in 1909, but as Gideon says:

"It has taken four years for these pennies to find their way into our town, but not even a month for the federal government to find us and send us"—he gestured to the forms—"this notice about the new income tax."

"Oh, dear." Amelia sank into the chair next to him and lifted the paper closest to her. "A full page of directions? How complicated this looks."

"Look at page number three."

She studied it. "Deductions? Do we have any?"

"We haven't any debt, so we haven't paid interest on any loans. And no losses due to shipwreck. I do believe lines three—that's the school tax—and the last one, number six, are the only ones that apply to us."

She ran her finger several inches down the page and read number six aloud. "*Amount representing a reasonable allowance for the exhaustion, wear, and tear of property arising out of its use or employment in the business.* What wear and tear?"

"I thought I might list the number of items of mine the Surratt's goats have eaten."

She laughed at his droll tone. "You bought several implements during the past year. Surely they could be listed on line number one." She picked up the other page and studied both sides. "Four pages altogether. Why did they have to make this so complicated?" Amelia screwed her face into that patently fake grimace he loved so much. "One per cent," she read. "That does seem excessive."

"Be glad we did not make $500,000, for then we would have to pay …"—he leaned over and bumped his shoulder against hers and she joined him in reading the amount for that category—"six per cent."

Taxes between 1 and 6 percent — one entire page of instructions — what do you suppose they would have said if they'd seen ahead 105 years?

~ ~ ~

Kindsight

Tuesday November 13, 2018 — I love this thought. "What was I learning?" rather than "What was I thinking?"

As I write my own memoirs, I want to keep this in mind. I have, after all, learned a great deal over the years.

Are you being kind to yourself? What have you learned?

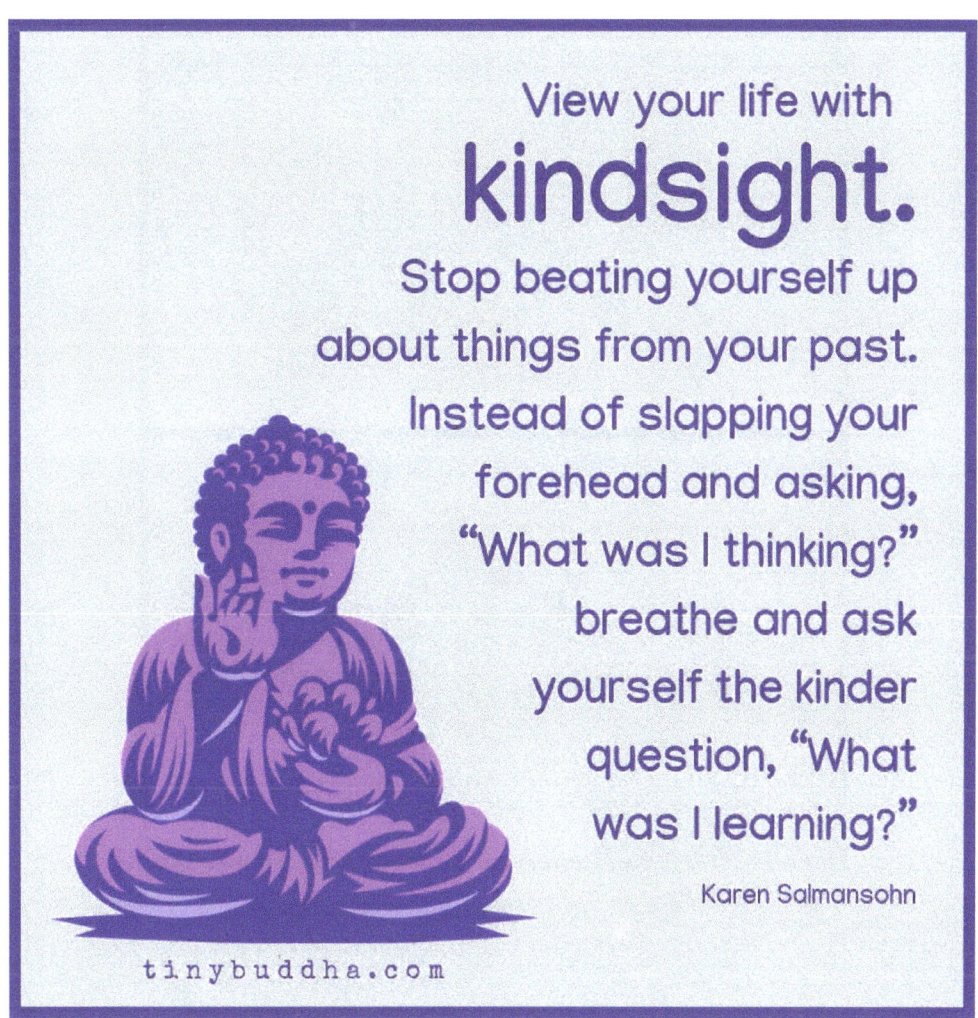

~ ~ ~

Nine Lives

Wednesday November 14, 2018 — Yesterday a friend of mine shared one of those "hilarious" videos from the Internet where the creator declared, "You're gonna die laughing about these funny cats." I will not reproduce all the egregious exclamation points. I've found that the more exclamation points, the worse the video is liable to be.

I watched it anyway. I'm sorry I did.

Fran Stewart

Why on earth do people think it's funny to watch a cat with the handle of a plastic bag twisted around its neck? The poor thing was obviously panicked as it tore around the kitchen careening into everything, while its humans laughed their unthinking heads off. Other scenes were just as bad, and I quickly shut it off.

If I'm looking for funny things about cats, I'd rather see a cartoon like this one. I'm glad this cat still has two to go …

~ ~ ~

Trish Terrell and Zoom

Thursday November 15, 2018 — Tuesday evening I had the honor of hosting p.m. terrell, the guest author for the Atlanta Chapter of Sisters in Crime's "Virtual Book Club." We used a conference program called Zoom, which is the same one I'll be using when I begin my webinars next April, helping you learn how to write your memoirs. Check it out at zoom.us.

At any rate, Trish Terrell (whose pen name is pm terrell) is not only a suspense writer, she has a degree in marketing and a website called The Novel Business where writers can learn the how's and why's of promoting their books. I wish I'd known about her back when I first started writing my Biscuit McKee Mysteries.

She was a great guest and answered all our questions with ease and grace.

~ ~ ~

Fine Line

Friday November 16, 2018 — Playing with words has long been a favorite pastime of mine. And when numbers are combined in the mixture, the result is perfect. I remember Mr. Cooley, my seventh-grade math teacher at East Junior High School in Colorado Springs, who delighted in teaching and who encouraged my love of all things numerical.

I held that joy to myself, though. I probably could have talked of it with my dad, who had an incisive mind where figures were concerned, but it never occurred to me to share my burgeoning interest.

Who knows how my life might have been different if I had opened up such a discussion?

No regrets—just some wondering about that fine line.

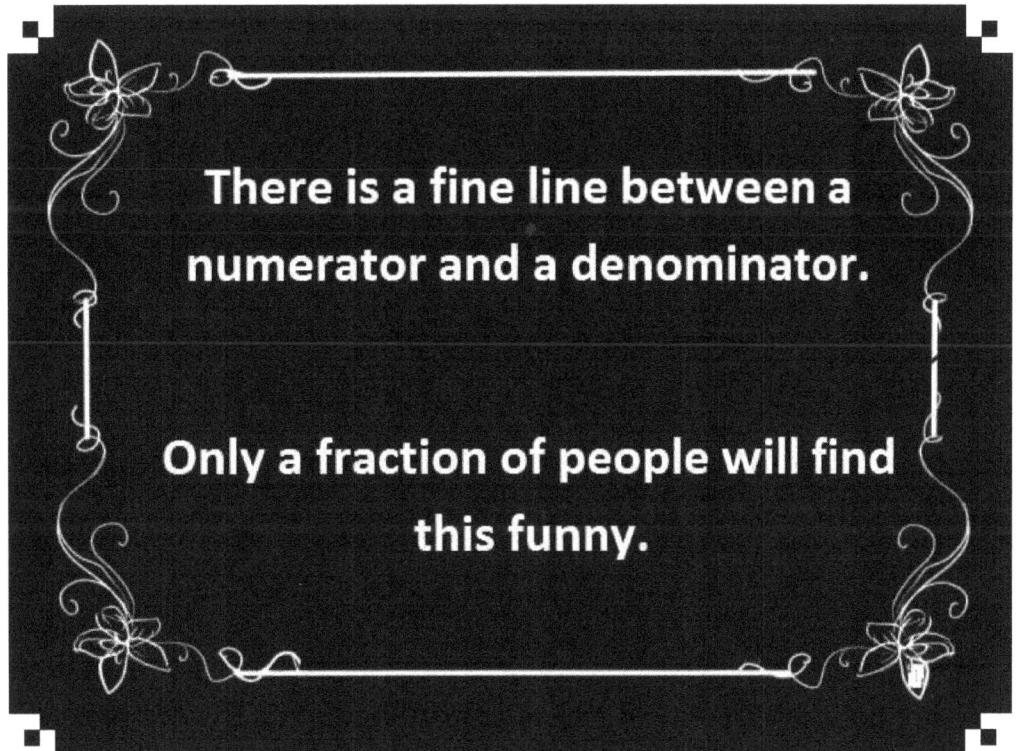

~ ~ ~

Gratitude

Saturday November 17, 2018 — At the beginning of this month, my friend Ingrid Krein put out a chal-

Fran Stewart

lenge to join her in a daily gratitude list. She said she'd be listing three things every day for which she was grateful. I took her up on that challenge and have had such fun sending her a FB message each morning.

It's a great way to start the day, so I'd like to invite you to take part as well. You can do it any way you want — either just list them in a notebook, email them to a friend you've invited to partake of the joy with you, or post them here on the Internet.

Keeping a gratitude list changed my life back in 1997, as I've already shared (probably several times) in these posts. It all started with this book, *Simple Abundance* by Sarah Ban Breathnach.

Give gratitude a try.

~ ~ ~

One Pushup

Monday November 19, 2018 — Why do we tend to wait for January first before we begin all those brave new projects? What's wrong with starting today?

One of the things I hear again and again in the memoirs classes I teach is, "I've always wanted to write these stories, but I just never knew how to do it or where to start."

"You've come to the right place," I tell them.

Now I'm delighted that I'll be offering these "Writing Your Life" classes as webinars, with a class for beginners starting in mid-March and an advanced class beginning in late April. The beginner's class will be a prerequisite to the advanced one.

A lot of you have expressed an interest, but I need to get some definite dates set up.

Now, here's the question: if you'd like to take the classes, would you prefer Tuesdays from 1:00 to 2:30 Eastern, or Sundays same time?

If there's enough interest, I'll do both days.

You can answer by leaving a comment here or send me a FB message. And please, feel free to share this post with friends who might be interested in writing the stories of their lives.

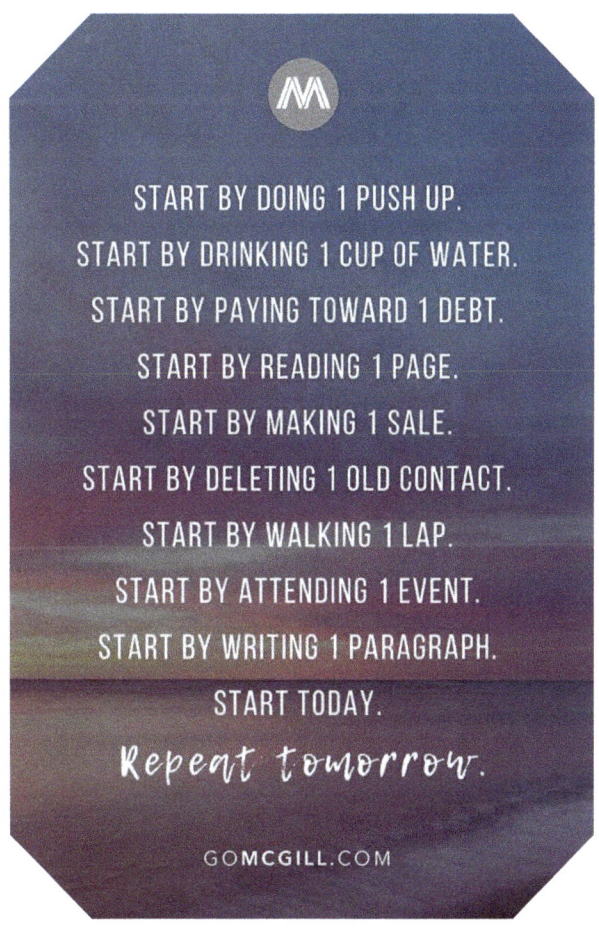

~ ~ ~

Your Heart Knows the Way

Tuesday November 20, 2018 — Yesterday was the 155th anniversary of the Gettysburg Address. Those 272 words are woven into the history of this country, despite Lincoln's assertion that "the world will little note nor long remember what we say here."

Writers who care about the words they create would like the world both to note and to remember those words, but what so often happens is that our words become lost in the myriad of books published each year, just as these Facebook posts of mine will undoubtedly be "available" on the Internet for years to come, but will in all likelihood be swamped by the multitude of other FB presences.

Will that discourage me?

No.

Why not? I'm glad you asked.

The reason is that I do not write for "the multitude" out there. I write for you. My heart does know the way, and I choose to run in that direction. As long as you read my words and perhaps carry them in your heart, I am noted and remembered. If my words are not worth remembering, if they cannot change your life for the better (even in the smallest way), then they deserve to be forgotten.

My final quadrilogy has been described as a living jigsaw puzzle because of the way all the pieces gradually fit together. I believe that in these last four books, I've written something that is worthy of being read, shared, remembered, and discussed for a good many years to come. If you disagree, I'm fine with that. If you agree, I'm delighted.

[**2020 Note:** It's for this very reason that I've chosen to compile all these FB posts into *Clear as Mud*. As you saw near the beginning of this book, I lost a year and a half of FB posts either to a technological glitch or to my own techie ineptitude. Hopefully these remaining words will not be lost.]

Clear as Mud

~ ~ ~

100 Milestone Documents https://www.ourdocuments.gov/content.php?flash=true&page=milestone

Wednesday November 21, 2018 — While we're talking about remembering words for hundreds of years, I thought I'd share with you this marvelous site called "100 Milestone Documents." It's purported to be a sort of lesson in the sweep of America's history, from 1776 to 1965.

An associated site declares that:

The decision not to include milestone documents since 1965 was a deliberate acknowledgement of the difficulty in examining more recent history. As stated in the guidelines for the National History Standards, developed by the National Center for History in the Schools, "Historians can never attain complete objectivity, but they tend to fall shortest of the goal when they deal with current or very recent events."

Smart move. That's one reason why, when I began writing my Biscuit McKee mysteries in 2002, I set them in the mid-1990s. We were too close to the events of September 11th for me to feel I could view them or write about them with any sort of objectivity, and I did not want the pall of that day to hang over Biscuit and her friends.

I plan to read through these 100 documents. Some of them I'm familiar with, of course, but many are new to me. It should be an exciting exploration. Want to join me?

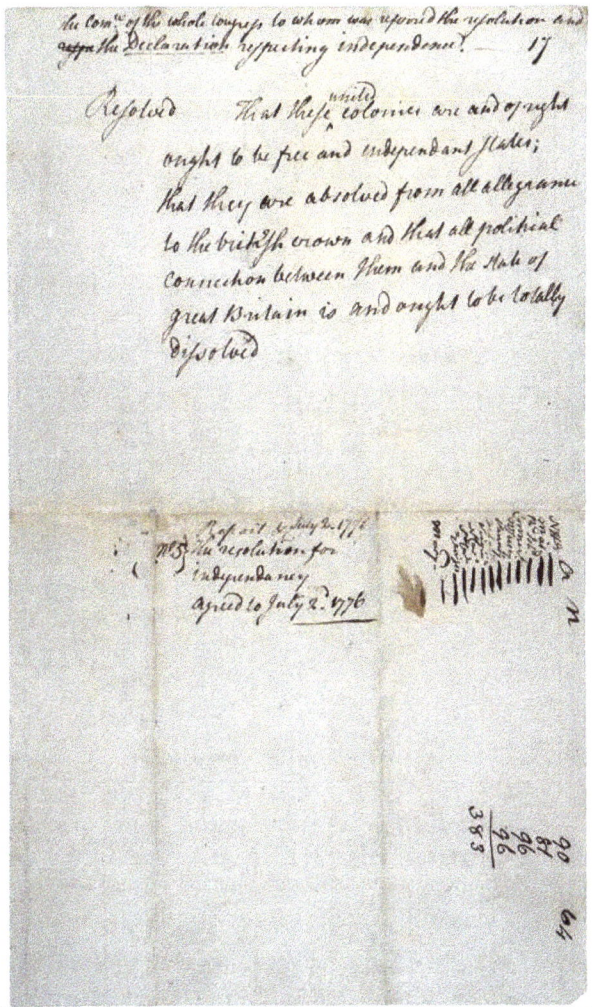

~ ~ ~

Look Up and Smile

Thursday November 22, 2018 — What more can I say?

Thank you on this Thanksgiving Day.

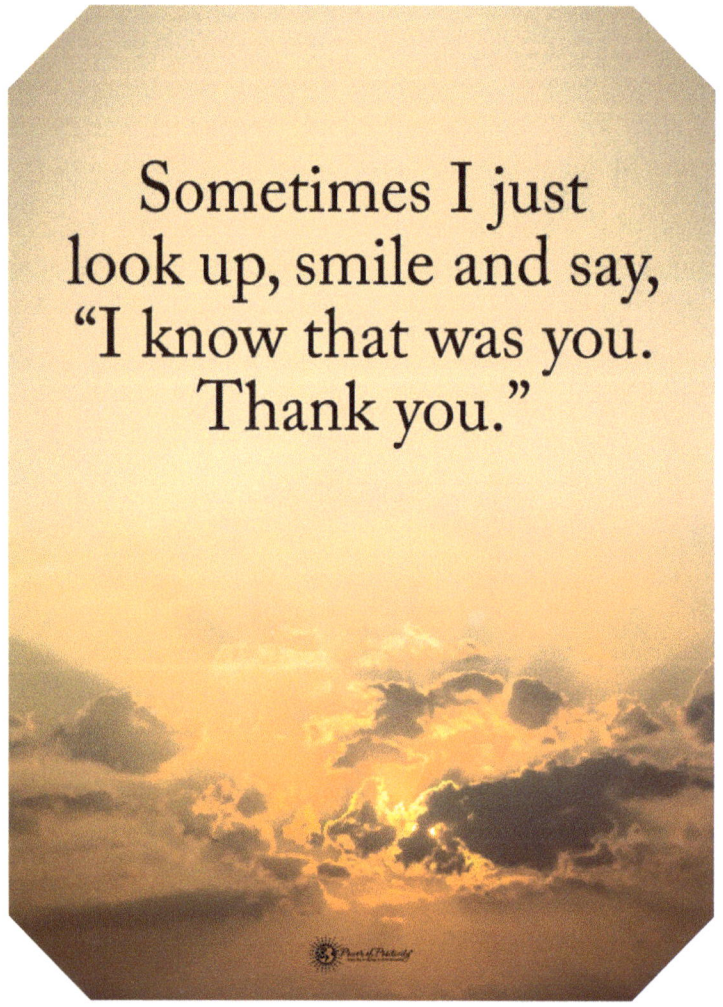

~ ~ ~

improve Your Argument

Friday November 23, 2018 — A couple of days ago I ended up being yelled at by an extremely rude young man who objected to my walking into Planned Parenthood, an organization he wanted to eviscerate.

The more I tried to reason with him, to explain my side of the story, the more he turned up his microphone. Yes, he had a portable microphone. Add that to the fact that he was yelling to begin with, it left my ears ringing. And most likely the ears of all the other folks within a hundred yards.

I was left with the distinct impression that he didn't have a good argument at all — but he obviously thought his volume made him more believable.

I was not impressed, but I offered him a handshake before I turned to leave. He recoiled as if I'd offered to hit him.

I sure would hate to live my life with that much suspicion.

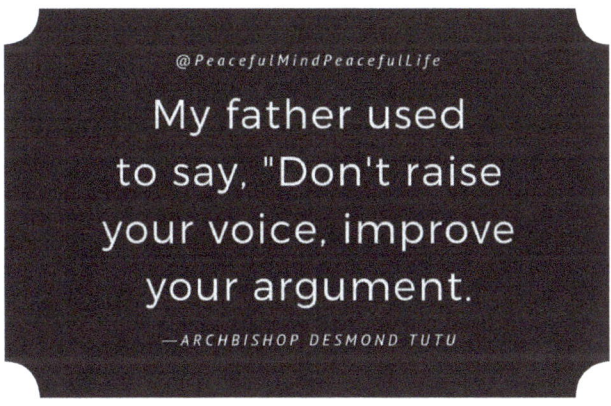

~ ~ ~

Possums

Saturday November 24, 2018 — In my WHITE AS ICE quadrilogy, I wrote several scenes about the possums visiting the bird feeders out in Biscuit and Bob's back yard. I rather like possums, particularly since I found out they can neither contract nor transmit rabies. It's something about their body chemistry.

Speaking of WHITE AS ICE, next weekend is the big launch for this final volume of my Biscuit McKee Mystery Series. I can't wait to begin hearing from you as to what you think about the ending. It's a big beautiful book, and I sincerely hope you'll feel it was well worth waiting for.

Fran Stewart

~ ~ ~

Someplace to Go

Monday November 26, 2018 — Over the Thanksgiving weekend, I went to Scotland and London.

The trip to Scotland came about through the eyes (and the pen) of Susanna Kearsley in *The Shadowy Horses*, her gripping tale of a (fictional) archeological dig in Eyemouth, looking for the Ninth Legion of Rome, which went missing 2,000 years ago. They were great folk to spend a couple of days with.

I then managed to tour 19th century London with Commander William Monk of the River Police and his stalwart wife, Hester, whom I had met in a number of previous tales. She served as a nurse during the Crimean War, and Anne Perry does her full justice in *Blind Justice*."

I've always felt sorry for people who say they don't like to read. Where, after all, can they go when they want to travel for a few hours (or a few days)?

[**2020 Note**: Particularly now, with the pandemic still in full swing, how can anyone not want to read?]

~ ~ ~

Where Do They Cross?

Tuesday November 27, 2018 — Do you find your eyes crossing when you look at this picture? I sure did when I first saw it.

I love optical illusions, even though occasionally they come close to driving me crazy. But even more than the pictures themselves, I love to try to figure out how someone could have come up with the idea in the first place.

And I have to admit that there's no answer to that, rather like when someone asks me where the ideas for my mysteries come from. They simply are there. I, like the optical illusionist, pick up my pen and begin to write.

Right?

To write is something like a rite, one that I never tire of.

~ ~ ~

Refill Your Own Cup

Wednesday November 28, 2018 — Last night I left book club early. I was thoroughly enjoying the conversation, but I realized I simply needed to get home. Why? No particular reason, but I'd known all day that I was going to need an early-to-bed night.

Fran Stewart

Of course, this morning I woke at 4:15. Wooly Bear was a little confused when I turned on the light, but she's always been up for a good scratch no matter what time of day.

I've already changed the sheets, washed my hair, done a load of laundry, and practiced playing my grandmother's march—I'm getting ready for my son's visit because I promised him I'd have the music written down by the time he got here. Now Fuzzy Britches is reminding me that I forgot to feed her, regardless of the fact that it's still half an hour before she usually gets fed.

What am I doing with all this time-shifting? Well, I feel like I'm refilling my cup. There's something about the early morning hours that feels so incredibly restful. Now I'm ready for the rest of the day.

~ ~ ~

Wake Up and Live

Thursday November 29, 2018 — There's a lot to be said for that children's prayer that contains the line, "If I should die before I wake."

Far too many people live their lives as if they're asleep, or as this quote for the day says, as if they need more sleep. They are enfolded in a boredom so deep it becomes mind-numbing.

Mary Webb, born in the palindromic year of 1881, was a poet who wrote, "The well of Providence is deep; it's the buckets we bring to it that are small."

Get a bigger bucket and fill it today. It's never too late to start to live.

Clear as Mud

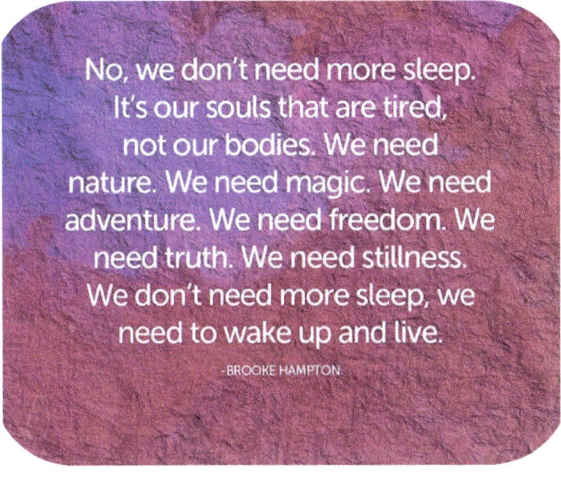

~ ~ ~

Sock Hanger

Friday November 30, 2018 — When I was a kid, helping with laundry, it was one of my chores to hang selected pieces of clothing on clothespin contraptions my father made. They were simple devices: an old wooden coat hanger, six clothespins, seven small eyehooks, and some sturdy string.

A month before I left for college, my father made me my very own. I'm still using it, since I don't like to put my hand-knitted socks in the dryer, and it would take them forever to dry on the line outside in this humid Georgia weather.

They used to make string a lot sturdier than they do nowadays. This is still—after 54 years—the original string. Maybe I should put the sock-hanger in my will. I'm sure it'll still be doing its job 30 years from now.

Only trouble is—who would want it?

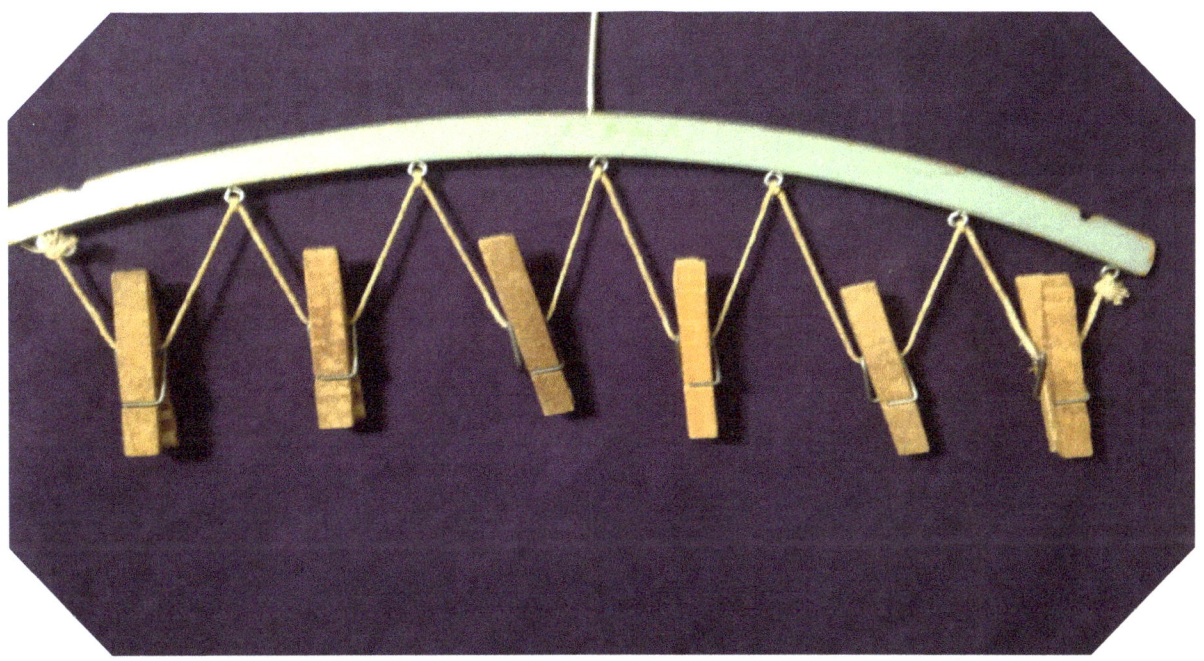

Fran Stewart

December 2018

No Remote

Saturday December 1, 2018 — HOORAY!!! Today is the initial launch of WHITE AS ICE, my final mystery. I've had so many people ask me why I'm not going to write more mysteries Someone else recently declared that he was certain I'd wake up some day and change my mind.

I know all those people love my books. I truly appreciate that. But it's time to change my life, to step into a new phase. I've already started the transition, and I'm delighted with where I'm headed and how I'm getting there.

Stay tuned. I'll be sharing my ongoing journey with you.

p.s. Today, I'm taking a plate of my Molasses Chewies to my book launch. Those are the cookies Biscuit McKee serves the guests who shelter with her during the ice storm.

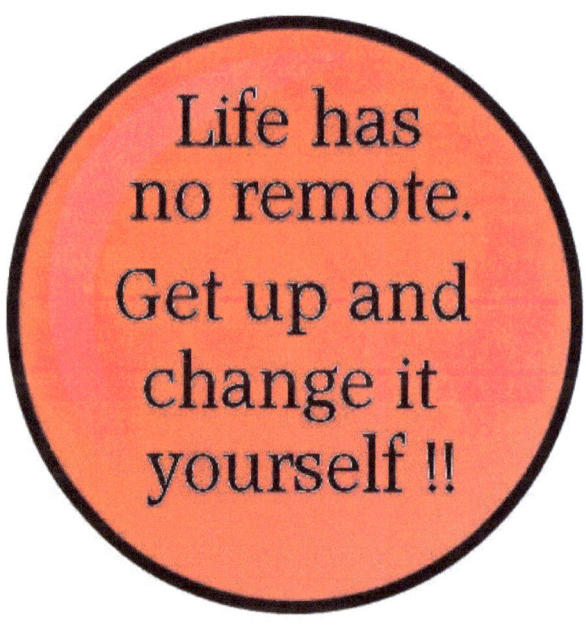

~ ~ ~

Pictures from the launches

Monday December 3, 2018 — I've had an exhilarating weekend, with two book launches, two unexpected family members showing up, two delightful gifts, and two satisfying dinners. No wonder I ignored my alarm cat this morning.

On Saturday, my son Eli who lives in California and my granddaughter who goes to UGA both appeared at

Liberty Books in Lawrenceville. Most of my book club was there, too, and Janice Adams Beene, a fan who has become a friend. Janice flew in from Indiana just to attend the launch. Eli had great fun talking with everybody. And everybody had fun eating my Molasses Chewy cookies—the same ones Biscuit serves to her guests during the ice storm.

My publisher, Darlene Carter, who is also a long-time dear friend (and a quilter) presented me with a lap quilt that featured fabric books—all my Biscuit McKee book covers—on the front, and cats (of course) on the back. I love its whimsical twisty-stitch border.

After the event, Darlene and Janice and I went to dinner at Dominick's Italian just up the street. Yum.

The next day, I was at Another Chapter Bookstore in Cumming, and a steady stream of people came. Janice was there (again—hooray!), and she brought me a lovely blank-paged journal for me to use for memoirs. The journal was wrapped in paper with stripes of all the colors of my books, and then, under that, with a number of layers of brightly colored tissue paper — orange, yellow, green, and blue. I had such fun opening it. The care she had taken with the wrapping was in itself a gift.

On the back of the envelope of the accompanying card, Janice had written: "If I were Marm, your name would be … HeartWords."

Those of you who have read any of my Biscuit McKee Mysteries will understand completely how very touched I was.

And then, of course, after the event, Janice and my friend Peggy Ann Dixon, both of whom have characters named after them in WHITE AS ICE, went to dinner at Tupelo's – Yummy!

So, I hope you'll enjoy the launches vicariously through these photos.

Clear as Mud

~ ~ ~

German Shepherd's Eyes

Tuesday December 4, 2018 — You'll never see a photo like this of a person with a cat. Why?

I'm glad you asked.

The answer is that cats can't move their eyeballs the way dogs can. It they want to look upward, they have to move their entire head. It's the white below an upraised eye that makes it look so soulful — and cats just don't have that ability.

Fran Stewart

Maybe the next time someone tells you that cats are aloof, you could explain to them about eyeballs.

Of course, anyone who's ever been owned by a cat already knows this.

~ ~ ~

Mother Ebbesen's Towel

Wednesday December 5, 2018 — When I was five, my family lived for a year at Shaw Field, South Carolina. "Aunt" Lucille and "Uncle" Martin lived next door. Aunt Lucille's mother lived with them. "Mother Ebbesen" had taken her last step the year I was born.

Every time I visited next door, Mother Ebbesen was doing needlework. With her body so bent, and her hands so gnarled and twisted, it was a miracle she could hold a needle, but she told me once years later that it was her needlework that had kept her sane for all those years.

This picture is of a section of a tea towel she embroidered. You have to understand that every stitch involved six steps. First, as she held the needle beneath the hoop that held the fabric taut, she would insert the needle at the beginning of the stitch. Then she would grasp the pointed end of the needle and pull it through the fabric until all the length of embroidery yarn was resting on the top of the fabric.

Next, she would insert the needle through the top of the fabric. Then, she'd use her forearms to grasp the whole piece and turn it upside down so she could see where the needle was coming out on the back side. This wasn't too hard when she was working on a tea towel, but it involved a great deal of effort when her project was a full-sized tablecloth.

The final two steps were to pull the needle and the length of thread through to the back and then, again using her forearms (because her hands weren't able to open wide enough to grasp the hoop and fabric), she would turn the whole thing upright again and find where the needle was to be inserted from the back to begin another stitch.

She went through these six steps for EVERY SINGLE STITCH.

Aunt Lucille always had to move the hoop from one section to another after her mother had finished in that area. And, of course, she had to thread the needle as well.

Uncle Martin was assigned to the same base in Germany as my dad was after our Shaw Field tour, so I visited often with them and was endlessly fascinated by this woman who was a font of fabulous stories. As I got older, I could move the hoop for her and thread her needles—it was such an honor!

And to this day, I treasure the few items I have from her loving hands.

~ ~ ~

Always Make Sure

Thursday December 6, 2018 — I vote for the optimistic thoughts today.

How about you? Will you join me in seeing the best? I'd like to join you in celebrating the positive. Let's light a candle, sing a song, pat ourselves on the back, smile for no other reason than that it feels good, and laugh out loud today!

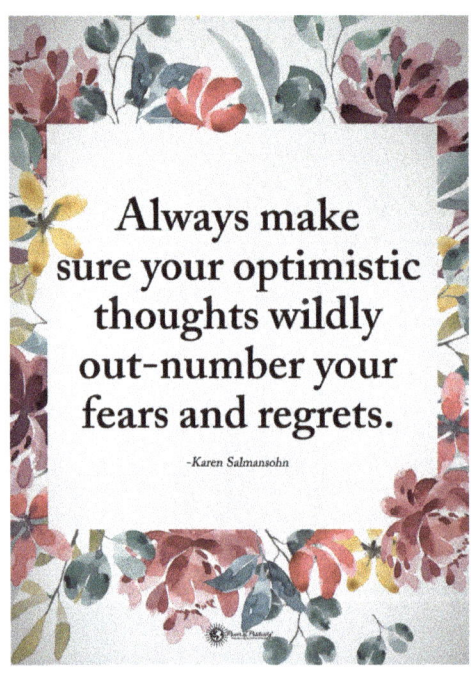

~ ~ ~

Licking the Paddles

Friday December 7, 2018 — Licking the ice cream paddle at Ben & Jerry's.

Yep! That's what I said.

You never know how much something's going to grow. Back in 1978, when Ben Cohen and Jerry Greenfield rented an abandoned gas station in downtown Burlington, Vermont and started their ice cream store, they had a huge old red motor-driven ice cream maker right there by the front windows. Nowadays OSHA would have a fit, but back then we all knew enough to stay away from the thing while it was cranking.

If we timed it just right, we'd get there when the ice cream was done. Ben or Jerry would lift out the paddle and pass it around so anyone there at the time could take a lick. Nowadays I imagine the EPA or the CDC or who knows what other organization would have a hissy fit, but we didn't worry too much about germs back then. After all, we were pretty sturdy folks.

Ben and Jerry needed to get the volume of their business higher, though, so they got hold of an ancient movie projector—the kind with the great big reels—and a bunch of old movies. We had to bring our own chairs, but each Friday night (or maybe it was Saturdays) in the summer, lots of us would gather on the pavement in front of the store and watch movies that were projected onto the white-painted two-story brick wall of the building next door. The picture looked a little wrinkly, but we didn't mind.

Every time they had to change a reel, we'd all go inside and buy ice cream. Lots of ice cream. I guess their marketing scheme worked, because eventually they outgrew the gas station.

I already told you (back in April) about the first time I tasted Cherry Garcia Ice Cream.

If you want to type all these letters and numbers into your browser, you can watch a quick video of how Ben & Jerry's originated—and how they grew.

https://www.youtube.com/watch?v=JNuDGsSdE0U

~ ~ ~

Depression Visible

Saturday December 8, 2018 — The holidays, unfortunately, are times when a lot of people go from feeling down to feeling worse.

It's bad enough if you're simply dealing with the (mostly self-imposed) stresses of high expectations, stretched budgets, and impossible deadlines.

Why do I say these stresses are self-imposed?

I'm glad you asked.

We could step back. We could say no. We could re-order our lives so that the things that truly matter are the things we pay attention to. We could refuse to buy into the marketing plans of corporations and turn our attention to the things that will truly matter in the years to come.

How many of you have given a gift only to have the recipient set it aside in their rush to open yet another package?

That happened to me once too often a number of years ago, and I haven't given a holiday gift since then. Not to anyone.

Does that mean I'm a Grinch or a Scrooge? Not at all. I give gifts throughout the year, ones that probably mean a lot more to the recipient that something that gets lost in a lot of holiday hoopla. The once-a-week "Grannie Days" that freed my daughter's time for the chores it's hard to accomplish when little ones are underfoot. The dog-sitting here and there throughout the year. The perfect article of clothing or piece of jewelry in April or June or August. The knitted scarves just before the cold weather settled in. The calendars I save for a friend who collects them. The notes I write by hand and mail with a stamp.

If you're dealing with a deeper depression, though, one that worsens during the holiday season but won't go away when the calendar turns, please check out *Depression Visible: The Ragged Edge*, written by my sister Diana Alishouse.

Fran Stewart

Her fabric art throughout the book shows what depression feels like. If you've ever felt like your stuffing was coming out, your edges were raveling, and you could never match up your buttons with your buttonholes—or if you know someone who fits that bill—then *Depression Visible* just might be the lifeline you need at this time of year.

~ ~ ~

Speed Limit Calculation

Monday December 10, 2018 — When my family traveled across country to visit my grandparents back in the fifties, we used to play games with road signs. One of my favorite games was the one where a sign would say this many miles to Town A and that many miles to Town B. Our mother always had us add the two distances together to find out how far it was to Town B. It took me years to figure out that both distances were calculated from where the sign was, so our answers were always wrong.

Still, it was a fun way to learn to add in my head and then to practice that skill even once I knew Town B was precisely as far away as the sign had said. I have to admit, I still do such calculations automatically when I'm on a road trip.

I wonder what I would have thought back then about a sign like this one.

~ ~ ~

Eating Customers

Tuesday December 11, 2018 — Today I'm not interested in eating any customers.

A dash or a period sure would have been helpful.

This sign comes via CaptainGrammarPants on Facebook.

Fran Stewart

~ ~ ~

Shakespeare Tavern

Wednesday December 12, 2018 — Last Sunday evening, I had the great pleasure of attending *A Christmas Carol* at Atlanta's very own Shakespeare Tavern with (from the left), my grandson Aiden, my daughter Veronica, my son Eli, and my daughter-of-the-heart Nima.

The production was an absolute delight. If you're ever in the Atlanta area, be sure to check out the Shakespeare Tavern, ShakespeareTavern.com.

I've been going to their shows religiously since 1992, when I saw *Julius Caesar*. Even having seen the same plays numerous times, there is something about superb live theater that sparks new insights with every new production.

It's rather like re-reading a well-written book. Insights galore. That's one reason I hope people will re-read my Biscuit McKee mysteries in order, beginning with ORANGE AS MARMALADE and proceeding through to book #11 — WHITE AS ICE.

And if you haven't read my three ScotShop Mysteries, feel free to pick those up at The Shakespeare Tavern—they sell them in their gift shop.

[**2020 Note:** Like all the other arts organizations in Atlanta (and of course around the globe), the Shakespeare Tavern has had to suspend live performances due to the COVID-19 pandemic, but they are maintaining an active online presence of education classes. Please support the arts in any way you can now when they need the help desperately.]

~ ~ ~

Your Mind is a Garden

Thursday December 13, 2018 — Today, I plan to plant flowers.

What about you?

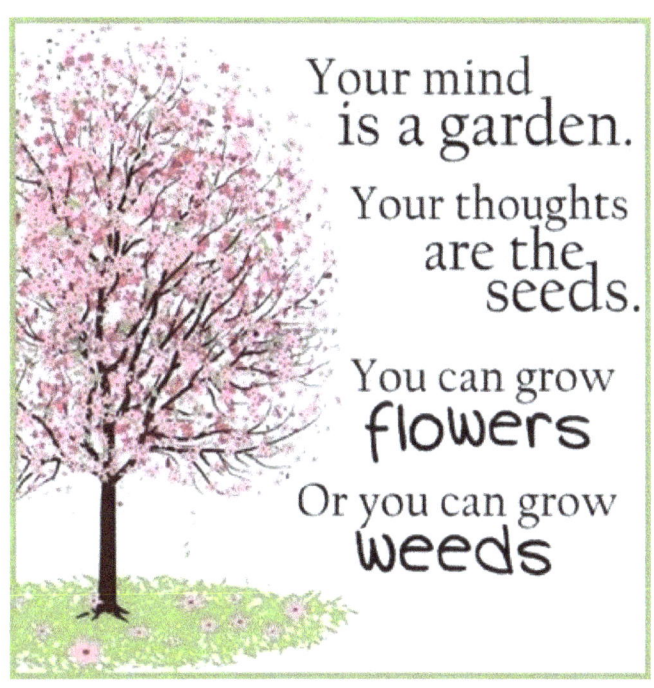

~ ~ ~

Top 10 Reasons to Procrastinate

Friday December 14, 2018 — Are you like I am when it comes to organization?

Some things I keep track of beautifully, either with calendar notes, lists, file folders, or my ubiquitous spreadsheets.

Then there are the other things that — doggone it — just don't get done. Like getting up on the roof to blow off the leaves that have accumulated there. Seems like every time I feel like I have the time to do it, it's raining. Or on days like yesterday when it was perfectly dry and I had the whole afternoon because my granddaughter, who had said she was going to drop by for a visit (and a round of cookie-baking) decided to stay at college for an extra day.

Did I say, "Oh, goody, this will give me time to clean off the roof?"

Nope.

I made a crockpot of soup, did some paperwork, played around with some cryptograms and some sudoku.

Then, when evening came on and it really was too dark to tackle the roof, I knitted while listening to an audio book.

<<sigh>> The leaves are still up there.

The good news? Savannah said she'd drop by later today.

~ ~ ~

Find a Way

Saturday December 15, 2018 — Today's saying sort of goes along with yesterday's note about procrastination.

As to the state of my roof (see yesterday's whining if you're not sure what I'm talking about), when my granddaughter was here yesterday afternoon, I mentioned the leaves on the roof.

"Grannie! You can't get up there!"

She didn't say "not at your age," but it seemed to be implied.

I told her I'd been cleaning off my own roof for the past 25 years and I didn't see any reason to stop now.

Very quick to volunteer her brother, she told me, "Aiden would love to get up there and clean off your leaves."

And then came a discussion of how difficult it has always been for me to ask for help, largely based on a memory from my childhood in which I overheard my mother telling my grandmother (over the steaming canning jars), "We don't come to visit more often because you always work us to death while we're here." I think I swore then that I'd never put somebody in that position.

To be fair, though, I must admit there's a big difference between my dad having to replace fence poles, dig up stumps, and build a new cover for the cistern during his "vacation," compared to the fun of climbing

Grannie's ladder and blowing off a pile of leaves …

[**2020 Note**: As I was compiling these posts for this book, I remembered that a few years ago my son came for a visit and I asked him to dig a ditch for me—a LONG ditch—so I could lay an extension to my downspout. The idea was to take the roof run-off and funnel it into what would become a water garden. It worked, but when I think of all the sweating he did during that endeavor, I think maybe I was channeling my grandmother. Sorry, Eli. But I DID truly appreciate the effort you put into it.]

At any rate, I told Savannah that if her brother wanted to get up on my roof, he might want to call me and volunteer.

I'll let you know what happens.

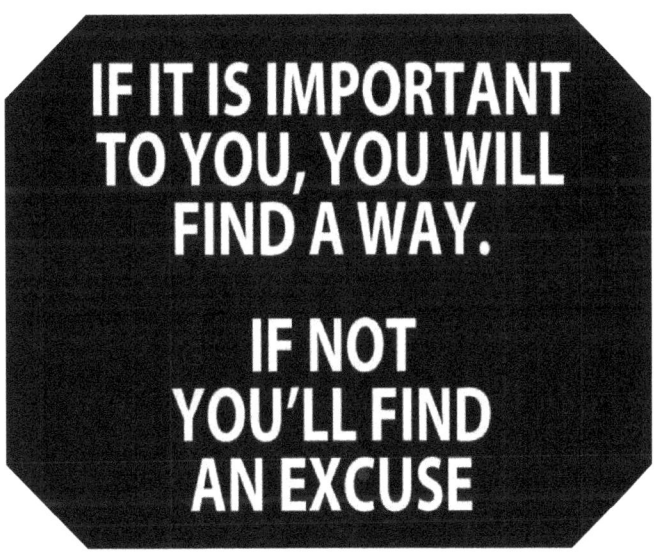

~ ~ ~

Adventures, Not Toys

Monday December 17, 2018 — I used to take my kids on nature walks when they were small. They each started out with a bucket, so they could pick up interesting treasures, and I had a bag with me so I could pick up any wayside trash we came across.

After we got home, we'd inspect, talk about, and make up stories about their stones and pieces of wood (nothing alive was allowed in a bucket—snails and salamanders and snakes and frogs and minnows were just for looking at). Eventually, the treasures all ended up out among the trees in our yard. I wonder now if my grownup offspring even remember those walks.

Longfellow wrote a poem about leaving seashells in place, since the beauty of a shell was made more lovely when it was encompassed by the sand and shore. Rather like what Anne Morrow Lindbergh said in *Gift From the Sea*, in which she wrote about how she collected shells like crazy when she first went on her retreat in a small cabin beside the ocean, but she gradually found that she paid no attention to them when they sat, sterile, on a shelf.

Fran Stewart

Instead, she borrowed just one example of each type of shell to meditate on, to derive a life-lesson from, to gain insights about.

I'm going to go wander through the woods in my back yard. No telling what I'll find to write about or think about or sing to.

"Nuttin' For Christmas"

Tuesday December 18, 2018 — Last week the Pen Women organization I belong to (NLAPW.org and AtlantPenWomen.org) had its annual holiday music program, featuring performances by a number of our Atlanta members of songs that reflected the diversity of their various heritages. About half the women sang songs they had written themselves, while the others sang songs from their childhood or songs that represented where their families had come from.

Then there was me. Although Scot genes and Cherokee genes feature prominently in my background, my father used to say my sister and I came from a long line of horse thieves, so I figured I could get away with singing "I'm Gettin' Nuttin' for Christmas ('cause I ain't been nuttin' but bad)", written in 1955 by Sid Tepper and Roy C. Bennett.

If you're familiar with the lyrics, you'll know that the chorus begins with a great big "So," which I strung out to ridiculous lengths each time it came around. Here I am at the start of the final chorus.

Fran Stewart

~ ~ ~

Silly Grannie on the Roof

Wednesday December 19, 2018 — Remember last week when I talked about not having the leaves swept off my roof yet?

The weather's been dry for a few days, so I decided I might as well do it myself instead of waiting for my grandson to call. Everything was fine until I got ready to climb down, and the ladder slipped. I tried to reposition it, but I couldn't get it stable enough — and I didn't particularly want to risk breaking my neck.

So, I called my neighbors—nobody was home. I called my daughter—who didn't answer her phone. I finally called my granddaughter, who's home from college for the winter break. She and a friend were our walking a nature trail. They drove to my house, repositioned the ladder, and held it firmly.

But first, she had to take a picture, which she gleefully labeled "Silly Grannie."

It was dark before any of my neighbors returned. I would have been up there a LONG time if Savannah hadn't been around.

~ ~ ~

Thursday December 20, 2018 — Nothing posted until 1/1/2019

Sick for the first four days of this time, then just took a vacation from posting.

Didn't tell anybody, and nobody seemed to notice.

Hmmm … Is this telling me something?

~ ~ ~

Thus ends *Clear as Mud*. I'll be resuming this daily journey with the 2019 and 2020 posts in *Clearly Me*, due to be published in early 2021.

I hope you've enjoyed the journey so far. I hope you've gotten something out of these meanderings of mine—either something profound or at least something to laugh about. I know I've learned a lot about myself just through the act of writing down my thoughts and my stories.

I encourage you to write your stories, whether you ever want anyone else to read them or not. No telling what all you'll find.

    --Fran

    From my house beside a creek

    on the other side of Hog Mountain

    September 2020.

www.ingramcontent.com/pod-product-compliance
Lightning Source LLC
Chambersburg PA
CBHW051353110526
44592CB00024B/2967